THE ULTIMATE PUBLIC CAMPGROUND

Corps of Engineers Camping

Directory of 942 Camping Areas in 35 States

Corps of Engineers Camping, copyright © 2022 by Ted Houghton. Printed and bound in the United States of America. All rights reserved. No part of this publication may be reproduced in any form without the prior written permission from the publisher.

Although efforts are made to ensure the accuracy of this publication, the author and Roundabout Publications shall have neither liability nor responsibility to any person or entity with respect to any loss or damage caused, or alleged to be caused, directly or indirectly by the information contained in this publication.

Published by:

Roundabout Publications
PO Box 569
LaCygne, KS 66040

Phone: 800-455-2207
Internet: www.RoundaboutPublications.com

Library of Congress Control Number: 2022934904

ISBN-10: 1-885464-82-7
ISBN-13: 978-1-885464-82-8

Table of Contents

Introduction	4
Alabama	5
Arkansas	8
California	19
Connecticut	22
Florida	24
Georgia	26
Idaho	30
Illinois	33
Iowa	36
Kansas	39
Kentucky	44
Louisiana	48
Maryland	51
Massachusetts	53
Minnesota	55
Mississippi	57
Missouri	61
Montana	67
Nebraska	70
New Mexico	72
North Carolina	74
North Dakota	76
Ohio	78
Oklahoma	80
Oregon	88
Pennsylvania	90
South Carolina	93
South Dakota	95
Tennessee	97
Texas	101
Vermont	108
Virginia	110
Washington	112
West Virginia	115
Wisconsin	117

Introduction

Huge portions of public lands, managed by a variety of government agencies, are available to the general public for recreational use. This book will guide you to 942 camping areas available from the U.S. Army Corps of Engineers projects in 35 states.

Corps of Engineers Camping

The U.S. Army Corps of Engineers is one of the nation's leading federal providers of outdoor recreation with more than 400 lake and river projects. These areas offer recreational opportunities at campgrounds, lakes and marinas across the country. Common activities include hiking, boating, fishing, camping and hunting. The more adventurous will find snorkeling, windsurfing, whitewater rafting, mountain biking and geo-caching. To learn more about the Corps of Engineers, visit their website: www.usace.army.mil. Recreation information including activities, amenities, discounts, directions and fees is available at the *Corps Lakes Gateway* website: www.corpslakes.com.

Using This Guide

This guide is especially helpful when used along with Google Maps, Windows Maps, or a GPS device for locating and navigating to each camping area.

State Maps

A state map is provided to aid you in locating the camping areas. A grid overlay on each map is used when cross-referencing with each camping area.

Map Grid Chart & Alphabetical List

Following the state map is a chart showing the camping area ID number(s) located within a map grid. Following this chart is an alphabetical list of each camping area, which is especially helpful when you already know the name of an area. This list provides each location's ID number and map grid location.

Camping Area Details

Camping area details include information about each public camping area within the state. Preceding each location's name is the ID number and map grid location, which is used when referencing the state map.

Details for each camping area generally include the following information:

- Total number of sites or dispersed camping
- Number of RV sites
- Sites with electric hookups
- Full hookup sites, if available
- Water (central location or spigots at site)
- Showers
- RV dump station
- Toilets (flush, pit/vault, or none)
- Laundry facilities
- Camp store
- Maximum RV size limits (if any)
- Reservation information (accepted, not accepted, recommended or required)
- Generator use and hours (if limited)
- Operating season
- Camping fees charged
- Miscellaneous notes
- Length of stay limit
- Elevation in feet and meters
- Telephone number
- Nearby city or town
- GPS coordinates

The Ultimate Public Campground Project

Data for this publication is from *The Ultimate Public Campground Project*, which was established in 2008 to provide a consolidated and comprehensive source for public campgrounds of all types. Please note that despite our best efforts, there will always be errors to be found in the data. With over 45,000 records in the database, it is impossible to ensure that each one is always up-to-date.

Happy Camping!

Common Abbreviations Used

ATV	All-Terrain Vehicle
CG	Campground
CR	County Road
HMU	Habitat Management Unit
FSR	Forest Service Road
LTVA	Long Term Visitors Area
NCA	National Conservation Area
OHV	Off-Highway Vehicle
OHVA	Off-Highway Vehicle Area
ORV	Off-Road Vehicle
RA	Recreation Area
RMA	Recreation Management Area
TH	Trail Head
WA	Wildlife Area
WMA	Wildlife Management Area

Alabama

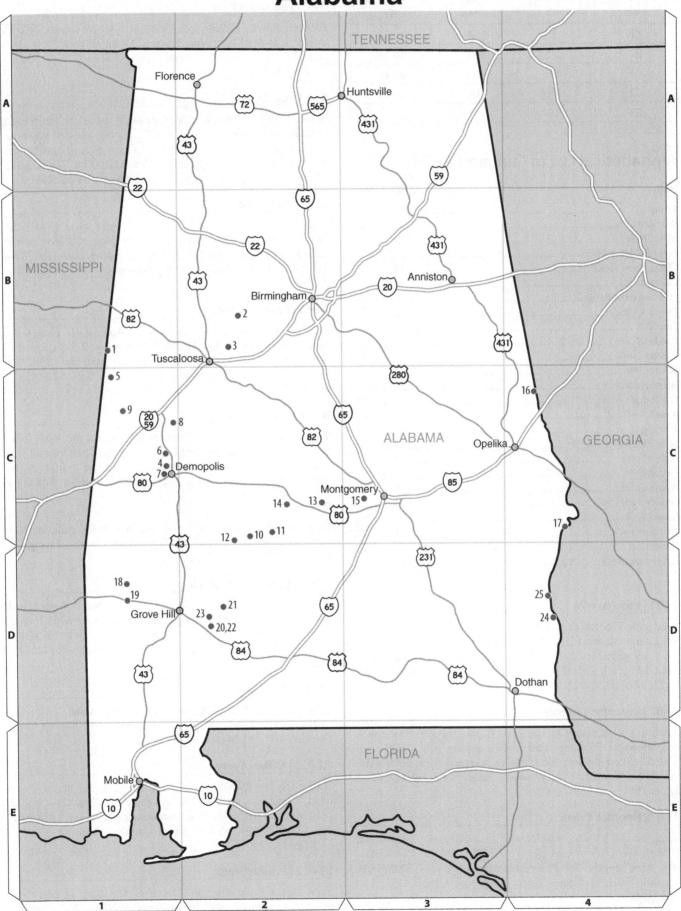

Map	ID	Map	ID
B1	1	C4	16-17
B2	2-3	D1	18-19
C1	4-9	D2	20-23
C2	10-14	D4	24-25
C3	15		

Alphabetical List of Camping Areas

Name	ID	Map
Amity	16	C4
Belmont Park	4	C1
Bluff Creek	17	C4
Burchfield Branch	2	B2
Chilatchee Creek	10	C2
Cochrane	5	C1
Damsite West Bank	20	D2
Deerlick Creek	3	B2
Elm Bluff	11	C2
Forkland	6	C1
Foscue Creek	7	C1
Gunter Hill	15	C3
Haines Island	21	D2
Hardridge Creek	24	D4
Isaac Creek	22	D2
Jennings Ferry	8	C1
Lenoir Landing	18	D1
Millers Ferry	12	C2
Pickensville	1	B1
Prairie Creek	13	C2
Service Park	19	D1
Silver Creek	23	D2
Six Mile Creek	14	C2
Sumter	9	C1
White Oak Creek	25	D4

1 • B1 | Pickensville

Total sites: 176, RV sites: 176, Elec sites: 176, Water at site, Flush toilet, Free showers, RV dump, Tent & RV camping: $20-28, Open all year, Max Length: 140ft, Reservations accepted, Elev: 194ft/59m, Tel: 205-373-6328, Nearest town: Carrollton. GPS: 33.236977, -88.303223

2 • B2 | Burchfield Branch

Total sites: 37, RV sites: 36, Elec sites: 37, Water at site, Flush toilet, Free showers, RV dump, Tent & RV camping: $28-30, Open all year, Max Length: 95ft, Reservations accepted, Elev: 266ft/81m, Tel: 205-497-9828, Nearest town: Adger. GPS: 33.447742, -87.366197

3 • B2 | Deerlick Creek

Total sites: 46, RV sites: 40, Elec sites: 40, Water at site, Flush toilet, Free showers, RV dump, Tents: $20/RVs: $28-30, Open Mar-Nov, Max Length: 40ft, Reservations accepted, Elev: 322ft/98m, Tel: 205-759-1591, Nearest town: Tuscaloosa. GPS: 33.257331, -87.433945

4 • C1 | Belmont Park

Dispersed sites, Central water, Vault/pit toilet, No showers, No RV dump, Tent & RV camping: Fee unk, Open all year, Elev: 118ft/36m, Tel: 334-289-3540, Nearest town: Belmont. GPS: 32.552378, -87.876981

5 • C1 | Cochrane

Total sites: 60, RV sites: 60, Elec sites: 60, Water at site, Flush toilet, Free showers, RV dump, Tent & RV camping: $16-18, Stay limit: 14 days, Generator hours: 0600-2200, Open all year, Max Length: 65+ft, Reservations not accepted, Elev: 128ft/39m, Tel: 205-373-8806, Nearest town: Aliceville. GPS: 33.081299, -88.264404

6 • C1 | Forkland

Total sites: 42, RV sites: 42, Elec sites: 42, Water at site, Flush toilet, Free showers, RV dump, Tent & RV camping: $20-26, Open all year, Max Length: 107ft, Reservations accepted, Elev: 167ft/51m, Tel: 334-289-5530, Nearest town: Demopolis. GPS: 32.627315, -87.882975

7 • C1 | Foscue Creek

Total sites: 54, RV sites: 54, Elec sites: 54, Water at site, Flush toilet, Free showers, RV dump, Tent & RV camping: $28-30, Open all year, Max Length: 153ft, Reservations accepted, Elev: 89ft/27m, Tel: 334-289-5535, Nearest town: Demopolis. GPS: 32.514557, -87.868784

8 • C1 | Jennings Ferry

Total sites: 52, RV sites: 52, Elec sites: 52, Water at site, Flush toilet, Free showers, RV dump, Tent & RV camping: $28, Open all year, Max Length: 168ft, Reservations accepted, Elev: 151ft/46m, Tel: 205-372-1217, Nearest town: Eutaw. GPS: 32.805664, -87.812256

9 • C1 | Sumter

Dispersed sites, No water, No toilets, Tent & RV camping: $10, Elev: 131ft/40m, Tel: 662-327-2142, Nearest town: Livingston. GPS: 32.872476, -88.184782

10 • C2 | Chilatchee Creek

Total sites: 33, RV sites: 33, Elec sites: 33, Water at site, Flush toilet, Free showers, RV dump, Tent & RV camping: $26, Open all year, Max Length: 85ft, Reservations accepted, Elev: 125ft/38m, Tel: 334-573-2562, Nearest town: Alberta. GPS: 32.142334, -87.275391

11 • C2 | Elm Bluff

Total sites: 11, RV sites: 8, No water, Vault/pit toilet, Tent & RV camping: $10, Open all year, Elev: 102ft/31m, Nearest town: Camden. GPS: 32.164342, -87.115402

12 • C2 | Millers Ferry

Total sites: 66, RV sites: 66, Elec sites: 66, Water at site, Flush toilet, Free showers, RV dump, Tent & RV camping: $26, Open all year, Max Length: 100ft, Reservations accepted, Elev: 121ft/37m, Tel: 334-682-4191, Nearest town: Camden. GPS: 32.117657, -87.389612

13 • C2 | Prairie Creek

Total sites: 62, RV sites: 55, Elec sites: 62, Water at site, Flush toilet, Free showers, RV dump, Tents: $22/RVs: $26, Open all year, Max Length: 115ft, Reservations accepted, Elev: 151ft/46m, Tel: 334-418-4916, Nearest town: Lowndesboro. GPS: 32.337646, -86.769531

14 • C2 | Six Mile Creek

Total sites: 31, RV sites: 31, Elec sites: 31, Water at site, Flush toilet, Free showers, RV dump, Tent & RV camping: $26, Open Apr-Sep, Max Length: 123ft, Reservations accepted, Elev: 138ft/42m, Tel: 334-875-6228, Nearest town: Selma. GPS: 32.326587, -87.015538

15 • C3 | Gunter Hill

Total sites: 142, RV sites: 142, Elec sites: 142, Water at site, Flush toilet, Free showers, RV dump, Tent & RV camping: $26-30, 75 full hookups, Open all year, Max Length: 138ft, Reservations accepted, Elev: 158ft/48m, Tel: 334-269-1053, Nearest town: Montgomery. GPS: 32.364061, -86.457316

16 • C4 | Amity

Total sites: 96, RV sites: 93, Elec sites: 93, Water at site, Flush toilet, Free showers, RV dump, Tent & RV camping: $30, Open Apr-Sep, Max Length: 55ft, Reservations accepted, Elev: 738ft/225m, Tel: 334-499-2404, Nearest town: Lanett. GPS: 32.977567, -85.210689

17 • C4 | Bluff Creek

Total sites: 88, RV sites: 88, Elec sites: 88, Water at site, Flush toilet, Free showers, RV dump, Tent & RV camping: $26, Open Mar-Sep, Max Length: 40ft, Reservations accepted, Elev: 240ft/73m, Tel: 256-855-2746, Nearest town: Pittsview. GPS: 32.181485, -85.011499

18 • D1 | Lenoir Landing

Total sites: 6, RV sites: 6, Central water, Vault/pit toilet, No showers, No RV dump, Tent & RV camping: Free, Open all year, Elev: 66ft/20m, Nearest town: Womack Hill. GPS: 31.856288, -88.159288

19 • D1 | Service Park

Total sites: 32, RV sites: 30, Elec sites: 30, Water at site, Flush toilet, Free showers, RV dump, Tents: $18/RVs: $26, Open Mar-Nov, Max Length: 97ft, Reservations accepted, Elev: 52ft/16m, Tel: 251-754-9338, Nearest town: Demopolis. GPS: 31.755393, -88.148722

20 • D2 | Damsite West Bank

Total sites: 2, RV sites: 2, Central water, Vault/pit toilet, No showers, No RV dump, Tent & RV camping: Free, Open all year, Max Length: 20ft, Elev: 108ft/33m, Nearest town: Gosport. GPS: 31.615003, -87.556498

21 • D2 | Haines Island

Total sites: 12, RV sites: 12, No water, Vault/pit toilet, Tent & RV camping: Free, Open all year, Max Length: 40ft, Reservations not accepted, Elev: 69ft/21m, Nearest town: Camden. GPS: 31.725393, -87.469253

22 • D2 | Isaac Creek

Total sites: 66, RV sites: 66, Elec sites: 66, Water at site, Flush toilet, Free showers, RV dump, Tent & RV camping: $26, Open Jan-Oct, Max Length: 86ft, Reservations accepted, Elev: 102ft/31m, Tel: 251-282-4254, Nearest town: Camden. GPS: 31.621670, -87.550030

23 • D2 | Silver Creek

Total sites: 8, RV sites: 8, Central water, Vault/pit toilet, No showers, No RV dump, Tent & RV camping: Free, Open all year, Max Length: 20ft, Elev: 62ft/19m, Tel: 334-682-4244, Nearest town: Gosport. GPS: 31.664809, -87.572921

24 • D4 | Hardridge Creek

Total sites: 74, RV sites: 74, Elec sites: 40, Water at site, Flush toilet, Free showers, RV dump, Tent & RV camping: $26-28, 20 full hookups, Open Mar-Sep, Max Length: 30ft, Reservations accepted, Elev: 220ft/67m, Tel: 334-585-5945, Nearest town: Ft Gaines GA. GPS: 31.643699, -85.102895

25 • D4 | White Oak Creek

Total sites: 129, RV sites: 129, Elec sites: 129, Water at site, Flush toilet, Free showers, RV dump, Tent & RV camping: $26, Open all year, Max Length: 40ft, Reservations accepted, Elev: 249ft/76m, Tel: 334-687-3101, Nearest town: Eufaula. GPS: 31.774901, -85.143727

Arkansas

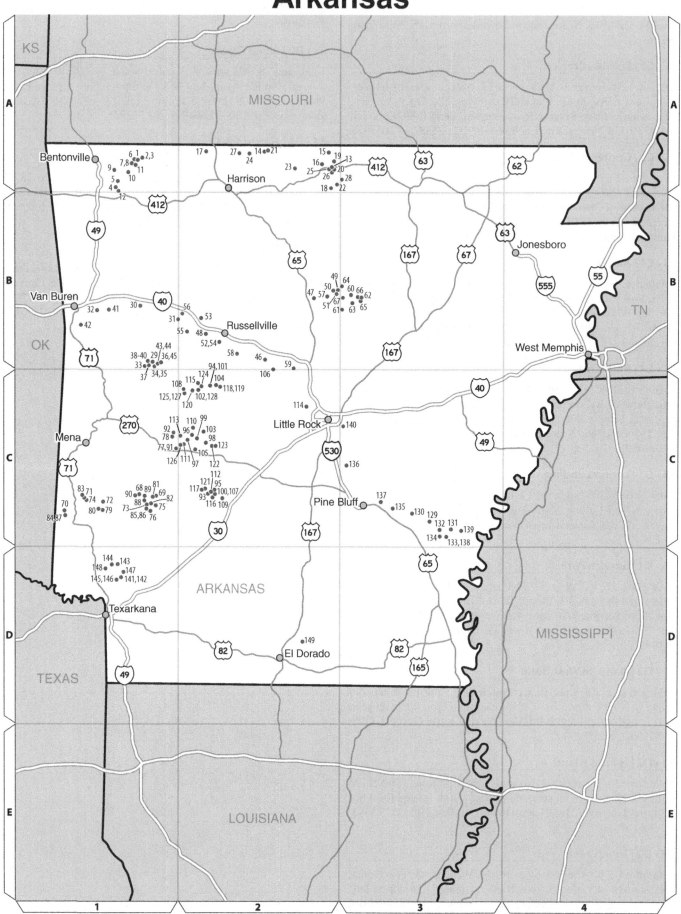

Map	ID	Map	ID
A1	1-12	C1	68-92
A2	13-27	C2	93-128
A3	28	C3	129-140
B1	29-45	D1	141-148
B2	46-59	D2	149
B3	60-67		

Alphabetical List of Camping Areas

Name	ID	Map
Alpine Ridge	93	C2
Anderson Branch	94	C2
Arlie Moore	95	C2
Arrowhead Point	68	C1
Ashley Creek	29	B1
Aux Arc	30	B1
Avant	96	C2
Bear Creek	69	C1
Beard's Bluff	141	D1
Beard's Lake	142	D1
Bellah Mine	70	C1
Bidwell Point	13	A2
Big Bayou Meto	129	C3
Big Coon Creek	71	C1
Big Fir	97	C2
Blue Ridge	72	C1
Brady Mountain	98	C2
Buck Creek	14	A2
Buckhorn	73	C1
Buckville	99	C2
Caddo Drive	100	C2
Calamity Beach	15	A2
Cane Creek	31	B1
Carter Cove	101	C2
Casa Camp	102	C2
Cedar Fourche	103	C2
Cherokee	60	B3
Cherokee Park	46	B2
Choctaw	47	B2
Clear Creek	32	B1
Cossatot Reefs	74	C1
Cottonshed Landing	143	D1
County Line	104	C2
Cove Creek	61	B3
Cowhide Cove	75	C1
Cranfield	16	A2
Cricket Creek	17	A2
Crystal Springs	105	C2
Cypress Creek	106	C2
Dam Area	76	C1
Dam Site	62	B3
Dam Site - Quarry Cove	18	A2
Dam Site Lake	1	A1
Dam Site Park - Parker Bottoms	2	A1
Dam Site River	3	A1
Delaware Park	48	B2
Denby Point	77	C1
Devils Fork	49	B2
Edgewood	107	C2
Gamaliel	19	A2
Heber Springs	63	B3
Henderson	20	A2
Hickory Creek	4	A1
Highway 125	21	A2
Highway 27	78	C1
Hill Creek	64	B3
Hise Hill	33	B1
Hog Farm	108	C2
Horseshoe Bend	5	A1
Horseshoe Bend	79	C1
Indian Creek	6	A1
Iron Mountain	109	C2
Irons Fork	110	C2
Jefferson Ridge COE	80	C1
John F Kennedy	65	B3
Joplin	111	C2
Jordan Island (Sand Island)	22	A2
Kerley Point	28	A3
Kirby Landing	81	C1
Lakeview	23	A2
Laurel Creek	82	C1
Lead Hill	24	A2
Lease Three	34	B1
Lenox Marcus	112	C2
Lick Creek	35	B1
Little Bayou Meto	130	C3
Little Coon Creek	83	C1
Little Fir	113	C2
Lock and Dam No. 8	149	D2
Lost Bridge North	7	A1
Lost Bridge South	8	A1
Maumelle Park	114	C2
Merrisach Lake Park	131	C3
Mill Creek	50	B2
Moore Bayou	132	C3
Narrows	51	B2
Norman Hill	115	C2
Notrebes Bend	133	C3
Oak Grove	84	C1
Old Hwy 25	66	B3
Old Post Road Park	52	B2
Outlet Area	36	B1
Ozan Point	116	C2
Panther Bay	25	A2
Paraloma Landing	144	D1
Parker Creek	85	C1
Pendleton Bend	134	C3
Persimmion Point #1	37	B1
Persimmion Point #2	38	B1
Persimmion Point #3	39	B1
Persimmion Point #4	40	B1
Pikeville	86	C1
Pine Ridge	87	C1
Piney Bay	53	B2
Point Cedar	117	C2
Prairie Creek	9	A1
Quarry Cove	118	C2
Rising Star	135	C3
River Ridge	41	B1

Name	Page	Grid
River Road	119	C2
River Run East	145	D1
River Run West	146	D1
Riverview Park	54	B2
Robinson Point	26	A2
Rock Creek	88	C1
Rocky Branch	10	A1
Rover Landing	120	C2
Saratoga Landing	147	D1
Self Creek	89	C1
Shiloh	67	B3
Shoal Bay	55	B2
Shouse Ford	121	C2
Spadra Park	56	B2
Spillway Group	122	C2
Springhill	42	B1
Star of the West	90	C1
Starkey	11	A1
Stephens Park	123	C2
Sugar Loaf	57	B2
Sunlight Bay	124	C2
Sweeden Island Park	58	B2
Tar Camp	136	C3
The Big Island	43	B1
The Big Rock	125	C2
The Slide	44	B1
Toad Suck Park	59	B2
Tompkins Bend	126	C2
Trulock	137	C3
Tucker Hollow	27	A2
Twin Creek	91	C1
Twin Lakes	127	C2
War Eagle	12	A1
Wards Crossing	128	C2
Washita	92	C1
Waveland Park	45	B1
White Cliffs	148	D1
Wilbur D Mills	138	C3
Wild Goose Bayou	139	C3
Willow Beach	140	C3

1 • A1 | Dam Site Lake

Total sites: 47, RV sites: 47, Elec sites: 42, Central water, Flush toilet, Free showers, RV dump, Tent & RV camping: $22-29, Open Apr-Oct, Max Length: 82ft, Reservations accepted, Elev: 1106ft/337m, Tel: 479-253-5828, Nearest town: Eureka. GPS: 36.420419, -93.856236

2 • A1 | Dam Site Park - Parker Bottoms

Total sites: 7, RV sites: 7, Elec sites: 7, Central water, Flush toilet, Free showers, Tent & RV camping: Fee unk, Reservations not accepted, Elev: 946ft/288m, Tel: 417-336-5083, Nearest town: Busch. GPS: 36.434824, -93.822314

3 • A1 | Dam Site River

Total sites: 58, RV sites: 58, Elec sites: 58, Central water, Flush toilet, Free showers, RV dump, Tent & RV camping: $21-29, Open Apr-Oct, Max Length: 96ft, Reservations accepted, Elev: 961ft/293m, Tel: 479-253-9865, Nearest town: Eureka. GPS: 36.430293, -93.836085

4 • A1 | Hickory Creek

Total sites: 55, RV sites: 55, Elec sites: 55, Central water, Flush toilet, Free showers, RV dump, Tent & RV camping: $24, Open Apr-Oct, Max Length: 82ft, Elev: 1138ft/347m, Tel: 479-750-2943, Nearest town: Springdale. GPS: 36.241001, -94.036333

5 • A1 | Horseshoe Bend

Total sites: 138, RV sites: 135, Elec sites: 135, Central water, Flush toilet, Free showers, RV dump, Tents: $16/RVs: $22-26, Open Apr-Oct, Max Length: 60ft, Reservations accepted, Elev: 1198ft/365m, Tel: 479-925-2561, Nearest town: Rogers. GPS: 36.283855, -94.024021

6 • A1 | Indian Creek

Total sites: 33, RV sites: 33, Elec sites: 33, Central water, Flush toilet, Free showers, RV dump, Tent & RV camping: $22, Open May-Sep, Max Length: 62ft, Reservations accepted, Elev: 1142ft/348m, Tel: 479-656-3145, Nearest town: Gateway. GPS: 36.418741, -93.886641

7 • A1 | Lost Bridge North

Total sites: 48, RV sites: 48, Elec sites: 48, Central water, Flush toilet, Free showers, RV dump, Tent & RV camping: $22, Group site: $40, Open Apr-Sep, Max Length: 52ft, Reservations accepted, Elev: 1138ft/347m, Tel: 479-359-3312, Nearest town: Rogers. GPS: 36.412621, -93.894961

8 • A1 | Lost Bridge South

Total sites: 36, RV sites: 36, Elec sites: 36, Central water, Flush toilet, Free showers, RV dump, Tent & RV camping: $22-24, Open May-Sep, Max Length: 45ft, Reservations accepted, Elev: 1148ft/350m, Tel: 479-359-3755, Nearest town: Rogers. GPS: 36.395508, -93.903076

9 • A1 | Prairie Creek

Total sites: 107, RV sites: 106, Elec sites: 106, Central water, Flush toilet, Free showers, RV dump, Tents: $20/RVs: $22-29, Open Apr-Oct, Max Length: 70ft, Reservations accepted, Elev: 1168ft/356m, Tel: 479-925-3957, Nearest town: Rogers. GPS: 36.353831, -94.053766

10 • A1 | Rocky Branch

Total sites: 41, RV sites: 41, Elec sites: 41, Central water, Flush toilet, Free showers, RV dump, Tent & RV camping: $22-29, Open May-Oct, Max Length: 51ft, Reservations accepted, Elev: 1257ft/383m, Tel: 479-925-2526, Nearest town: Rogers. GPS: 36.338571, -93.935147

11 • A1 | Starkey

Total sites: 23, RV sites: 23, Elec sites: 23, Central water, Flush toilet, Free showers, RV dump, Tents: $22/RVs: $22-28, Open May-Sep, Max Length: 50ft, Reservations accepted, Elev: 1299ft/396m, Tel: 479-253-5866, Nearest town: Eureka Springs. GPS: 36.391830, -93.877670

12 • A1 | War Eagle

Total sites: 26, RV sites: 26, Elec sites: 26, Central water, Flush toilet, Free showers, RV dump, Tent & RV camping: $22, Open May-Sep, Max Length: 43ft, Reservations accepted, Elev:

1240ft/378m, Tel: 479-750-4722, Nearest town: Springdale. GPS: 36.218530, -94.016060

13 • A2 | Bidwell Point

Total sites: 48, RV sites: 48, Elec sites: 46, Central water, Flush toilet, Free showers, RV dump, Tent & RV camping: $21-22, Open May-Oct, Max Length: 70ft, Reservations accepted, Elev: 581ft/177m, Tel: 870-467-5375, Nearest town: Mountain Home. GPS: 36.385986, -92.237793

14 • A2 | Buck Creek

Total sites: 38, RV sites: 38, Elec sites: 36, Central water, Flush toilet, Free showers, RV dump, Tents: $14/RVs: $21-22, Open May-Oct, Max Length: 36ft, Reservations accepted, Elev: 705ft/215m, Tel: 417-785-4313, Nearest town: Protem. GPS: 36.488481, -92.794341

15 • A2 | Calamity Beach

Dispersed sites, No water, No toilets, Tent & RV camping: Free, Permit required, Elev: 614ft/187m, Tel: 870-425-2700, Nearest town: Howards Ridge. GPS: 36.476575, -92.258567

16 • A2 | Cranfield

Total sites: 66, RV sites: 66, Elec sites: 66, Central water, Flush toilet, Free showers, RV dump, Tents: $14/RVs: $20-22, Open Apr-Oct, Max Length: 60ft, Reservations accepted, Elev: 554ft/169m, Tel: 870-492-4191, Nearest town: Mountain Home. GPS: 36.403076, -92.321289

17 • A2 | Cricket Creek

Total sites: 36, RV sites: 36, Elec sites: 36, Central water, Flush toilet, Free showers, RV dump, Tents: $21/RVs: $21-23, Open Apr-Sep, Max Length: 80ft, Reservations accepted, Elev: 1004ft/306m, Tel: 870-426-3331, Nearest town: Branson, MO. GPS: 36.484072, -93.294048

18 • A2 | Dam Site - Quarry Cove

Total sites: 68, RV sites: 68, Elec sites: 68, Central water, Flush toilet, Free showers, RV dump, Tents: $21-22/RVs: $20-22, Group site $65, Open all year, Max Length: 64ft, Reservations accepted, Elev: 417ft/127m, Tel: 870-499-7216, Nearest town: Norfolk. GPS: 36.248176, -92.243665

19 • A2 | Gamaliel

Total sites: 63, RV sites: 63, Elec sites: 63, Central water, Flush toilet, Free showers, RV dump, Tent & RV camping: $20-21, Open Apr-Oct, Max Length: 40ft, Reservations accepted, Elev: 679ft/207m, Tel: 870-467-5680, Nearest town: Gamaliel. GPS: 36.420576, -92.220407

20 • A2 | Henderson

Total sites: 38, RV sites: 38, Elec sites: 38, Water at site, No toilets, No showers, RV dump, Tent & RV camping: $20-21, Open May-Sep, Max Length: 50ft, Reservations accepted, Elev: 577ft/176m, Tel: 870-425-2700, Nearest town: Mountain Home. GPS: 36.375244, -92.233643

21 • A2 | Highway 125

Total sites: 39, RV sites: 39, Elec sites: 39, Central water, Flush toilet, Free showers, RV dump, Tent & RV camping: $21-22, Open Apr-Oct, Max Length: 50ft, Reservations accepted, Elev: 742ft/226m, Tel: 870-436-5711, Nearest town: Yellville. GPS: 36.491666, -92.772944

22 • A2 | Jordan Island (Sand Island)

Dispersed sites, No water, No toilets, Tents only: Free, Boat-in, Elev: 525ft/160m, Tel: 870-425-2700. GPS: 36.273586, -92.197795

23 • A2 | Lakeview

Total sites: 78, RV sites: 78, Elec sites: 78, Central water, Flush toilet, Free showers, RV dump, Tent & RV camping: $21-22, Open all year, Max Length: 42ft, Reservations accepted, Elev: 669ft/204m, Tel: 870-431-8116, Nearest town: Mountain Home. GPS: 36.376709, -92.547119

24 • A2 | Lead Hill

Total sites: 62, RV sites: 62, Elec sites: 62, Central water, Flush toilet, Free showers, RV dump, Tent & RV camping: $20-22, 2 group sites $18-$40, Open Apr-Oct, Max Length: 50ft, Reservations accepted, Elev: 653ft/199m, Tel: 870-422-7555, Nearest town: Lead Hill. GPS: 36.473028, -92.922468

25 • A2 | Panther Bay

Total sites: 15, RV sites: 15, Elec sites: 15, Central water, Flush toilet, Free showers, RV dump, Tent & RV camping: $18, Open May-Sep, Reservations not accepted, Elev: 584ft/178m, Tel: 870-425-2700, Nearest town: Mountain Home. GPS: 36.372070, -92.250977

26 • A2 | Robinson Point

Total sites: 102, RV sites: 102, Elec sites: 102, Central water, Flush toilet, Free showers, RV dump, Tent & RV camping: $20-22, Open Apr-Oct, Max Length: 70ft, Reservations accepted, Elev: 571ft/174m, Tel: 870-492-6853, Nearest town: Mountain Home. GPS: 36.351563, -92.239014

27 • A2 | Tucker Hollow

Total sites: 28, RV sites: 28, Elec sites: 28, Central water, Flush toilet, Free showers, RV dump, Tent & RV camping: $22, Open May-Sep, Max Length: 42ft, Reservations accepted, Elev: 705ft/215m, Tel: 870-436-5622, Nearest town: Lead Hill. GPS: 36.475120, -93.008490

28 • A3 | Kerley Point

Dispersed sites, No water, No toilets, Tent & RV camping: Free, Permit required, Reservations not accepted, Elev: 558ft/170m, Tel: 870-425-2700, Nearest town: Ellizabeth. GPS: 36.306170, -92.156910

29 • B1 | Ashley Creek

Total sites: 10, RV sites: 10, Central water, Vault/pit toilet, No showers, No RV dump, Tent & RV camping: Free, Open all year, Elev: 443ft/135m, Tel: 479-947-2372, Nearest town: Booneville. GPS: 35.107422, -93.709229

30 • B1 | Aux Arc

Total sites: 61, RV sites: 61, Elec sites: 57, Water at site, Flush toilet, Free showers, RV dump, Tents: $10/RVs: $18-20, Open all year,

Max Length: 86ft, Reservations accepted, Elev: 384ft/117m, Tel: 479-667-1100, Nearest town: Ozark. GPS: 35.473445, -93.818772

31 • B1 | Cane Creek
Total sites: 9, RV sites: 9, No water, Vault/pit toilet, No showers, No RV dump, Tent & RV camping: Free, Open Mar-Oct, Reservations not accepted, Elev: 371ft/113m, Tel: 479-968-5008, Nearest town: Scranton. GPS: 35.388359, -93.502854

32 • B1 | Clear Creek
Total sites: 41, RV sites: 41, Elec sites: 25, Central water, Flush toilet, Free showers, RV dump, Tents: $10/RVs: $18, Open all year, Reservations not accepted, Elev: 446ft/136m, Tel: 479-632-4882, Nearest town: Alma. GPS: 35.436905, -94.169732

33 • B1 | Hise Hill
Total sites: 9, RV sites: 9, Central water, Vault/pit toilet, No showers, No RV dump, Tent & RV camping: Free, Reservations not accepted, Elev: 430ft/131m, Tel: 479-947-2372, Nearest town: Waveland. GPS: 35.083449, -93.773086

34 • B1 | Lease Three
Dispersed sites, No water, Vault/pit toilet, Tent & RV camping: Free, Permit required, Reservations not accepted, Elev: 396ft/121m, Tel: 501-324-5551, Nearest town: Waveland. GPS: 35.089622, -93.698288

35 • B1 | Lick Creek
Total sites: 7, RV sites: 7, Central water, Vault/pit toilet, No showers, No RV dump, Tent & RV camping: Free, Reservations not accepted, Elev: 459ft/140m, Tel: 479-947-2372, Nearest town: Waveland. GPS: 35.093015, -93.688040

36 • B1 | Outlet Area
Total sites: 26, RV sites: 26, Elec sites: 26, Water at site, Flush toilet, Free showers, RV dump, Tent & RV camping: $18-20, Open all year, Max Length: 72ft, Reservations accepted, Elev: 413ft/126m, Tel: 479-947-2101, Nearest town: Waveland. GPS: 35.100586, -93.652588

37 • B1 | Persimmion Point #1
Dispersed sites, No water, Vault/pit toilet, Tent & RV camping: Free, Permit required, Reservations not accepted, Elev: 410ft/125m, Tel: 501-324-5551, Nearest town: Magazine. GPS: 35.093176, -93.737098

38 • B1 | Persimmion Point #2
Dispersed sites, No water, Vault/pit toilet, Tent & RV camping: Free, Permit required, Reservations not accepted, Elev: 391ft/119m, Tel: 501-324-5551, Nearest town: Magazine. GPS: 35.104876, -93.739768

39 • B1 | Persimmion Point #3
Dispersed sites, No water, Vault/pit toilet, Tent & RV camping: Free, Permit required, Reservations not accepted, Elev: 419ft/128m, Tel: 501-324-5551, Nearest town: Magazine. GPS: 35.107413, -93.742663

40 • B1 | Persimmion Point #4
Dispersed sites, No water, Vault/pit toilet, Tent & RV camping: Free, Permit required, Reservations not accepted, Elev: 418ft/127m, Tel: 501-324-5551, Nearest town: Magazine. GPS: 35.107288, -93.746492

41 • B1 | River Ridge
Total sites: 18, RV sites: 18, Central water, Vault/pit toilet, No showers, No RV dump, Tent & RV camping: $11, Can park in lot overnight in winter, Open Apr-Sep, Reservations not accepted, Elev: 390ft/119m, Tel: 479-667-2129, Nearest town: Cecil. GPS: 35.443761, -94.071103

42 • B1 | Springhill
Total sites: 47, RV sites: 47, Elec sites: 44, Water at site, Flush toilet, Free showers, RV dump, Tents: $10/RVs: $18-20, Group site: $30, Open all year, Max Length: 113ft, Reservations accepted, Elev: 446ft/136m, Tel: 479-452-4598, Nearest town: Van Buren. GPS: 35.343018, -94.296143

43 • B1 | The Big Island
Dispersed sites, No water, Vault/pit toilet, Tents only: Free, Boat-in, Permit required, Reservations not accepted, Elev: 412ft/126m, Tel: 501-324-5551, Nearest town: Waveland. GPS: 35.106021, -93.675412

44 • B1 | The Slide
Dispersed sites, No water, Vault/pit toilet, Tents only: Free, Hike-in/boat-in, .2 mi, Permit required, Reservations not accepted, Elev: 396ft/121m, Tel: 501-324-5551, Nearest town: Waveland. GPS: 35.101348, -93.675045

45 • B1 | Waveland Park
Total sites: 38, RV sites: 38, Elec sites: 38, Water at site, Flush toilet, Free showers, RV dump, Tent & RV camping: $18-20, Open all year, Max Length: 70ft, Reservations accepted, Elev: 486ft/148m, Tel: 479-947-2102, Nearest town: Waveland. GPS: 35.107910, -93.655518

46 • B2 | Cherokee Park
Total sites: 33, RV sites: 33, Elec sites: 33, Water at site, Flush toilet, Free showers, RV dump, Tent & RV camping: $18-20, Open Mar-Oct, Elev: 308ft/94m, Tel: 501-329-2986, Nearest town: Morrilton. GPS: 35.131263, -92.779845

47 • B2 | Choctaw
Total sites: 146, RV sites: 146, Elec sites: 91, Central water, Flush toilet, Free showers, RV dump, Tents: $16/RVs: $18-20, Open all year, Reservations accepted, Elev: 538ft/164m, Tel: 501-745-8320, Nearest town: Heber Springs. GPS: 35.532959, -92.380371

48 • B2 | Delaware Park
Total sites: 13, RV sites: 13, Central water, Vault/pit toilet, No showers, No RV dump, Tent & RV camping: $10, Open Mar-Oct, Reservations not accepted, Elev: 453ft/138m, Tel: 479-968-5008, Nearest town: Dardanelle. GPS: 35.297363, -93.274658

49 • B2 | Devils Fork
Total sites: 55, RV sites: 55, Elec sites: 55, Central water, Flush toilet, Free showers, RV dump, Tent & RV camping: $18-24,

Open all year, Max Length: 70ft, Reservations accepted, Elev: 489ft/149m, Tel: 501-825-8618, Nearest town: Greers Ferry. GPS: 35.587646, -92.185059

50 • B2 | Mill Creek

Total sites: 39, RV sites: 39, Central water, Vault/pit toilet, No showers, No RV dump, Tent & RV camping: $16, Open May-Sep, Reservations not accepted, Elev: 512ft/156m, Tel: 501-362-2416, Nearest town: Bee Branch. GPS: 35.582514, -92.217921

51 • B2 | Narrows

Total sites: 59, RV sites: 59, Elec sites: 59, Central water, Flush toilet, Free showers, RV dump, Tent & RV camping: $18, Open May-Sep, Max Length: 70ft, Reservations accepted, Elev: 504ft/154m, Tel: 501-825-7602, Nearest town: Greers Ferry. GPS: 35.563965, -92.198242

52 • B2 | Old Post Road Park

Total sites: 40, RV sites: 40, Elec sites: 40, Water at site, Flush toilet, Free showers, RV dump, Tent & RV camping: $20, Open all year, Max Length: 83ft, Reservations accepted, Elev: 338ft/103m, Tel: 479-968-7962, Nearest town: Dardanelle. GPS: 35.247369, -93.162659

53 • B2 | Piney Bay

Total sites: 91, RV sites: 91, Elec sites: 85, Central water, Flush toilet, Free showers, RV dump, Tents: $10/RVs: $16-20, Open Mar-Oct, Max Length: 80ft, Reservations accepted, Elev: 374ft/114m, Tel: 479-885-3029, Nearest town: Russelville. GPS: 35.398163, -93.317234

54 • B2 | Riverview Park

Total sites: 18, RV sites: 18, Elec sites: 8, Water at site, Vault/pit toilet, No showers, No RV dump, Tents: $10/RVs: $18, Open Mar-Oct, Reservations not accepted, Elev: 314ft/96m, Tel: 479-968-5008, Nearest town: Dardanelle. GPS: 35.243783, -93.170413

55 • B2 | Shoal Bay

Total sites: 82, RV sites: 82, Elec sites: 82, Water at site, Flush toilet, Free showers, RV dump, Tent & RV camping: $16-20, Open Mar-Oct, Max Length: 64ft, Reservations accepted, Elev: 423ft/129m, Tel: 479-938-7335, Nearest town: Dardanelle. GPS: 35.308594, -93.429932

56 • B2 | Spadra Park

Total sites: 29, RV sites: 29, Elec sites: 24, Water at site, Flush toilet, Free showers, RV dump, Tents: $12/RVs: $18, Open all year, Reservations not accepted, Elev: 368ft/112m, Tel: 479-754-6438, Nearest town: Clarksville. GPS: 35.425537, -93.473877

57 • B2 | Sugar Loaf

Total sites: 94, RV sites: 94, Elec sites: 57, Central water, Flush toilet, Free showers, RV dump, Tent & RV camping: $16-18, Open May-Sep, Max Length: 88ft, Reservations accepted, Elev: 512ft/156m, Tel: 501-654-2267, Nearest town: Choctaw. GPS: 35.545898, -92.272461

58 • B2 | Sweeden Island Park

Total sites: 28, RV sites: 22, Elec sites: 22, Central water, No toilets, No showers, RV dump, Tents: $10-12/RVs: $16-18, Open all year, Max Length: 30ft, Elev: 354ft/108m, Tel: 870-246-5501, Nearest town: Atkins. GPS: 35.168945, -93.011475

59 • B2 | Toad Suck Park

Total sites: 48, RV sites: 48, Elec sites: 48, Water at site, Flush toilet, Free showers, RV dump, Tent & RV camping: $18-20, Open all year, Max Length: 85ft, Reservations accepted, Elev: 285ft/87m, Tel: 501-759-2005, Nearest town: Conway. GPS: 35.075928, -92.545166

60 • B3 | Cherokee

Total sites: 33, RV sites: 33, Elec sites: 17, Water at site, No toilets, No showers, RV dump, Tent & RV camping: $16-18, Open May-Sep, Reservations not accepted, Elev: 512ft/156m, Tel: 501-362-2416, Nearest town: Greers Ferry. GPS: 35.554443, -92.076416

61 • B3 | Cove Creek

Total sites: 63, RV sites: 63, Elec sites: 31, Central water, Flush toilet, Free showers, RV dump, Tents: $16/RVs: $18-24, Open May-Sep, Reservations not accepted, Elev: 495ft/151m, Tel: 501-362-2416, Nearest town: Heber Springs. GPS: 35.463135, -92.152344

62 • B3 | Dam Site

Total sites: 252, RV sites: 252, Elec sites: 148, Water at site, Flush toilet, Free showers, RV dump, Tents: $16/RVs: $18-24, Open all year, Max Length: 120ft, Reservations accepted, Elev: 548ft/167m, Tel: 501-362-5233, Nearest town: Heber Springs. GPS: 35.528813, -92.000547

63 • B3 | Heber Springs

Total sites: 136, RV sites: 136, Elec sites: 101, Central water, Flush toilet, Free showers, RV dump, Tents: $16/RVs: $18-20, Open Mar-Oct, Max Length: 100ft, Reservations accepted, Elev: 466ft/142m, Tel: 501-250-0485, Nearest town: Heber Springs. GPS: 35.503906, -92.066650

64 • B3 | Hill Creek

Total sites: 40, RV sites: 40, Elec sites: 30, Central water, Flush toilet, Free showers, RV dump, Tents: $16/RVs: $16-18, Open May-Sep, Max Length: 72ft, Reservations accepted, Elev: 554ft/169m, Tel: 870-948-2419, Nearest town: Greers Ferry. GPS: 35.611328, -92.149170

65 • B3 | John F Kennedy

Total sites: 68, RV sites: 68, Elec sites: 68, Central water, Flush toilet, Free showers, RV dump, Tent & RV camping: $18-24, Open all year, Max Length: 80ft, Reservations accepted, Elev: 400ft/122m, Tel: 501-250-0481, Nearest town: Heber Springs. GPS: 35.516357, -91.995850

66 • B3 | Old Hwy 25

Total sites: 120, RV sites: 120, Elec sites: 84, Central water, Flush toilet, Free showers, RV dump, Tents: $16/RVs: $18-20, Group site $150, Open Mar-Oct, Max Length: 96ft, Reservations accepted, Elev: 561ft/171m, Tel: 501-250-0483, Nearest town: Heber Springs. GPS: 35.538280, -92.017940

67 • B3 | Shiloh

Total sites: 116, RV sites: 116, Elec sites: 60, Central water, Flush toilet, Free showers, RV dump, Tent & RV camping: $16-18,

Group site $150, Open May-Sep, Max Length: 90ft, Reservations accepted, Elev: 489ft/149m, Tel: 501-825-8619, Nearest town: Greers Ferry. GPS: 35.536621, -92.146240

68 • C1 | Arrowhead Point

Total sites: 23, RV sites: 23, Central water, Vault/pit toilet, Tent & RV camping: $6, Nov-Feb: Free, Open Mar-Nov, Max Length: 35ft, Reservations not accepted, Elev: 633ft/193m, Tel: 870-285-2151, Nearest town: Kirby. GPS: 34.244629, -93.801025

69 • C1 | Bear Creek

Total sites: 19, RV sites: 9, Central water, Vault/pit toilet, No showers, No RV dump, Tent & RV camping: $5, Nov-Feb: Free, Open all year, Reservations not accepted, Elev: 636ft/194m, Tel: 870-285-2151, Nearest town: Kirby. GPS: 34.237305, -93.667969

70 • C1 | Bellah Mine

Total sites: 24, RV sites: 24, Elec sites: 24, Central water, Flush toilet, Free showers, RV dump, Tent & RV camping: $16-18, Open all year, Max Length: 120ft, Reservations accepted, Elev: 495ft/151m, Tel: 870-386 7511, Nearest town: DeQueen. GPS: 34.127437, -94.398739

71 • C1 | Big Coon Creek

Total sites: 31, RV sites: 31, Elec sites: 31, Water at site, Flush toilet, Free showers, RV dump, Tents: $16-18/RVs: $18-24, Open all year, Max Length: 132ft, Reservations accepted, Elev: 551ft/168m, Tel: 870-584-4161, Nearest town: Wickes. GPS: 34.221617, -94.243264

72 • C1 | Blue Ridge

Total sites: 22, RV sites: 22, Elec sites: 22, Water at site, Flush toilet, Free showers, No RV dump, Tent & RV camping: $14, $10 Nov-Feb, Open all year, Reservations not accepted, Elev: 614ft/187m, Tel: 870-286-2346, Nearest town: Dierks. GPS: 34.193791, -94.094561

73 • C1 | Buckhorn

Total sites: 9, RV sites: 4, No water, Vault/pit toilet, No showers, No RV dump, Tent & RV camping: $5, Nov-Feb: Free, Open all year, Reservations not accepted, Elev: 620ft/189m, Tel: 870-285-2151, Nearest town: Murfreesboro. GPS: 34.178600, -93.730700

74 • C1 | Cossatot Reefs

Total sites: 30, RV sites: 28, Elec sites: 28, Central water, Flush toilet, Free showers, RV dump, Tent & RV camping: $16-18, Walk-to sites, 2 walk-in sites, Open all year, Max Length: 78ft, Reservations accepted, Elev: 476ft/145m, Tel: 870-584-4161, Nearest town: Gillham. GPS: 34.203705, -94.227408

75 • C1 | Cowhide Cove

Total sites: 50, RV sites: 48, Elec sites: 48, Central water, Flush toilet, Free showers, RV dump, Tents: $16/RVs: $20-22, Open Mar-Dec, Max Length: 54ft, Reservations accepted, Elev: 604ft/184m, Tel: 870-285-2151, Nearest town: Kirby. GPS: 34.174817, -93.667401

76 • C1 | Dam Area

Total sites: 24, RV sites: 24, Elec sites: 16, Central water, Flush toilet, Free showers, RV dump, Tents: $10/RVs: $10-18, Also cabins, Open Mar-Oct, Reservations accepted, Elev: 742ft/226m, Tel: 870-285-2151, Nearest town: Murfreesboro. GPS: 34.149900, -93.713600

77 • C1 | Denby Point

Total sites: 67, RV sites: 58, Elec sites: 58, Central water, Flush toilet, Free showers, RV dump, Tents: $14-16/RVs: $18-30, 2 group sites $60-$65, Open Mar-Oct, Max Length: 70ft, Reservations accepted, Elev: 604ft/184m, Tel: 501-767-2108, Nearest town: Mount Ida. GPS: 34.552246, -93.494141

78 • C1 | Highway 27

Total sites: 18, RV sites: 18, Elec sites: 18, Central water, Flush toilet, RV dump, Tents: $4/RVs: $12, Open all year, Reservations not accepted, Elev: 623ft/190m, Nearest town: Story. GPS: 34.625636, -93.541066

79 • C1 | Horseshoe Bend

Total sites: 11, RV sites: 11, Elec sites: 11, Water at site, Flush toilet, Free showers, Tent & RV camping: $14, Open all year, Reservations not accepted, Elev: 469ft/143m, Tel: 870-286-2346, Nearest town: Dierck. GPS: 34.139686, -94.093735

80 • C1 | Jefferson Ridge COE

Total sites: 85, RV sites: 85, Elec sites: 85, Water at site, Flush toilet, Free showers, RV dump, Tent & RV camping: $16-18, Open all year, Max Length: 124ft, Reservations accepted, Elev: 581ft/177m, Tel: 870-286-3214, Nearest town: Dierks. GPS: 34.147892, -94.123704

81 • C1 | Kirby Landing

Total sites: 105, RV sites: 105, Elec sites: 105, Water at site, Flush toilet, Free showers, RV dump, Tent & RV camping: $20-22, Open all year, Max Length: 75ft, Reservations accepted, Elev: 594ft/181m, Tel: 870-285-2151, Nearest town: Kirby. GPS: 34.231689, -93.693848

82 • C1 | Laurel Creek

Total sites: 24, RV sites: 12, No water, Vault/pit toilet, No showers, No RV dump, Tent & RV camping: $5, Free Nov-Feb, Open all year, Reservations not accepted, Elev: 614ft/187m, Tel: 870-285-2151, Nearest town: Kirby. GPS: 34.187012, -93.706787

83 • C1 | Little Coon Creek

Total sites: 10, RV sites: 10, Elec sites: 10, Water at site, Flush toilet, Free showers, No RV dump, Tent & RV camping: $14-16, $10 Nov-Feb, Open all year, Reservations not accepted, Elev: 614ft/187m, Tel: 870-584-4161, Nearest town: Wickes. GPS: 34.229091, -94.257018

84 • C1 | Oak Grove

Total sites: 36, RV sites: 36, Elec sites: 36, Central water, Flush toilet, Free showers, RV dump, Tent & RV camping: $14-18, Open all year, Max Length: 122ft, Reservations accepted, Elev: 554ft/169m, Tel: 870-584-4161, Nearest town: DeQueen. GPS: 34.098202, -94.394404

85 • C1 | Parker Creek

Total sites: 63, RV sites: 60, Elec sites: 49, Central water, Flush toilet, Free showers, RV dump, Tents: $16/RVs: $16-22, Open

Mar-Dec, Max Length: 50ft, Reservations accepted, Elev: 584ft/178m, Tel: 870-285-2151, Nearest town: Murfreesboro. GPS: 34.158691, -93.739502

86 • C1 | Pikeville

Total sites: 12, RV sites: 12, No water, Vault/pit toilet, Tent & RV camping: Free, Open all year, Reservations not accepted, Elev: 591ft/180m, Tel: 870-285-2151, Nearest town: Murfreesboro. GPS: 34.169189, -93.729248

87 • C1 | Pine Ridge

Total sites: 45, RV sites: 45, Elec sites: 17, Central water, Flush toilet, Free showers, RV dump, Tent & RV camping: $14-18, Open all year, Max Length: 84ft, Reservations accepted, Elev: 495ft/151m, Tel: 870-584-4161, Nearest town: DeQueen. GPS: 34.104541, -94.397043

88 • C1 | Rock Creek

Total sites: 14, RV sites: 0, No water, Vault/pit toilet, Tents only: Free, Open all year, Reservations not accepted, Elev: 571ft/174m, Tel: 870-285-2151, Nearest town: Murfreesboro. GPS: 34.208733, -93.759498

89 • C1 | Self Creek

Total sites: 76, RV sites: 76, Elec sites: 41, Central water, Flush toilet, Free showers, RV dump, Tent & RV camping: $10-18, Also cabins, Reservations not accepted, Elev: 577ft/176m, Tel: 870-285-2151, Nearest town: Daisy. GPS: 34.236330, -93.758500

90 • C1 | Star of the West

Total sites: 21, RV sites: 21, Central water, Vault/pit toilet, No showers, No RV dump, Tent & RV camping: $5, Nov-Feb: Free, Open all year, Reservations not accepted, Elev: 614ft/187m, Tel: 870-285-2151, Nearest town: Kirby. GPS: 34.239014, -93.825195

91 • C1 | Twin Creek

Total sites: 15, RV sites: 15, Central water, Flush toilet, No showers, No RV dump, Tent & RV camping: $12-16, Open all year, Max Length: 20ft, Reservations not accepted, Elev: 623ft/190m, Tel: 501-767-2101, Nearest town: Mount Ida. GPS: 34.549525, -93.510653

92 • C1 | Washita

Total sites: 70, RV sites: 70, No water, Vault/pit toilet, Tent & RV camping: Free, Open all year, Reservations not accepted, Elev: 614ft/187m, Tel: 501-767-2101, Nearest town: Story. GPS: 34.649691, -93.531228

93 • C2 | Alpine Ridge

Total sites: 49, RV sites: 49, Elec sites: 49, Central water, Flush toilet, Free showers, RV dump, Tent & RV camping: $20, Open Mar-Nov, Max Length: 66ft, Reservations accepted, Elev: 463ft/141m, Tel: 870-246-5501, Nearest town: Arkadelphia. GPS: 34.259677, -93.235379

94 • C2 | Anderson Branch

Dispersed sites, No water, Vault/pit toilet, Tent & RV camping: Free, Permit required, No large RVs, Reservations not accepted, Elev: 367ft/112m, Tel: 479-272-4324, Nearest town: Plainview. GPS: 34.955888, -93.232761

95 • C2 | Arlie Moore

Total sites: 87, RV sites: 68, Elec sites: 87, Central water, Flush toilet, Free showers, RV dump, Tent & RV camping: $16, Open all year, Max Length: 60ft, Reservations accepted, Elev: 564ft/172m, Tel: 870-246-5501, Nearest town: Arkadelphia. GPS: 34.273574, -93.197058

96 • C2 | Avant

Total sites: 70, RV sites: 70, No water, Vault/pit toilet, Tent & RV camping: Free, Open all year, Elev: 650ft/198m, Tel: 501-767-2101. GPS: 34.636579, -93.383142

97 • C2 | Big Fir

Total sites: 17, RV sites: 17, Central water, Vault/pit toilet, No showers, No RV dump, Tent & RV camping: $10-14, Open all year, Reservations not accepted, Elev: 633ft/193m, Tel: 501-767-2101, Nearest town: Mount Ida. GPS: 34.605872, -93.413842

98 • C2 | Brady Mountain

Total sites: 74, RV sites: 57, Elec sites: 57, Central water, Flush toilet, Free showers, RV dump, Tents: $16/RVs: $20-30, Open Mar-Sep, Max Length: 70ft, Reservations accepted, Elev: 591ft/180m, Tel: 501-767-2108, Nearest town: Hot Springs. GPS: 34.588135, -93.264893

99 • C2 | Buckville

Total sites: 30, RV sites: 30, Central water, Vault/pit toilet, No showers, No RV dump, Tent & RV camping: Free, Open all year, Max Length: 20ft, Reservations not accepted, Elev: 663ft/202m, Tel: 501-767-2101, Nearest town: Avant. GPS: 34.612958, -93.342172

100 • C2 | Caddo Drive

Total sites: 72, RV sites: 45, Elec sites: 45, Central water, Flush toilet, Free showers, RV dump, Tent & RV camping: $16, Open Mar-Oct, Max Length: 58ft, Reservations accepted, Elev: 450ft/137m, Tel: 870-246-5501, Nearest town: Arkadelphia. GPS: 34.258057, -93.194580

101 • C2 | Carter Cove

Total sites: 34, RV sites: 34, Elec sites: 34, Central water, Flush toilet, Free showers, RV dump, Tent & RV camping: $18-20, Open all year, Max Length: 75ft, Reservations accepted, Elev: 383ft/117m, Tel: 479-272-4983, Nearest town: Plainview. GPS: 34.961499, -93.238592

102 • C2 | Casa Camp

Dispersed sites, No water, Vault/pit toilet, Tent & RV camping: Free, Permit required, No large RVs, Reservations not accepted, Elev: 585ft/178m, Tel: 479-272-4324, Nearest town: Plainview. GPS: 34.929512, -93.332822

103 • C2 | Cedar Fourche

Total sites: 30, RV sites: 30, No water, Vault/pit toilet, No showers, Tent & RV camping: Free, Open all year, Reservations not accepted, Elev: 614ft/187m, Tel: 501-767-2101, Nearest town: Lena. GPS: 34.662625, -93.283621

104 • C2 | County Line

Total sites: 21, RV sites: 21, Elec sites: 21, Central water, Flush toilet, Free showers, RV dump, Tent & RV camping: $16-18, Open Mar-Oct, Max Length: 30ft, Reservations not accepted, Elev: 430ft/131m, Tel: 479-272-4945, Nearest town: Plainview. GPS: 34.962830, -93.185000

105 • C2 | Crystal Springs

Total sites: 74, RV sites: 63, Elec sites: 63, Water at site, Flush toilet, Free showers, RV dump, Tents: $14/RVs: $22-30, Group site: $80, Open all year, Max Length: 78ft, Reservations accepted, Elev: 607ft/185m, Tel: 501-767-2108, Nearest town: Hot Springs. GPS: 34.542433, -93.353141

106 • C2 | Cypress Creek

Total sites: 9, RV sites: 9, Central water, Vault/pit toilet, No showers, No RV dump, Tent & RV camping: Free, Open Mar-Oct, Max Length: 40ft, Elev: 331ft/101m, Tel: 501-329-2986, Nearest town: Houston. GPS: 35.068675, -92.717199

107 • C2 | Edgewood

Total sites: 51, RV sites: 45, Elec sites: 49, Central water, Flush toilet, Free showers, RV dump, Tent & RV camping: $20, Open Mar-Oct, Max Length: 84ft, Reservations accepted, Elev: 466ft/142m, Tel: 870-246-5501, Nearest town: Arkadelphia. GPS: 34.254966, -93.183041

108 • C2 | Hog Farm

Dispersed sites, No water, Vault/pit toilet, Tent & RV camping: Free, Permit required, No large RVs, Reservations not accepted, Elev: 391ft/119m, Tel: 479-272-4324, Nearest town: Plainview. GPS: 34.924933, -93.451124

109 • C2 | Iron Mountain

Total sites: 69, RV sites: 69, Elec sites: 69, Central water, Flush toilet, Free showers, RV dump, Tent & RV camping: $16, Open May-Sep, Max Length: 85ft, Reservations accepted, Elev: 518ft/158m, Tel: 870-246-5501, Nearest town: Arkadelphia. GPS: 34.227303, -93.126075

110 • C2 | Irons Fork

Total sites: 5, RV sites: 5, No water, Vault/pit toilet, Tent & RV camping: Free, Open all year, Reservations not accepted, Elev: 627ft/191m, Tel: 501-984-5313, Nearest town: Story. GPS: 34.686299, -93.372717

111 • C2 | Joplin

Total sites: 59, RV sites: 36, Elec sites: 57, Central water, Flush toilet, Free showers, RV dump, Tents: $16-18/RVs: $16-24, Not recommended for large RVs, Open all year, Max Length: 90ft, Reservations accepted, Elev: 610ft/186m, Tel: 501-767-2108, Nearest town: Mount Ida. GPS: 34.575928, -93.440918

112 • C2 | Lenox Marcus

Dispersed sites, Central water, Vault/pit toilet, No showers, No RV dump, Tent & RV camping: Free, Open all year, Reservations not accepted, Elev: 433ft/132m, Tel: 870-246-5501, Nearest town: Lambert. GPS: 34.267116, -93.217566

113 • C2 | Little Fir

Total sites: 29, RV sites: 29, Elec sites: 29, Water at site, Flush toilet, Pay showers, RV dump, Tent & RV camping: $18, Group site $30, Open all year, Elev: 600ft/183m, Tel: 501-767-2101, Nearest town: Mount Ida. GPS: 34.633182, -93.472326

114 • C2 | Maumelle Park

Total sites: 98, RV sites: 98, Elec sites: 98, Water at site, Flush toilet, Free showers, RV dump, Tent & RV camping: $22-26, Open all year, Max Length: 100ft, Reservations accepted, Elev: 253ft/77m, Tel: 501-868-9477, Nearest town: Little Rock. GPS: 34.832119, -92.433307

115 • C2 | Norman Hill

Dispersed sites, No water, Vault/pit toilet, Tent & RV camping: Free, Permit required, No large RVs, Reservations not accepted, Elev: 370ft/113m, Tel: 479-272-4324, Nearest town: Plainview. GPS: 34.976393, -93.336502

116 • C2 | Ozan Point

Total sites: 50, RV sites: 50, Central water, Flush toilet, No showers, No RV dump, Tent & RV camping: $10, Max Length: 15ft, Reservations not accepted, Elev: 440ft/134m, Tel: 870-246-5501, x4005, Nearest town: Bismarck. GPS: 34.238632, -93.205191

117 • C2 | Point Cedar

Total sites: 62, RV sites: 62, Central water, Flush toilet, No showers, No RV dump, Tent & RV camping: $10, Reservations not accepted, Elev: 459ft/140m, Tel: 870-246-5501, x4005, Nearest town: Bismarck. GPS: 34.281738, -93.289795

118 • C2 | Quarry Cove

Total sites: 31, RV sites: 31, Elec sites: 31, Central water, Flush toilet, Free showers, RV dump, Tent & RV camping: $18-20, Open Mar-Oct, Max Length: 70ft, Reservations accepted, Elev: 433ft/132m, Tel: 479-272-4233, Nearest town: Plainview. GPS: 34.957233, -93.165274

119 • C2 | River Road

Total sites: 21, RV sites: 21, Elec sites: 21, Central water, Flush toilet, Free showers, RV dump, Tent & RV camping: $17-20, Open all year, Max Length: 78ft, Reservations accepted, Elev: 390ft/119m, Tel: 479-272-4835, Nearest town: Ola. GPS: 34.950415, -93.157334

120 • C2 | Rover Landing

Dispersed sites, No water, Vault/pit toilet, Tent & RV camping: Free, Permit required, No large RVs, Reservations not accepted, Elev: 367ft/112m, Tel: 479-272-4324, Nearest town: Plainview. GPS: 34.926247, -93.383203

121 • C2 | Shouse Ford

Total sites: 100, RV sites: 100, Elec sites: 100, Central water, Flush toilet, Free showers, RV dump, Tent & RV camping: $16, Open May-Sep, Max Length: 72ft, Reservations accepted, Elev: 456ft/139m, Tel: 870-246-5501, Nearest town: Bismarck. GPS: 34.289551, -93.268066

122 • C2 | Spillway Group

Total sites: 6, Central water, Vault/pit toilet, Group site: $30, Reservations made at local USACE office, Open Mar-Oct, Reservations accepted, Elev: 594ft/181m, Tel: 501-767-2101. GPS: 34.570124, -93.216745

123 • C2 | Stephens Park

Total sites: 9, RV sites: 9, Elec sites: 9, Central water, No toilets, No showers, No RV dump, Tent & RV camping: $30, 9 full hookups, Open all year, Max Length: 60ft, Reservations accepted, Elev: 430ft/131m, Tel: 501-767-2101, Nearest town: Hot Springs. GPS: 34.568480, -93.192180

124 • C2 | Sunlight Bay

Total sites: 29, RV sites: 29, Elec sites: 29, Central water, Flush toilet, Free showers, RV dump, Tent & RV camping: $18-20, Open Mar-Nov, Max Length: 72ft, Reservations accepted, Elev: 407ft/124m, Tel: 479-272-4234, Nearest town: Plainview. GPS: 34.954834, -93.304199

125 • C2 | The Big Rock

Dispersed sites, No water, Vault/pit toilet, Tent & RV camping: Free, Permit required, No large RVs, Reservations not accepted, Elev: 398ft/121m, Tel: 479-272-4324, Nearest town: Plainview. GPS: 34.909212, -93.454788

126 • C2 | Tompkins Bend

Total sites: 74, RV sites: 63, Elec sites: 63, Water at site, Flush toilet, Free showers, RV dump, Tents: $14-16/RVs: $22-30, Open all year, Max Length: 70ft, Reservations accepted, Elev: 597ft/182m, Tel: 501-767-2108, Nearest town: Mount Ida. GPS: 34.573242, -93.468994

127 • C2 | Twin Lakes

Dispersed sites, No water, Vault/pit toilet, Tent & RV camping: Free, Permit required, No large RVs, Reservations not accepted, Elev: 386ft/118m, Tel: 479-272-4324, Nearest town: Plainview. GPS: 34.914943, -93.440092

128 • C2 | Wards Crossing

Dispersed sites, No water, Vault/pit toilet, Tent & RV camping: Free, Permit required, No large RVs, Reservations not accepted, Elev: 345ft/105m, Tel: 479-272-4324, Nearest town: Plainview. GPS: 34.944049, -93.327622

129 • C3 | Big Bayou Meto

Dispersed sites, No water, Vault/pit toilet, Tent & RV camping: Free, Reservations not accepted, Elev: 171ft/52m, Tel: 870-548-2291, Nearest town: Gillett. GPS: 34.081947, -91.441684

130 • C3 | Little Bayou Meto

Dispersed sites, No water, Vault/pit toilet, Tent & RV camping: Free, Open all year, Reservations not accepted, Elev: 181ft/55m, Tel: 870-548-2291, Nearest town: Reydell. GPS: 34.134197, -91.579016

131 • C3 | Merrisach Lake Park

Total sites: 67, RV sites: 67, Elec sites: 62, Water at site, Flush toilet, Free showers, RV dump, Tents: $11-12/RVs: $16-19, Open all year, Max Length: 103ft, Reservations accepted, Elev: 190ft/58m, Tel: 870-548-2291, Nearest town: Dumas. GPS: 34.030029, -91.266357

132 • C3 | Moore Bayou

Dispersed sites, No water, Vault/pit toilet, Tent & RV camping: Free, Open all year, Reservations not accepted, Elev: 164ft/50m, Tel: 870-548-2291, Nearest town: Gillett. GPS: 34.025611, -91.362056

133 • C3 | Notrebes Bend

Total sites: 30, RV sites: 30, Elec sites: 30, Water at site, Flush toilet, Free showers, RV dump, Tent & RV camping: $19, Open Mar-Oct, Max Length: 50ft, Reservations accepted, Elev: 187ft/57m, Tel: 870-548-2291, Nearest town: Gillett. GPS: 33.987793, -91.309326

134 • C3 | Pendleton Bend

Total sites: 31, RV sites: 31, Elec sites: 31, Water at site, Flush toilet, Free showers, RV dump, Tent & RV camping: $16-19, Open all year, Max Length: 115ft, Reservations accepted, Elev: 190ft/58m, Tel: 870-548-2291, Nearest town: Dumas. GPS: 33.989323, -91.358857

135 • C3 | Rising Star

Total sites: 25, RV sites: 25, Elec sites: 25, Water at site, Flush toilet, Free showers, RV dump, Tent & RV camping: $19, Open Mar-Oct, Max Length: 90ft, Reservations accepted, Elev: 203ft/62m, Tel: 870-534-0451, Nearest town: Grady. GPS: 34.168826, -91.737454

136 • C3 | Tar Camp

Total sites: 53, RV sites: 53, Elec sites: 45, Water at site, Flush toilet, Free showers, RV dump, Tents: $9/RVs: $19, Open Mar-Oct, Max Length: 98ft, Reservations accepted, Elev: 226ft/69m, Tel: 501-397-5101, Nearest town: Redfield. GPS: 34.450065, -92.111506

137 • C3 | Trulock

Dispersed sites, Central water, Vault/pit toilet, No showers, No RV dump, Tent & RV camping: Free, Open Mar-Oct, Elev: 223ft/68m, Tel: 870-534-0451, Nearest town: Pine Bluff. GPS: 34.210039, -91.832913

138 • C3 | Wilbur D Mills

Total sites: 21, RV sites: 21, Elec sites: 21, Water at site, Flush toilet, Free showers, RV dump, Tent & RV camping: $16, Open Mar-Oct, Max Length: 60ft, Reservations accepted, Elev: 148ft/45m, Tel: 870-548-2291, Nearest town: Dumas. GPS: 33.977124, -91.305895

139 • C3 | Wild Goose Bayou

Dispersed sites, No water, Vault/pit toilet, Tent & RV camping: Free, Reservations not accepted, Elev: 142ft/43m, Tel: 870-548-2291, Nearest town: Tichnor. GPS: 34.021014, -91.188577

140 • C3 | Willow Beach

Total sites: 23, RV sites: 23, Elec sites: 23, Water at site, Flush toilet, Free showers, RV dump, Tent & RV camping: $19, Open all year, Max Length: 84ft, Reservations accepted, Elev: 246ft/75m, Tel: 501-534-0451, Nearest town: Scott. GPS: 34.701161, -92.138878

141 • D1 | Beard's Bluff

Total sites: 23, RV sites: 23, Elec sites: 21, Water at site, Flush toilet, Free showers, RV dump, Tents: $12/RVs: $15-21, Open all year, Reservations accepted, Elev: 377ft/115m, Tel: 870-388-9556, Nearest town: Ashdown. GPS: 33.704346, -93.939209

142 • D1 | Beard's Lake

Total sites: 8, RV sites: 5, Elec sites: 5, Water at site, Flush toilet, Free showers, No RV dump, Tents: $10/RVs: $13, $10 Nov-Feb w/ no hookups, Open all year, Reservations not accepted, Elev: 262ft/80m, Tel: 870-898-3343, Nearest town: Ashdown. GPS: 33.697394, -93.942125

143 • D1 | Cottonshed Landing

Total sites: 43, RV sites: 43, Elec sites: 43, Water at site, Flush toilet, Free showers, RV dump, Tent & RV camping: $15, Open all year, Max Length: 75ft, Reservations accepted, Elev: 305ft/93m, Tel: 870-898-3343, Nearest town: Mineral Springs. GPS: 33.792236, -93.965088

144 • D1 | Paraloma Landing

Total sites: 34, RV sites: 34, Elec sites: 34, Water at site, Flush toilet, Free showers, RV dump, Tent & RV camping: $13, Open Mar-Oct, Reservations not accepted, Elev: 322ft/98m, Tel: 870-898-3343, Nearest town: Mineral Springs. GPS: 33.786865, -94.009766

145 • D1 | River Run East

Total sites: 8, RV sites: 8, No water, Vault/pit toilet, Tent & RV camping: $8, Open all year, Reservations not accepted, Elev: 259ft/79m, Tel: 870-898-3343, Nearest town: Ashdown. GPS: 33.690858, -93.962575

146 • D1 | River Run West

Total sites: 4, RV sites: 4, No water, Vault/pit toilet, Tent & RV camping: $8, Open all year, Reservations not accepted, Elev: 259ft/79m, Tel: 870-898-3343, Nearest town: Ashdown. GPS: 33.691306, -93.966513

147 • D1 | Saratoga Landing

Total sites: 17, RV sites: 17, Elec sites: 17, Water at site, Flush toilet, Free showers, No RV dump, Tent & RV camping: $13, Open Mar-Oct, Reservations not accepted, Elev: 308ft/94m, Tel: 870-898-3343, Nearest town: Saratoga. GPS: 33.738913, -93.919854

148 • D1 | White Cliffs

Total sites: 25, RV sites: 25, Elec sites: 25, Water at site, Flush toilet, Free showers, RV dump, Tent & RV camping: $15-21, Open all year, Max Length: 60ft, Reservations accepted, Elev: 335ft/102m, Tel: 870-898-3343, Nearest town: Mineral Springs. GPS: 33.760682, -94.058544

149 • D2 | Lock and Dam No. 8

Total sites: 7, RV sites: 7, No water, Vault/pit toilet, Tent & RV camping: Free, Open all year, Reservations not accepted, Elev: 95ft/29m, Tel: 601-631-5000, Nearest town: El Dorado. GPS: 33.300169, -92.461527

California

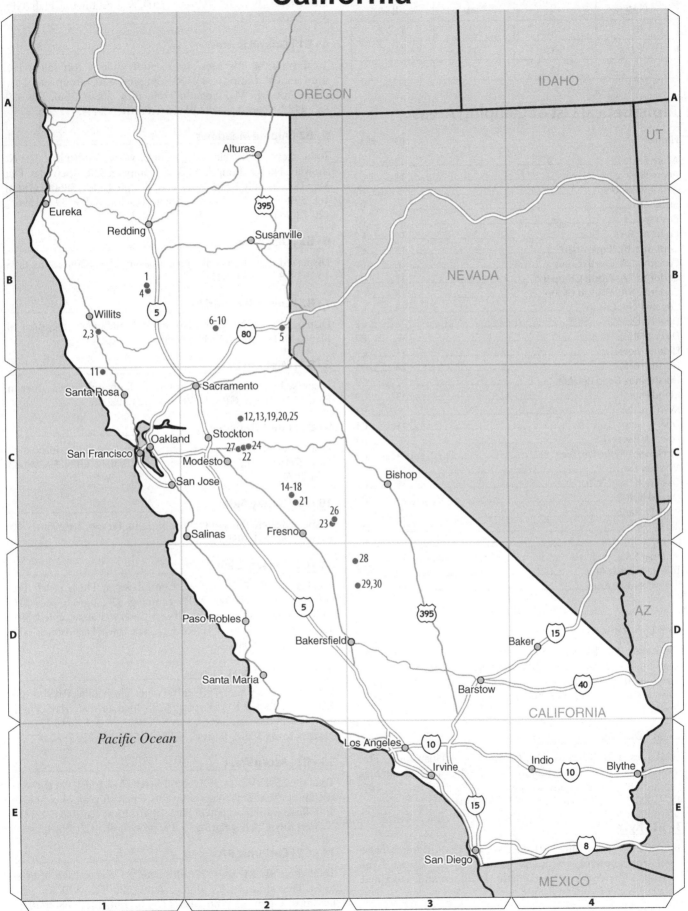

Map	ID	Map	ID
B1	1-4	C2	12-27
B2	5-10	D3	28-30
C1	11		

Alphabetical List of Camping Areas

Name	ID	Map
Acorn East	12	C2
Acorn West	13	C2
Alpine Meadows	5	B2
Buckhorn	1	B1
Bushay	2	B1
Codorniz RA	14	C2
Codorniz RA - Equestrian	15	C2
Codorniz RA - North Group A	16	C2
Codorniz RA - North Group B	17	C2
Codorniz RA - Wildcat Group	18	C2
Coyote Point Group	19	C2
Deer Flat	20	C2
Dixon Hill	6	B2
Hidden View	21	C2
Horse Creek	28	D3
Horsheshoe Road Rec Area	22	C2
Island Park	23	C2
Kyen	3	B1
Liberty Glen	11	C1
Lower Missouri Bar	7	B2
McHenry Avenue Rec Area	24	C2
Missouri Bar	8	B2
Oak Knoll	25	C2
Orland Buttes	4	B1
Point Defiance	9	B2
Rocky Hill	29	D3
Sunny Side	10	B2
Trimmer RA	26	C2
Tule Recreation Area	30	D3
Valley Oak Rec Area	27	C2

1 • B1 | Buckhorn

Total sites: 92, RV sites: 87, Central water, Flush toilet, Free showers, RV dump, Tent & RV camping: $18-20, Also walk-to sites, Open all year, Max Length: 150ft, Reservations accepted, Elev: 508ft/155m, Tel: 530-865-4781, Nearest town: Orland. GPS: 39.811426, -122.366035

2 • B1 | Bushay

Total sites: 166, RV sites: 163, Central water, Flush toilet, Free showers, RV dump, Tents: $25-30/RVs: $25-35, Open all year, Max Length: 78ft, Reservations accepted, Elev: 856ft/261m, Tel: 707-467-4200, Nearest town: Ukiah. GPS: 39.230469, -123.166016

3 • B1 | Kyen

Total sites: 101, RV sites: 101, Elec sites: 1, Central water, Flush toilet, Free showers, RV dump, Tents: $25/RVs: $25-30, 1 full hookups, Open Apr-Sep, Max Length: 35ft, Reservations accepted, Elev: 784ft/239m, Tel: 707-467-4200, Nearest town: Ukiah. GPS: 39.235107, -123.177979

4 • B1 | Orland Buttes

Total sites: 34, RV sites: 34, Central water, Flush toilet, Free showers, RV dump, Tent & RV camping: $20, Group site: $130, Open Apr-Sep, Max Length: 115ft, Elev: 508ft/155m, Tel: 530-865-4781, Nearest town: Orland. GPS: 39.772444, -122.352875

5 • B2 | Alpine Meadows

Total sites: 25, RV sites: 25, Central water, Vault/pit toilet, No showers, No RV dump, Tent & RV camping: $20, Open May-Oct, Max Length: 30ft, Reservations not accepted, Elev: 5860ft/1786m, Tel: 530-587-8113, Nearest town: Truckee. GPS: 39.321596, -120.122111

6 • B2 | Dixon Hill

Dispersed sites, Tents only: Free, Boat-in, Elev: 620ft/189m. GPS: 39.293818, -121.214827

7 • B2 | Lower Missouri Bar

Dispersed sites, No water, No toilets, Tents only: Free, Boat-in, Elev: 620ft/189m. GPS: 39.299955, -121.206731

8 • B2 | Missouri Bar

Dispersed sites, No water, No toilets, Tents only: Free, Boat-in, Elev: 551ft/168m. GPS: 39.301913, -121.202006

9 • B2 | Point Defiance

Dispersed sites, No water, Tents only: Free, Hike-in/boat-in, Elev: 571ft/174m, Nearest town: Grass Valley. GPS: 39.298063, -121.207337

10 • B2 | Sunny Side

Dispersed sites, Tents only: Free, Boat-in, Elev: 673ft/205m. GPS: 39.303168, -121.199032

11 • C1 | Liberty Glen

Total sites: 96, RV sites: 96, Central water, Flush toilet, Free showers, RV dump, Tent & RV camping: $25, 2 group sites: $50-$100, 1 equestrian site, Open all year, Reservations accepted, Elev: 1076ft/328m, Tel: 707-431-4533, Nearest town: Healdsburg. GPS: 38.716212, -123.060627

12 • C2 | Acorn East

Total sites: 70, RV sites: 70, Central water, Flush toilet, Pay showers, RV dump, Tent & RV camping: $20, Open all year, Max Length: 40ft, Reservations accepted, Elev: 732ft/223m, Tel: 209-772-1343, Nearest town: Valley Springs. GPS: 38.175208, -120.793548

13 • C2 | Acorn West

Total sites: 59, RV sites: 59, Central water, Flush toilet, Pay showers, RV dump, Tent & RV camping: $20, Open all year, Max Length: 40ft, Reservations accepted, Elev: 705ft/215m, Tel: 209-772-1343, Nearest town: Valley Springs. GPS: 38.175341, -120.798682

14 • C2 | Codorniz RA

Total sites: 81, RV sites: 77, Elec sites: 35, Central water, Flush toilet, Free showers, RV dump, Tents: $20/RVs: $20-30, 5 full hookups, Open all year, Max Length: 75ft, Elev: 686ft/209m,

Tel: 559-689-3255, Nearest town: Chowchilla. GPS: 37.213509, -119.967032

15 • C2 | Codorniz RA - Equestrian

Total sites: 4, RV sites: 4, Central water, Flush toilet, Free showers, Tent & RV camping: $20, Max Length: 55ft, Reservations accepted, Elev: 748ft/228m, Tel: 559-689-3255, Nearest town: Chowchilla. GPS: 37.207439, -119.961854

16 • C2 | Codorniz RA - North Group A

Total sites: 1, RV sites: 0, Central water, Flush toilet, Free showers, No RV dump, Group site: $80-$100, Reservations accepted, Elev: 709ft/216m, Tel: 559-689-3255, Nearest town: Chowchilla. GPS: 37.214599, -119.963710

17 • C2 | Codorniz RA - North Group B

Total sites: 1, RV sites: 0, Central water, Flush toilet, Free showers, No RV dump, Group site: $80-$100, Reservations accepted, Elev: 682ft/208m, Tel: 559-689-3255, Nearest town: Chowchilla. GPS: 37.215991, -119.963684

18 • C2 | Codorniz RA - Wildcat Group

Total sites: 1, RV sites: 0, Central water, Vault/pit toilet, No showers, No RV dump, Group site: $80-$100, Reservations accepted, Elev: 742ft/226m, Tel: 559-689-3255, Nearest town: Chowchilla. GPS: 37.213606, -119.962591

19 • C2 | Coyote Point Group

Total sites: 1, RV sites: 1, Central water, Flush toilet, Pay showers, RV dump, Group site: $130, Open May-Sep, Reservations accepted, Elev: 709ft/216m, Tel: 209-772-1343, Nearest town: Valley Springs. GPS: 38.175147, -120.785603

20 • C2 | Deer Flat

Total sites: 30, No water, Vault/pit toilet, Tents only: $12, Boat-in, Open May-Sep, Reservations not accepted, Elev: 731ft/223m, Tel: 209-772-1343. GPS: 38.152288, -120.792274

21 • C2 | Hidden View

Total sites: 53, RV sites: 41, Elec sites: 22, Central water, Flush toilet, Free showers, RV dump, Tents: $20/RVs: $20-30, 2 group sites $100, Open all year, Max Length: 90ft, Reservations accepted, Elev: 597ft/182m, Tel: 559-673-5151, Nearest town: Madera. GPS: 37.123381, -119.893468

22 • C2 | Horsheshoe Road Rec Area

Dispersed sites, No water, No toilets, Tents only: $20, Hike-in/boat-in, Elev: 167ft/51m. GPS: 37.806778, -120.719858

23 • C2 | Island Park

Total sites: 90, RV sites: 75, Elec sites: 22, Central water, Flush toilet, Pay showers, RV dump, Tents: $20/RVs: $20-30, Group fee: $100, Open all year, Max Length: 99ft, Reservations accepted, Elev: 955ft/291m, Tel: 559-787-2589, Nearest town: Fresno. GPS: 36.864301, -119.315675

24 • C2 | McHenry Avenue Rec Area

Total sites: 19, RV sites: 0, Central water, Vault/pit toilet, No showers, No RV dump, Tents only: $20, Walk-to/boat-in sites, Reservations not accepted, Elev: 202ft/62m, Tel: 209-881-3517, Nearest town: Modesto. GPS: 37.818232, -120.663742

25 • C2 | Oak Knoll

Total sites: 49, RV sites: 47, Central water, Flush toilet, Pay showers, RV dump, Tent & RV camping: $20, Open May-Sep, Max Length: 40ft, Reservations accepted, Elev: 748ft/228m, Tel: 209-772-1343, Nearest town: Valley Springs. GPS: 38.181827, -120.791954

26 • C2 | Trimmer RA

Total sites: 10, RV sites: 5, Central water, Flush toilet, Free showers, No RV dump, Tent & RV camping: $20, Open all year, Max Length: 40ft, Reservations accepted, Elev: 965ft/294m, Tel: 559-787-2589, Nearest town: Fresno. GPS: 36.903914, -119.291241

27 • C2 | Valley Oak Rec Area

Dispersed sites, No water, Vault/pit toilet, Tents only: $20, Walk-to sites, Reservations not accepted, Elev: 134ft/41m, Tel: 209-881-3517, Nearest town: Oakdale. GPS: 37.786143, -120.803152

28 • D3 | Horse Creek

Total sites: 83, RV sites: 83, Central water, Flush toilet, Free showers, RV dump, Tent & RV camping: $20, 4 equestrian sites, Often floods winter/spring limiting site availability, Generator hours: 0600-2200, Open all year, Max Length: 40ft, Reservations accepted, Elev: 682ft/208m, Tel: 559-597-2301, Nearest town: Visalia. GPS: 36.389150, -118.954831

29 • D3 | Rocky Hill

Dispersed sites, No water, Vault/pit toilet, Tent & RV camping: Fee unk, Elev: 656ft/200m, Tel: 559-784-0215, Nearest town: Porterville. GPS: 36.068000, -118.922000

30 • D3 | Tule Recreation Area

Total sites: 103, RV sites: 103, Elec sites: 29, Central water, Flush toilet, Free showers, RV dump, Tents: $20/RVs: $20-30, Open all year, Max Length: 80ft, Reservations accepted, Elev: 692ft/211m, Tel: 559-784-0215, Nearest town: Porterville. GPS: 36.079910, -118.902530

Connecticut

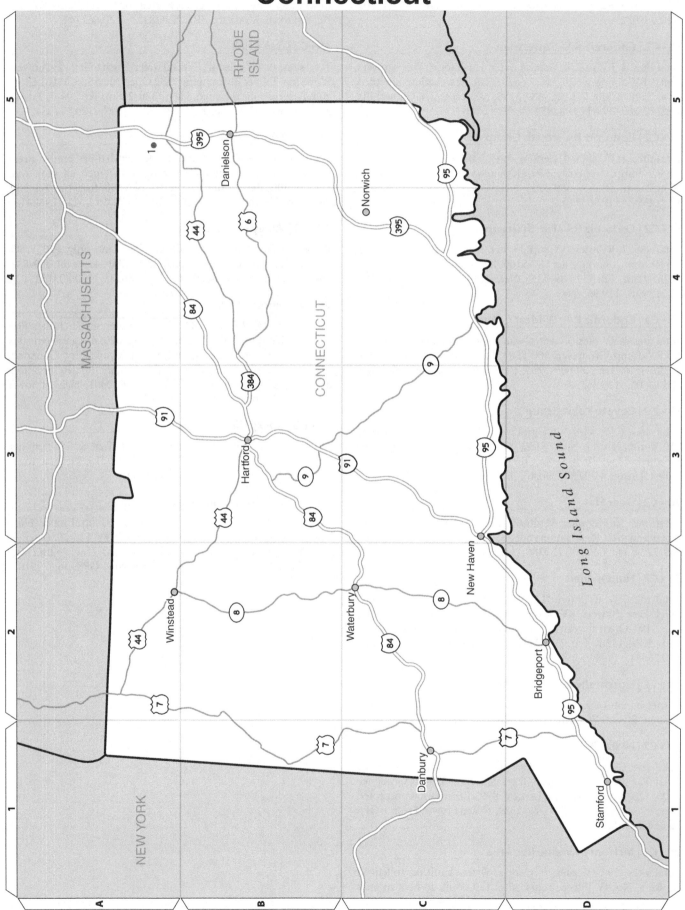

Map	ID	Map	ID
A5	1		

Alphabetical List of Camping Areas

Name   **ID**   **Map**

West Thompson Lake..1............A5

1 • A5 | West Thompson Lake

Total sites: 24, RV sites: 22, Elec sites: 11, Water at site, Flush toilet, Free showers, RV dump, Tents: $15/RVs: $15-30, Shelters available, Open May-Sep, Max Length: 40ft, Reservations accepted, Elev: 433ft/132m, Tel: 860-923-2982, Nearest town: North Grosvenordale. GPS: 41.955924, -71.898763

Florida

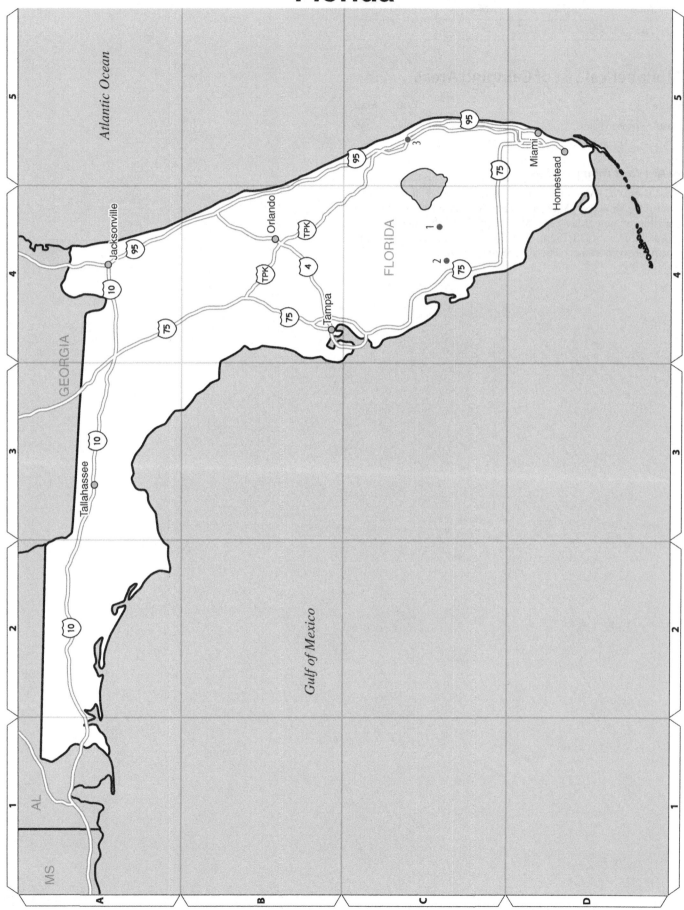

Map	ID	Map	ID
C4	1-2	C5	3

Alphabetical List of Camping Areas

Name	ID	Map
Ortona South	1	C4
St Lucie Lock South	3	C5
W. P. Franklin North	2	C4

1 • C4 | Ortona South

Total sites: 51, RV sites: 51, Elec sites: 51, Water at site, Flush toilet, Free showers, RV dump, Tent & RV camping: $30, Open all year, Max Length: 45ft, Reservations accepted, Elev: 36ft/11m, Tel: 863-675-8400, Nearest town: Labelle. GPS: 26.787598, -81.303223

2 • C4 | W. P. Franklin North

Total sites: 29, RV sites: 29, Elec sites: 28, Water at site, Flush toilet, Free showers, RV dump, Tent & RV camping: $30, Also boat-in sites, Also 8 boat elec/water hookups, Generator hours: 0600-2200, Open all year, Max Length: 35ft, Elev: 16ft/5m, Tel: 239-694-8770, Nearest town: Alva. GPS: 26.723756, -81.692819

3 • C5 | St Lucie Lock South

Total sites: 20, RV sites: 17, Elec sites: 17, Flush toilet, Free showers, RV dump, Tents: $20/RVs: $30, Also boat-in sites, Open all year, Max Length: 45ft, Reservations accepted, Elev: 20ft/6m, Tel: 772-287-1382, Nearest town: Stuart. GPS: 27.109419, -80.286032

26 • Georgia   Corps of Engineers Camping

Georgia

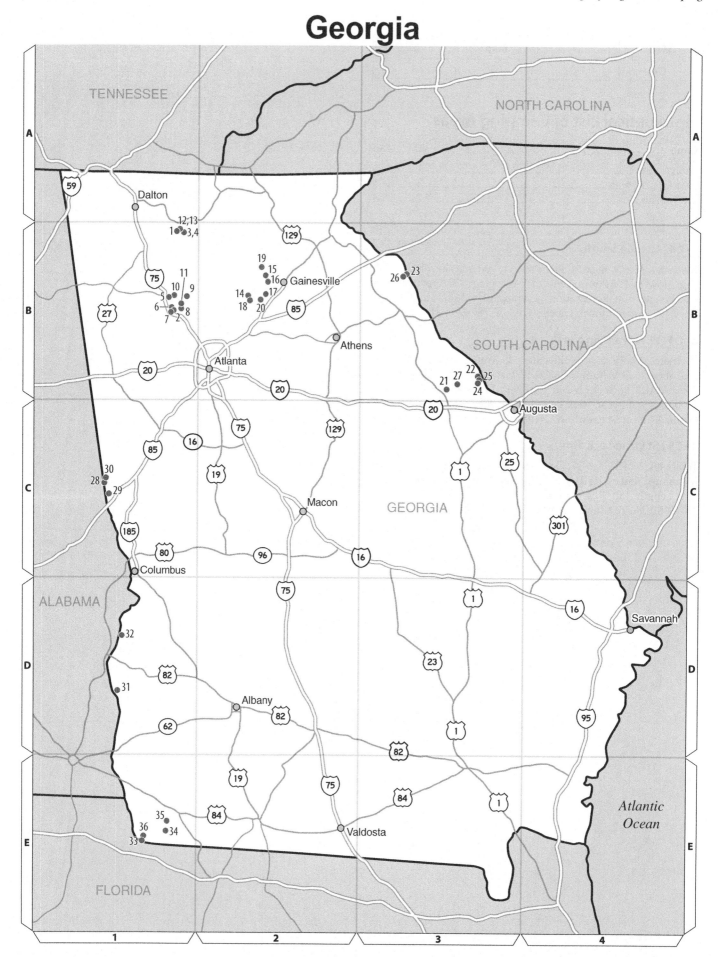

Map	ID	Map	ID
B1	1-13	C1	28-30
B2	14-20	D1	31-32
B3	21-27	E1	33-36

Alphabetical List of Camping Areas

Name	ID	Map
Bald Ridge	14	B2
Big Hart	21	B3
Bolding Mill	15	B2
Bussey Point	22	B3
Carters Lake Back-country	1	B1
Clark Creek North	2	B1
Cotton Hill	31	D1
Doll Mountain	3	B1
Duckett Mill	16	B2
Eastbank	33	E1
Faceville Landing	34	E1
Georgia River	23	B3
Hales Landing	35	E1
Harris Branch	4	B1
Holiday Park	28	C1
McKaskey Creek	5	B1
McKinney	6	B1
Old Federal	17	B2
Old Highway 41 #3	7	B1
Payne	8	B1
Petersburg	24	B3
R Shaefer Heard	29	C1
Ridge Road	25	B3
River Junction	36	E1
Rood Creek	32	D1
Sawnee	18	B2
Sweetwater Creek	9	B1
Toto Creek	19	B2
Upper Stamp Creek	10	B1
Van Pugh South	20	B2
Victoria	11	B1
Watsadler	26	B3
Whitetail Ridge Park	30	C1
Winfield	27	B3
Woodring Branch	12	B1
Woodring Branch Primitive	13	B1

1 • B1 | Carters Lake Back-country

Dispersed sites, No water, Vault/pit toilet, Tents only: Free, Hike-in/boat-in, Open all year, Reservations not accepted, Elev: 1089ft/332m, Tel: 706-334-2248, Nearest town: Oakman. GPS: 34.616976, -84.653994

2 • B1 | Clark Creek North

Total sites: 24, RV sites: 24, Elec sites: 24, Water at site, Flush toilet, Free showers, RV dump, Tent & RV camping: $28, Generator hours: 0600-2200, Open May-Sep, Max Length: 40ft, Reservations accepted, Elev: 902ft/275m, Tel: 678-721-6700, Nearest town: Cartersville. GPS: 34.103548, -84.683027

3 • B1 | Doll Mountain

Total sites: 65, RV sites: 39, Elec sites: 39, Water at site, Flush toilet, Free showers, RV dump, Tents: $18-24/RVs: $24-28, Steep hill, Open Apr-Oct, Max Length: 40ft, Reservations accepted, Elev: 1145ft/349m, Tel: 706-276-4413, Nearest town: Oakman. GPS: 34.603721, -84.612295

4 • B1 | Harris Branch

Total sites: 10, RV sites: 10, Central water, Flush toilet, Free showers, RV dump, Tent & RV camping: $18, Group site: $60, Open May-Sep, Reservations not accepted, Elev: 1194ft/364m, Tel: 706-276-4545, Nearest town: Oakman. GPS: 34.602783, -84.623779

5 • B1 | McKaskey Creek

Total sites: 50, RV sites: 31, Elec sites: 31, Water at site, Flush toilet, Free showers, RV dump, Tents: $24/RVs: $30-34, Open Mar-Sep, Max Length: 35ft, Reservations accepted, Elev: 899ft/274m, Tel: 678-721-6700, Nearest town: Cartersville. GPS: 34.191650, -84.720947

6 • B1 | McKinney

Total sites: 150, RV sites: 150, Elec sites: 150, Water at site, Flush toilet, Free showers, RV dump, Tent & RV camping: $30-34, Open Mar-Oct, Max Length: 55ft, Reservations accepted, Elev: 909ft/277m, Tel: 678-721-6700, Nearest town: Cartersville. GPS: 34.112809, -84.699392

7 • B1 | Old Highway 41 #3

Total sites: 44, RV sites: 44, Elec sites: 44, Water at site, Flush toilet, Free showers, RV dump, Tent & RV camping: $28-36, Open May-Sep, Max Length: 50ft, Reservations accepted, Elev: 942ft/287m, Tel: 678-721-6700, Nearest town: Cartersville. GPS: 34.091771, -84.710203

8 • B1 | Payne

Total sites: 60, RV sites: 60, Elec sites: 49, Water at site, Flush toilet, Free showers, RV dump, Tents: $22/RVs: $28-32, Open Mar-Sep, Max Length: 70ft, Reservations accepted, Elev: 889ft/271m, Tel: 678-721-6700, Nearest town: Cartersville. GPS: 34.121052, -84.619565

9 • B1 | Sweetwater Creek

Total sites: 160, RV sites: 118, Elec sites: 118, Water at site, Flush toilet, Free showers, RV dump, Tents: $22/RVs: $28-32, Group site available - $270, Open Mar-Sep, Max Length: 78ft, Reservations accepted, Elev: 892ft/272m, Tel: 678-721-6700, Nearest town: Cartersville. GPS: 34.196052, -84.577185

10 • B1 | Upper Stamp Creek

Total sites: 20, RV sites: 18, Elec sites: 18, Water at site, Flush toilet, Free showers, RV dump, Tents: $24/RVs: $30-34, Open May-Sep, Max Length: 33ft, Reservations accepted, Elev: 896ft/273m, Tel: 678-721-6700, Nearest town: Cartersville. GPS: 34.202879, -84.677987

11 • B1 | Victoria

Total sites: 74, RV sites: 74, Elec sites: 74, Water at site, Flush toilet, Free showers, RV dump, Tents: $24/RVs: $30-34, Open Mar-Oct, Max Length: 80ft, Reservations accepted, Elev: 906ft/276m, Tel:

678-721-6700, Nearest town: Cartersville. GPS: 34.150759, -84.617894

12 • B1 | Woodring Branch

Total sites: 39, RV sites: 28, Elec sites: 28, Water at site, Flush toilet, Free showers, RV dump, Tents: $18/RVs: $24-28, Group tent site: $20, Open May-Sep, Max Length: 40ft, Reservations accepted, Elev: 1201ft/366m, Tel: 706-276-6050, Nearest town: Oakman. GPS: 34.616066, -84.643382

13 • B1 | Woodring Branch Primitive

Total sites: 12, RV sites: 0, Central water, Vault/pit toilet, No showers, No RV dump, Tents only: $10, Open Apr-Oct, Reservations not accepted, Elev: 1164ft/355m, Tel: 706-276-6050, Nearest town: Oakman. GPS: 34.624798, -84.638053

14 • B2 | Bald Ridge

Total sites: 82, RV sites: 82, Elec sites: 82, Water at site, Flush toilet, Free showers, RV dump, Tent & RV camping: $26-36, $10 weekend surcharge, Open Mar-Oct, Max Length: 109ft, Reservations accepted, Elev: 1099ft/335m, Tel: 770-889-1591, Nearest town: Cumming. GPS: 34.207453, -84.086518

15 • B2 | Bolding Mill

Total sites: 97, RV sites: 88, Elec sites: 88, Water at site, Flush toilet, Free showers, RV dump, Tents: $20-30/RVs: $26-36, $10 weekend surcharge, Open Mar-Oct, Max Length: 80ft, Reservations accepted, Elev: 1102ft/336m, Tel: 770-532-3650, Nearest town: Fort Gaines. GPS: 34.336914, -83.950195

16 • B2 | Duckett Mill

Total sites: 111, RV sites: 97, Elec sites: 97, Water at site, Flush toilet, Free showers, RV dump, Tents: $20-30/RVs: $26-36, $10 weekend surcharge, Open Mar-Sep, Max Length: 75ft, Reservations accepted, Elev: 1125ft/343m, Tel: 770-532-9802, Nearest town: Fort Gaines. GPS: 34.304199, -83.935059

17 • B2 | Old Federal

Total sites: 91, RV sites: 63, Elec sites: 63, Water at site, Flush toilet, Free showers, RV dump, Tents: $20-32/RVs: $26-36, Also walk-to sites, 7 walk-to sites, $10 weekend surcharge, Open Mar-Oct, Max Length: 160ft, Reservations accepted, Elev: 1138ft/347m, Tel: 770-967-6757, Nearest town: Flowery Branch. GPS: 34.222412, -83.949219

18 • B2 | Sawnee

Total sites: 52, RV sites: 42, Elec sites: 42, Water at site, Flush toilet, Free showers, RV dump, Tents: $20-32/RVs: $24-36, Weekend surcharge: $10, Open Mar-Sep, Max Length: 85ft, Reservations accepted, Elev: 1112ft/339m, Tel: 770-887-0592, Nearest town: Cumming. GPS: 34.176758, -84.075195

19 • B2 | Toto Creek

Total sites: 9, RV sites: 0, Central water, Vault/pit toilet, No showers, No RV dump, Tents only: $16, Open Mar-Sep, Max Length: 35ft, Reservations accepted, Elev: 1ft/0m, Tel: 770-945-9531, Nearest town: Dawsonville. GPS: 34.393406, -83.983522

20 • B2 | Van Pugh South

Total sites: 55, RV sites: 37, Elec sites: 37, Water at site, Flush toilet, Free showers, No RV dump, Tents: $18/RVs: $22, Open Mar-Sep, Max Length: 26ft, Reservations accepted, Elev: 1112ft/339m, Tel: 770-967-6315, Nearest town: Buford. GPS: 34.183048, -83.988724

21 • B3 | Big Hart

Total sites: 31, RV sites: 31, Elec sites: 31, Water at site, Flush toilet, Free showers, RV dump, Tent & RV camping: $24-26, Open Apr-Oct, Max Length: 60ft, Reservations accepted, Elev: 394ft/120m, Tel: 706-595-8613, Nearest town: Thomson. GPS: 33.616032, -82.505199

22 • B3 | Bussey Point

Total sites: 14, RV sites: 14, Central water, Vault/pit toilet, No showers, No RV dump, Tent & RV camping: $10, Equestrian facilities, Open all year, Reservations accepted, Elev: 426ft/130m, Tel: 478-825-6354, Nearest town: Lincolnton. GPS: 33.701416, -82.263428

23 • B3 | Georgia River

Total sites: 15, RV sites: 15, Central water, Vault/pit toilet, No showers, No RV dump, Tent & RV camping: $10, Open May-Sep, Max Length: 20ft, Elev: 486ft/148m, Tel: 706-856-0300, Nearest town: Hartwell. GPS: 34.354145, -82.818382

24 • B3 | Petersburg

Total sites: 93, RV sites: 93, Elec sites: 85, Water at site, Flush toilet, Free showers, RV dump, Tents: $18/RVs: $26-28, Open all year, Max Length: 45ft, Reservations accepted, Elev: 397ft/121m, Tel: 706-541-9464, Nearest town: Appling. GPS: 33.661296, -82.259488

25 • B3 | Ridge Road

Total sites: 69, RV sites: 69, Elec sites: 63, Water at site, Flush toilet, Free showers, RV dump, Tents: $18/RVs: $26-28, Open Mar-Oct, Max Length: 50ft, Reservations accepted, Elev: 397ft/121m, Tel: 706-541-0282, Nearest town: Appling. GPS: 33.680176, -82.258545

26 • B3 | Watsadler

Total sites: 49, RV sites: 49, Elec sites: 49, Water at site, Flush toilet, Free showers, RV dump, Tent & RV camping: $28, Open all year, Max Length: 50ft, Reservations accepted, Elev: 682ft/208m, Tel: 888-893-0678, Nearest town: Hartwell. GPS: 34.344727, -82.842529

27 • B3 | Winfield

Total sites: 80, RV sites: 80, Elec sites: 80, Water at site, Flush toilet, Free showers, RV dump, Tent & RV camping: $28, Open Mar-Oct, Max Length: 65ft, Reservations accepted, Elev: 338ft/103m, Tel: 706-541-0147, Nearest town: Appling. GPS: 33.650146, -82.417969

28 • C1 | Holiday Park

Total sites: 121, RV sites: 110, Elec sites: 110, Water at site, Flush toilet, Free showers, RV dump, Tents: $20/RVs: $30, Group site: $60-$170, Open Mar-Sep, Max Length: 83ft, Reservations accepted, Elev: 686ft/209m, Tel: 706-884-6818, Nearest town: West Point. GPS: 33.008234, -85.190053

29 • C1 | R Shaefer Heard

Total sites: 117, RV sites: 117, Elec sites: 117, Water at site, Flush toilet, Free showers, RV dump, Tent & RV camping: $30, Open all year, Max Length: 100ft, Reservations required, Elev: 645ft/197m, Tel: 706-645-2404, Nearest town: West Point. GPS: 32.928759, -85.161724

30 • C1 | Whitetail Ridge Park

Total sites: 58, RV sites: 58, Elec sites: 58, Water at site, Flush toilet, Free showers, RV dump, Tent & RV camping: $30, Open Mar-Oct, Max Length: 75ft, Reservations accepted, Elev: 728ft/222m, Tel: 706-882-8972, Nearest town: LaGrange. GPS: 33.020995, -85.182829

31 • D1 | Cotton Hill

Total sites: 101, RV sites: 91, Elec sites: 101, Water at site, Flush toilet, Free showers, RV dump, Tents: $24/RVs: $28, 91 full hookups, Open all year, Max Length: 45ft, Reservations accepted, Elev: 249ft/76m, Tel: 229-768-3061, Nearest town: Fort Gaines. GPS: 31.674561, -85.063965

32 • D1 | Rood Creek

Total sites: 34, RV sites: 34, No water, Vault/pit toilet, Tent & RV camping: Free, Open Mar-Oct, Elev: 230ft/70m, Nearest town: Georgetown. GPS: 32.026091, -85.036897

33 • E1 | Eastbank

Total sites: 65, RV sites: 63, Elec sites: 63, Water at site, Flush toilet, Free showers, RV dump, Tents: $14/RVs: $24, Open all year, Max Length: 100ft, Reservations accepted, Elev: 138ft/42m, Tel: 229-622-9273, Nearest town: Chattahoochee, FL. GPS: 30.717830, -84.851000

34 • E1 | Faceville Landing

Total sites: 7, RV sites: 3, No water, Vault/pit toilet, Tent & RV camping: $8, Open all year, Max Length: 40ft, Reservations not accepted, Elev: 108ft/33m, Tel: 229-662-2001, Nearest town: Bainbridge. GPS: 30.787656, -84.665883

35 • E1 | Hales Landing

Total sites: 25, RV sites: 25, Elec sites: 25, Water at site, Flush toilet, Free showers, No RV dump, Tent & RV camping: $20, Open all year, Reservations not accepted, Elev: 105ft/32m, Tel: 229-662-2001, Nearest town: Bainbridge. GPS: 30.847127, -84.661556

36 • E1 | River Junction

Total sites: 11, RV sites: 11, Elec sites: 11, Water at site, Flush toilet, Free showers, No RV dump, Tent & RV camping: $20, Open all year, Max Length: 40ft, Reservations not accepted, Elev: 167ft/51m, Tel: 229-662-2001, Nearest town: Chattahoochee, FL. GPS: 30.749266, -84.839516

Idaho

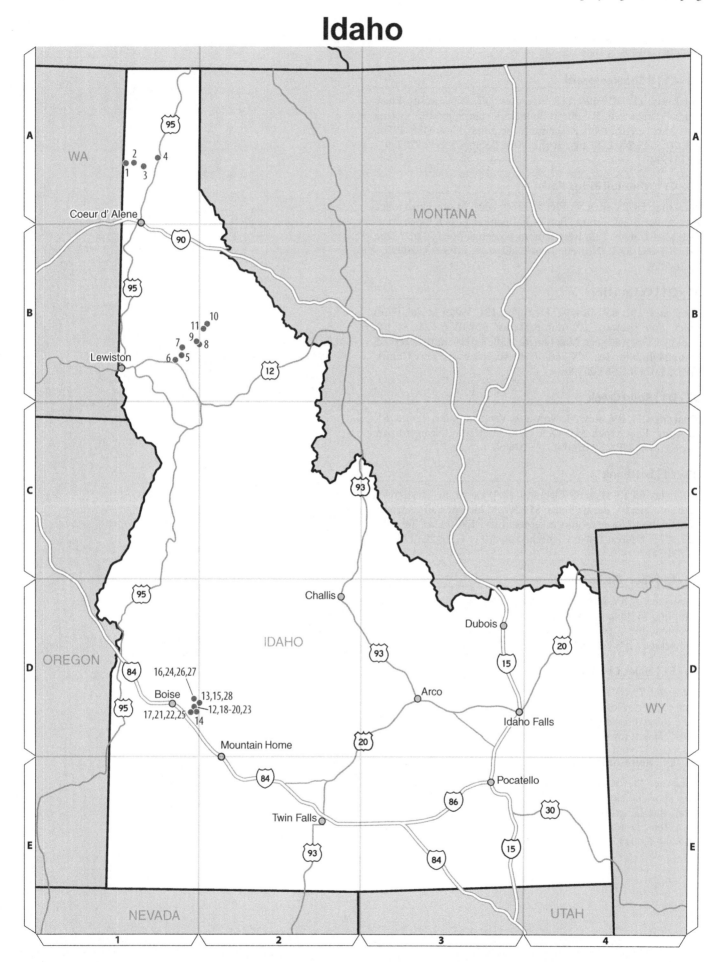

Map	ID	Map	ID
A1	1-4	D1	12-27
B1	5-9	D2	28
B2	10-11		

Alphabetical List of Camping Areas

Name	ID	Map
Albeni Cove	1	A1
Canyon Creek	5	B1
Dam View	6	B1
Dent Acres	7	B1
Grandad Creek	10	B2
Little Meadow Creek	11	B2
Lucky Peak Reservoir - Birch Creek Shelters 39-40	12	D1
Lucky Peak Reservoir - Brown's Gulch Shelter 49	13	D1
Lucky Peak Reservoir - Charcoal Flat Camp 15	14	D1
Lucky Peak Reservoir - Chimney Rock Shelters 41-48	15	D1
Lucky Peak Reservoir - Dead Dog Creek Creek Shelter 59	16	D1
Lucky Peak Reservoir - Deer Flat 67-85	17	D1
Lucky Peak Reservoir - Gooseneck Bay Shelter 1	18	D1
Lucky Peak Reservoir - Gooseneck Bay Shelter 6	19	D1
Lucky Peak Reservoir - Gooseneck Bay Shelters 2-5	20	D1
Lucky Peak Reservoir - Pipeline Gulch Camp 13	21	D1
Lucky Peak Reservoir - Pipeline Gulch Camps 9-12	22	D1
Lucky Peak Reservoir - Placer Point Shelters 32-38	23	D1
Lucky Peak Reservoir - Robie Creek Park	24	D1
Lucky Peak Reservoir - Sheep Creek Shelters 86-89	25	D1
Lucky Peak Reservoir - South Robie Creek Shelters 54-56	26	D1
Lucky Peak Reservoir - Turnaround Point Shelters 57-58	27	D1
Macks Creek	28	D2
Magnus Bay	8	B1
Priest River (Mudhole)	2	A1
Riley Creek	3	A1
Springy Point	4	A1
Swamp Creek	9	B1

1 • A1 | Albeni Cove

Total sites: 14, RV sites: 8, Central water, Flush toilet, Free showers, No RV dump, Tent & RV camping: $22, Rough access road - RVs not recommended, Open May-Sep, Max Length: 40ft, Reservations accepted, Elev: 2123ft/647m, Tel: 208-437-3133, Nearest town: Oldtown. GPS: 48.176017, -116.999089

2 • A1 | Priest River (Mudhole)

Total sites: 25, RV sites: 20, Central water, Flush toilet, Pay showers, RV dump, Tents: $10/RVs: $22, Open May-Sep, Max Length: 45ft, Reservations accepted, Elev: 2103ft/641m, Tel: 208-764-3682, Nearest town: Priest River. GPS: 48.178555, -116.890178

3 • A1 | Riley Creek

Total sites: 67, RV sites: 67, Elec sites: 67, Water at site, Flush toilet, Pay showers, RV dump, Tent & RV camping: $30, Open May-Sep, Max Length: 45ft, Reservations accepted, Elev: 2132ft/650m, Tel: 208-437-3133, Nearest town: Laclede. GPS: 48.159743, -116.773362

4 • A1 | Springy Point

Total sites: 38, RV sites: 37, Central water, Flush toilet, Pay showers, RV dump, Tent & RV camping: $22, Open May-Sep, Max Length: 40ft, Reservations accepted, Elev: 2129ft/649m, Tel: 208-437-3133, Nearest town: Sandpoint. GPS: 48.237061, -116.584473

5 • B1 | Canyon Creek

Total sites: 17, RV sites: 17, No water, Vault/pit toilet, Tent & RV camping: Free, Steep access road, Stay limit: 14 days, Generator hours: 0600-2200, Open Apr-Nov, Max Length: 10ft, Reservations not accepted, Elev: 1654ft/504m, Tel: 208-476-1255, Nearest town: Orofino. GPS: 46.555343, -116.233796

6 • B1 | Dam View

Total sites: 6, RV sites: 6, Water available, Vault/pit toilet, Tent & RV camping: Free, Generator hours: 0600-2200, Open Apr-Nov, Reservations not accepted, Elev: 1627ft/496m, Tel: 208-476-1255, Nearest town: Orofino. GPS: 46.516212, -116.305119

7 • B1 | Dent Acres

Total sites: 50, RV sites: 50, Elec sites: 50, Water at site, Flush toilet, Free showers, RV dump, Tent & RV camping: $20, Group site $50, 49 full hookups, Open Apr-Dec, Max Length: 35ft, Reservations accepted, Elev: 1785ft/544m, Tel: 208-476-9029, Nearest town: Orofino. GPS: 46.625509, -116.219289

8 • B1 | Magnus Bay

Dispersed sites, No water, No toilets, Tents only: Free, Boat-in, Reservations not accepted, Elev: 1606ft/490m, Tel: 208-476-1255, Nearest town: Headquarters. GPS: 46.651703, -116.008227

9 • B1 | Swamp Creek

Dispersed sites, No water, No toilets, Tents only: Free, Boat-in, Elev: 1632ft/497m, Nearest town: Orofino. GPS: 46.660927, -116.022942

10 • B2 | Grandad Creek

Total sites: 10, RV sites: 10, Central water, Vault/pit toilet, No showers, No RV dump, Tent & RV camping: Free, Stay limit: 14 days, Generator hours: 0600-2200, Open May-Sep, Max Length: 20ft, Reservations not accepted, Elev: 1552ft/473m, Tel: 208-476-1255, Nearest town: Headquarters. GPS: 46.824301, -115.913068

11 • B2 | Little Meadow Creek

Total sites: 6, RV sites: 6, No water, Vault/pit toilet, Tent & RV camping: Free, Open May-Sep, Reservations not accepted, Elev: 1626ft/496m, Tel: 208-476-1255, Nearest town: Orofino. GPS: 46.791284, -115.953797

12 • D1 | Lucky Peak Reservoir - Birch Creek Shelters 39-40

Total sites: 2, No water, Vault/pit toilet, No showers, No RV dump, Boat-to shelter: Free, Stay limit: 3 days, Generator hours: 0600-2200, Reservations not accepted, Elev: 3063ft/934m, Tel: 208-343-0671, Nearest town: Boise. GPS: 43.560082, -115.992373

13 • D1 | Lucky Peak Reservoir - Brown's Gulch Shelter 49

Total sites: 1, No water, Vault/pit toilet, No showers, No RV dump, Boat-to shelter: Free, Stay limit: 3 days, Generator hours: 0600-2200, Reservations not accepted, Elev: 3058ft/932m, Tel: 208-343-0671, Nearest town: Boise. GPS: 43.585475, -115.957785

14 • D1 | Lucky Peak Reservoir - Charcoal Flat Camp 15

Dispersed sites, No water, No toilets, Tents only: Free, Boat-in, Dock/shelter/picnic table, Water levels may impact access, Free marine pump-out at Spring Shores Marina, Stay limit: 3 days, Generator hours: 0600-2200, Reservations not accepted, Elev: 3063ft/934m, Tel: 208-343-0671, Nearest town: Boise. GPS: 43.53325, -115.99645

15 • D1 | Lucky Peak Reservoir - Chimney Rock Shelters 41-48

Total sites: 8, No water, Vault/pit toilet, No showers, No RV dump, Boat-to shelter: Free, Stay limit: 3 days, Generator hours: 0600-2200, Reservations not accepted, Elev: 3059ft/932m, Tel: 208-343-0671, Nearest town: Boise. GPS: 43.586445, -115.968641

16 • D1 | Lucky Peak Reservoir - Dead Dog Creek Creek Shelter 59

Total sites: 1, No water, Vault/pit toilet, No showers, No RV dump, Boat-to shelter: Free, Stay limit: 3 days, Generator hours: 0600-2200, Reservations not accepted, Elev: 3058ft/932m, Tel: 208-343-0671, Nearest town: Boise. GPS: 43.604892, -115.995755

17 • D1 | Lucky Peak Reservoir - Deer Flat 67-85

Total sites: 19, No water, Vault/pit toilet, No showers, No RV dump, Tents only: Free, Also boat-in sites, Stay limit: 3 days, Generator hours: 0600-2200, Reservations not accepted, Elev: 3071ft/936m, Tel: 208-343-0671, Nearest town: Boise. GPS: 43.537797, -116.020235

18 • D1 | Lucky Peak Reservoir - Gooseneck Bay Shelter 1

Total sites: 1, No water, Vault/pit toilet, No showers, No RV dump, Boat-to shelter: Free, Stay limit: 3 days, Generator hours: 0600-2200, Reservations not accepted, Elev: 3065ft/934m, Tel: 208-343-0671, Nearest town: Boise. GPS: 43.549381, -116.013764

19 • D1 | Lucky Peak Reservoir - Gooseneck Bay Shelter 6

Total sites: 1, No water, Vault/pit toilet, No showers, No RV dump, Boat-to shelter: Free, Stay limit: 3 days, Generator hours: 0600-2200, Reservations not accepted, Elev: 3068ft/935m, Tel: 208-343-0671, Nearest town: Boise. GPS: 43.559786, -116.009482

20 • D1 | Lucky Peak Reservoir - Gooseneck Bay Shelters 2-5

Total sites: 4, No water, Vault/pit toilet, No showers, No RV dump, Boat-to shelter: Free, Stay limit: 3 days, Generator hours: 0600-2200, Reservations not accepted, Elev: 3075ft/937m, Tel: 208-343-0671, Nearest town: Boise. GPS: 43.557125, -116.013245

21 • D1 | Lucky Peak Reservoir - Pipeline Gulch Camp 13

Dispersed sites, No water, No toilets, Tents only: Free, Boat-in, Dock/shelter/picnic table, Water levels may impact access, Free marine pump-out at Spring Shores Marina, Stay limit: 3 days, Open all year, Reservations not accepted, Elev: 3063ft/934m, Tel: 208-343-0671, Nearest town: Boise. GPS: 43.528259, -116.024222

22 • D1 | Lucky Peak Reservoir - Pipeline Gulch Camps 9-12

Dispersed sites, No water, No toilets, Tents only: Free, Boat-in, Stay limit: 3 days, Reservations not accepted, Elev: 3218ft/981m, Nearest town: Boise. GPS: 43.523539, -116.031046

23 • D1 | Lucky Peak Reservoir - Placer Point Shelters 32-38

Total sites: 7, No water, Vault/pit toilet, No showers, No RV dump, Boat-to shelter: Free, Stay limit: 3 days, Generator hours: 0600-2200, Reservations not accepted, Elev: 3060ft/933m, Tel: 208-343-0671, Nearest town: Boise. GPS: 43.555035, -116.004623

24 • D1 | Lucky Peak Reservoir - Robie Creek Park

Total sites: 7, No water, Vault/pit toilet, No showers, No RV dump, Tents only: Free, Also boat-in sites, Stay limit: 3 days, Generator hours: 0600-2200, Reservations not accepted, Elev: 3070ft/936m, Tel: 208-343-0671, Nearest town: Boise. GPS: 43.630103, -115.996585

25 • D1 | Lucky Peak Reservoir - Sheep Creek Shelters 86-89

Total sites: 5, No water, Vault/pit toilet, No showers, No RV dump, Tents only: Free, Also boat-in sites, Shelter at 1 site, Stay limit: 3 days, Generator hours: 0600-2200, Reservations not accepted, Elev: 3070ft/936m, Tel: 208-343-0671, Nearest town: Boise. GPS: 43.533166, -116.044592

26 • D1 | Lucky Peak Reservoir - South Robie Creek Shelters 54-56

Total sites: 3, No water, Vault/pit toilet, No showers, No RV dump, Boat-to shelter: Free, Stay limit: 3 days, Generator hours: 0600-2200, Reservations not accepted, Elev: 3058ft/932m, Tel: 208-343-0671, Nearest town: Boise. GPS: 43.622144, -116.003103

27 • D1 | Lucky Peak Reservoir - Turnaround Point Shelters 57-58

Total sites: 2, No water, Vault/pit toilet, No showers, No RV dump, Boat-to shelter: Free, Stay limit: 3 days, Generator hours: 0600-2200, Reservations not accepted, Elev: 3072ft/936m, Tel: 208-343-0671, Nearest town: Boise. GPS: 43.611856, -115.992242

28 • D2 | Macks Creek

Total sites: 15, RV sites: 5, Central water, Vault/pit toilet, No showers, No RV dump, Tent & RV camping: $10, Open May-Sep, Max Length: 35ft, Reservations accepted, Elev: 3159ft/963m, Tel: 208-343-0671, Nearest town: Boise. GPS: 43.610372, -115.937957

Illinois

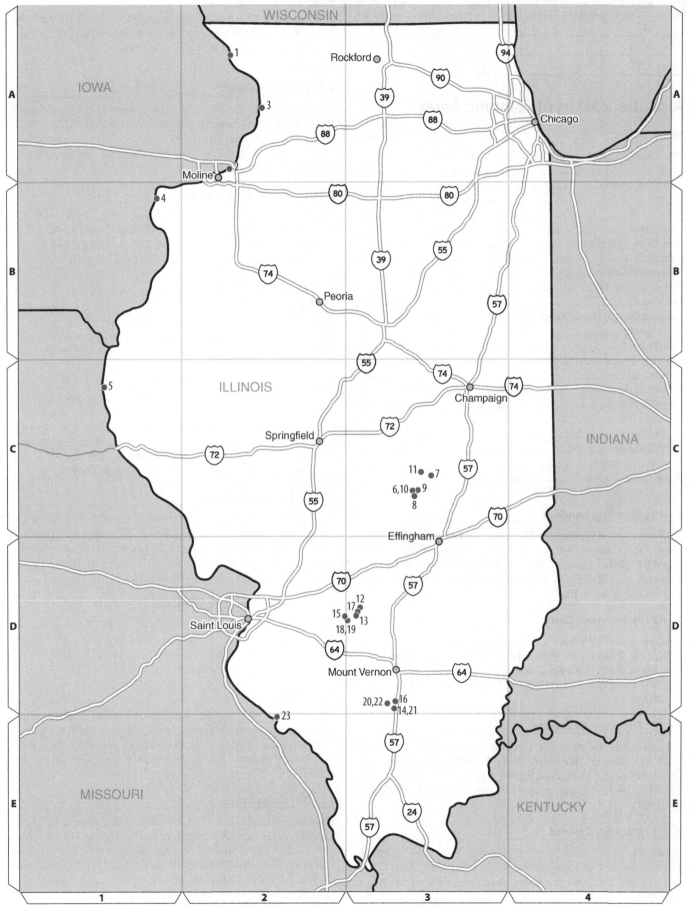

Map	ID	Map	ID
A2	1-3	C3	6-11
B1	4	D3	12-22
C1	5	E2	23

Alphabetical List of Camping Areas

Name	ID	Map
Bear Creek	5	C1
Blanchard Island	4	B1
Blanding Landing	1	A2
Boulder	12	D3
Coles Creek	13	D3
Coon Creek	6	C3
Dale Miller Youth Group	14	D3
Dam West	15	D3
Fisherman's Corner	2	A2
Forest W. Bo Wood	7	C3
Gun Creek	16	D3
Kaskaskia Jerry F. Costello Lock and Dam	23	E2
Lithia Springs	8	C3
Lone Point	9	C3
Lotus Group	17	D3
McNair	18	D3
McNair -East Spillway	19	D3
North Sandusky	20	D3
Opossum Creek	10	C3
South Marcum	21	D3
South Sandusky	22	D3
Thomson Causeway	3	A2
Wilborn Creek Group	11	C3

1 • A2 | Blanding Landing

Total sites: 37, RV sites: 37, Elec sites: 30, Central water, Flush toilet, Free showers, RV dump, Tents: $14/RVs: $14-20, Open May-Oct, Max Length: 40ft, Reservations accepted, Elev: 630ft/192m, Tel: 563-582-0881, Nearest town: Hanover. GPS: 42.286133, -90.402100

2 • A2 | Fisherman's Corner

Total sites: 56, RV sites: 51, Elec sites: 29, Central water, Flush toilet, Free showers, RV dump, Tents: $14/RVs: $20, Open May-Oct, Max Length: 80ft, Reservations accepted, Elev: 584ft/178m, Tel: 309-496-2720, Nearest town: Hampton. GPS: 41.569518, -90.390236

3 • A2 | Thomson Causeway

Total sites: 131, RV sites: 131, Elec sites: 126, Central water, Flush toilet, Free showers, RV dump, Tents: $14/RVs: $20, Open May-Oct, Max Length: 110ft, Reservations accepted, Elev: 587ft/179m, Tel: 815-259-2353, Nearest town: Thomson. GPS: 41.949759, -90.116995

4 • B1 | Blanchard Island

Total sites: 34, RV sites: 34, Vault/pit toilet, Tent & RV camping: $12, Open May-Oct, Reservations not accepted, Elev: 568ft/173m, Tel: 563-263-7913, Nearest town: Muscatine. GPS: 41.347900, -91.056396

5 • C1 | Bear Creek

Total sites: 30, RV sites: 30, Vault/pit toilet, Tent & RV camping: Free, Open Sep-Nov, Reservations not accepted, Elev: 492ft/150m, Tel: 563-263-7913, Nearest town: Marcelline. GPS: 40.111816, -91.479492

6 • C3 | Coon Creek

Total sites: 214, RV sites: 214, Elec sites: 214, Central water, Flush toilet, Free showers, RV dump, Tents: $18/RVs: $18-24, Open May-Oct, Max Length: 90ft, Reservations accepted, Elev: 676ft/206m, Tel: 217-774-2233, Nearest town: Shelbyville. GPS: 39.450843, -88.762539

7 • C3 | Forest W. Bo Wood

Total sites: 141, RV sites: 137, Central water, Flush toilet, Free showers, RV dump, Tents: $18/RVs: $18-24, Open Apr-Oct, Max Length: 150ft, Reservations accepted, Elev: 650ft/198m, Nearest town: Shelbyville. GPS: 39.552734, -88.619873

8 • C3 | Lithia Springs

Total sites: 115, RV sites: 115, Elec sites: 115, Central water, Flush toilet, Free showers, RV dump, Tent & RV camping: $18-24, Open Apr-Oct, Max Length: 100ft, Reservations accepted, Elev: 663ft/202m, Tel: 217-774-3951, Nearest town: Shelbyville. GPS: 39.434326, -88.761475

9 • C3 | Lone Point

Total sites: 64, RV sites: 64, Elec sites: 64, Central water, Flush toilet, Free showers, RV dump, Tents: $16/RVs: $16-24, 9 full hookups, Group site: $240, Open May-Sep, Max Length: 80ft, Reservations accepted, Elev: 659ft/201m, Tel: 217-774-3951, Nearest town: Shelbyville. GPS: 39.453471, -88.740273

10 • C3 | Opossum Creek

Total sites: 78, RV sites: 57, Elec sites: 57, Water at site, Flush toilet, Free showers, RV dump, Tent & RV camping: $16-24, 13 full hookups, Open May-Sep, Max Length: 100ft, Reservations accepted, Elev: 633ft/193m, Tel: 217-774-3951, Nearest town: Shelbyville. GPS: 39.446533, -88.773682

11 • C3 | Wilborn Creek Group

Total sites: 6, Central water, Vault/pit toilet, No showers, No RV dump, Group site: $120, Open May-Sep, Elev: 676ft/206m, Tel: 217-774-3951, Nearest town: Bethany. GPS: 39.573016, -88.706791

12 • D3 | Boulder

Total sites: 83, RV sites: 83, Elec sites: 83, Water available, Flush toilet, Free showers, RV dump, Tent & RV camping: $16-24, Open Apr-Oct, Max Length: 100ft, Reservations accepted, Elev: 466ft/142m, Tel: 618-594-5253, Nearest town: Carlyle. GPS: 38.693559, -89.237188

13 • D3 | Coles Creek

Total sites: 119, RV sites: 119, Elec sites: 119, Water at site, Flush toilet, Free showers, RV dump, Tent & RV camping: $16-24, Group sites: $150-$250, Open Apr-Sep, Max Length: 100ft, Reservations accepted, Elev: 466ft/142m, Tel: 618-226-3211, Nearest town: Carlyle. GPS: 38.652588, -89.266113

14 • D3 | Dale Miller Youth Group

Total sites: 1, RV sites: 1, Central water, Flush toilet, Free showers, RV dump, Group site: $100-$175, Open Apr-Nov, Reservations accepted, Elev: 443ft/135m, Tel: 618-724-2493, Nearest town: Rend City. GPS: 38.035114, -88.942978

15 • D3 | Dam West

Total sites: 109, RV sites: 109, Elec sites: 109, Central water, Flush toilet, Free showers, RV dump, Tents: $18/RVs: $18-26, Open Apr-Oct, Max Length: 138ft, Reservations accepted, Elev: 463ft/141m, Tel: 618-594-4410, Nearest town: Carlyle. GPS: 38.630799, -89.357844

16 • D3 | Gun Creek

Total sites: 100, RV sites: 100, Elec sites: 100, Central water, Flush toilet, Free showers, RV dump, Tents: $18/RVs: $18-26, 26 full hookups, Open Mar-Nov, Max Length: 96ft, Reservations accepted, Elev: 443ft/135m, Tel: 618-629-2338, Nearest town: Benton. GPS: 38.081055, -88.932129

17 • D3 | Lotus Group

Total sites: 1, RV sites: 0, Central water, Flush toilet, Free showers, RV dump, Group site: $125, Open May-Sep, Reservations accepted, Elev: 455ft/139m, Tel: 618-226-3211, Nearest town: Carlyle. GPS: 38.662288, -89.258244

18 • D3 | McNair

Total sites: 32, RV sites: 32, Central water, Flush toilet, Free showers, RV dump, Tent & RV camping: $16, Group site: $50, Open Apr-Nov, Max Length: 117ft, Reservations not accepted, Elev: 487ft/148m, Tel: 618-594-5253, Nearest town: Carlyle. GPS: 38.612789, -89.338052

19 • D3 | McNair -East Spillway

Total sites: 15, RV sites: 15, Elec sites: 10, Central water, No toilets, No showers, No RV dump, Tent & RV camping: $14, Open all year, Reservations not accepted, Elev: 426ft/130m, Tel: 618-594-5253, Nearest town: Carlyle. GPS: 38.615838, -89.354643

20 • D3 | North Sandusky

Total sites: 118, RV sites: 118, Elec sites: 118, Central water, Flush toilet, Free showers, RV dump, Tents: $18/RVs: $18-26, 16 full hookups, Open Apr-Oct, Max Length: 90ft, Reservations accepted, Elev: 450ft/137m, Tel: 618-625-6115, Nearest town: Benton. GPS: 38.067863, -88.999622

21 • D3 | South Marcum

Total sites: 160, RV sites: 146, Elec sites: 146, Water at site, Flush toilet, Free showers, RV dump, Tents: $16/RVs: $18-26, 46 full hookups, Open Apr-Nov, Max Length: 94ft, Reservations accepted, Elev: 446ft/136m, Tel: 618-435-3549, Nearest town: Benton. GPS: 38.037354, -88.937744

22 • D3 | South Sandusky

Total sites: 127, RV sites: 119, Elec sites: 119, Water at site, Flush toilet, Free showers, RV dump, Tents: $16/RVs: $18-26, 44 full hookups, Open Apr-Oct, Max Length: 99ft, Reservations accepted, Elev: 456ft/139m, Tel: 618-625-3011, Nearest town: Benton. GPS: 38.060303, -89.007080

23 • E2 | Kaskaskia Jerry F. Costello Lock and Dam

Total sites: 15, RV sites: 15, Elec sites: 15, Flush toilet, Tent & RV camping: $10, Reservations not accepted, Elev: 378ft/115m, Tel: 618-284-7160, Nearest town: Ellis Grove. GPS: 37.980278, -89.944624

Iowa

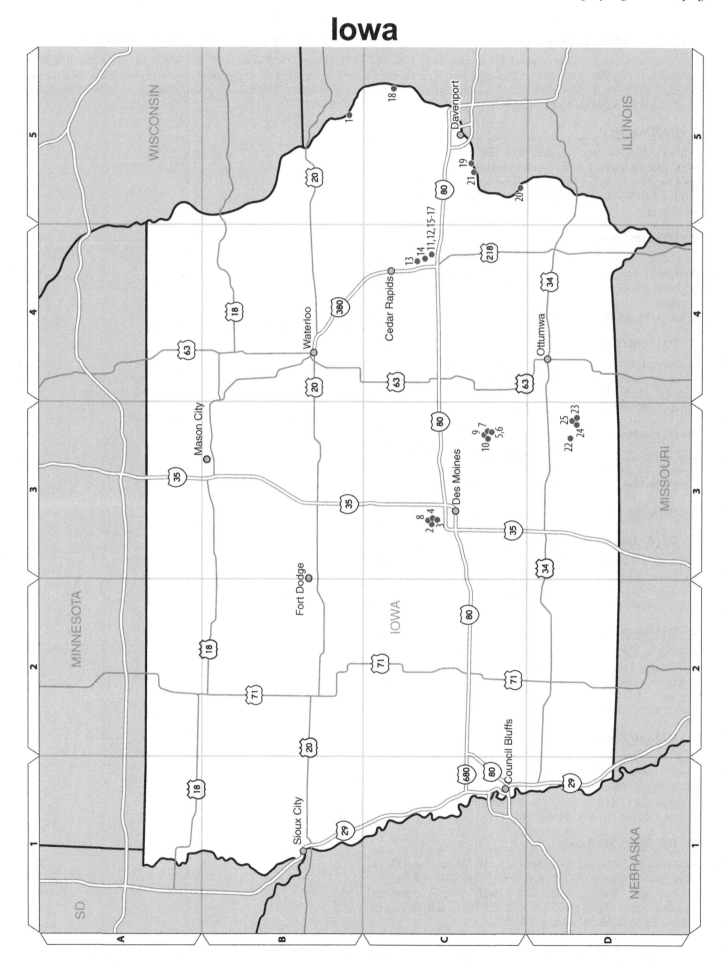

Map	ID	Map	ID
B5	1	C5	18-21
C3	2-10	D3	22-25
C4	11-17		

Alphabetical List of Camping Areas

Name	ID	Map
Acorn Valley	2	C3
Bob Shetler	3	C3
Bridgeview	22	D3
Buck Creek	23	D3
Bulger's Hollow	18	C5
Cherry Glen	4	C3
Clark's Ferry	19	C5
Cottonwood	11	C4
Ferry Landing	20	C5
Howell Station	5	C3
Island View	24	D3
Ivans	6	C3
Linder Point	12	C4
North Overlook	7	C3
Pleasant Creek	1	B5
Prairie Flower	8	C3
Prairie Ridge	25	D3
Sandy Beach	13	C4
Shady Creek	21	C5
Sugar Bottom	14	C4
Tailwater East	15	C4
Tailwater West	16	C4
Wallashuck	9	C3
West Overlook	17	C4
Whitebreast	10	C3

1 • B5 | Pleasant Creek

Total sites: 55, RV sites: 55, Central water, Vault/pit toilet, No showers, RV dump, Tent & RV camping: $12, Free 15 Oct-15 May, Open all year, Reservations not accepted, Elev: 636ft/194m, Tel: 563-582-0881, Nearest town: Dubuque. GPS: 42.211621, -90.382466

2 • C3 | Acorn Valley

Total sites: 94, RV sites: 29, Elec sites: 29, Central water, Flush toilet, Free showers, RV dump, Tents: $14/RVs: $22, Group sites: $35-$70, Open May-Oct, Max Length: 72ft, Reservations accepted, Elev: 932ft/284m, Tel: 515-276-0429, Nearest town: Des Moines. GPS: 41.737886, -93.720981

3 • C3 | Bob Shetler

Total sites: 67, RV sites: 67, Elec sites: 67, Central water, Flush toilet, Free showers, RV dump, Tent & RV camping: $20-22, Open May-Oct, Max Length: 70ft, Reservations accepted, Elev: 892ft/272m, Tel: 515-276-0873, Nearest town: Des Moines. GPS: 41.702411, -93.682649

4 • C3 | Cherry Glen

Total sites: 125, RV sites: 125, Elec sites: 125, Central water, Flush toilet, Free showers, RV dump, Tent & RV camping: $20-26, Open Apr-Oct, Max Length: 93ft, Reservations accepted, Elev: 915ft/279m, Tel: 515-964-8792, Nearest town: Des Moines. GPS: 41.730225, -93.681396

5 • C3 | Howell Station

Total sites: 143, RV sites: 143, Elec sites: 143, Central water, Flush toilet, Free showers, RV dump, Tent & RV camping: $22, Open Apr-Oct, Max Length: 80ft, Reservations accepted, Elev: 725ft/221m, Tel: 641-828-7522, Nearest town: Pella. GPS: 41.364746, -92.973633

6 • C3 | Ivans

Total sites: 21, RV sites: 21, Elec sites: 21, Central water, Flush toilet, Free showers, No RV dump, Tent & RV camping: $16, Open Apr-Sep, Reservations not accepted, Elev: 725ft/221m, Tel: 641-828-7522, Nearest town: Pella. GPS: 41.360352, -92.973145

7 • C3 | North Overlook

Total sites: 52, RV sites: 46, Elec sites: 46, Central water, Flush toilet, Free showers, RV dump, Tents: $14/RVs: $20, Open Apr-Oct, Max Length: 84ft, Reservations accepted, Elev: 827ft/252m, Tel: 641-828-7522, Nearest town: Pella. GPS: 41.380371, -92.969971

8 • C3 | Prairie Flower

Total sites: 242, RV sites: 242, Elec sites: 242, Central water, Flush toilet, Free showers, RV dump, Tent & RV camping: $20-22, 10 group sites: $80-$308, Open May-Oct, Max Length: 85ft, Reservations accepted, Elev: 932ft/284m, Tel: 515-984-6925, Nearest town: Des Moines. GPS: 41.748234, -93.688305

9 • C3 | Wallashuck

Total sites: 83, RV sites: 83, Elec sites: 83, Central water, Flush toilet, Free showers, RV dump, Tent & RV camping: $20, Open Apr-Oct, Max Length: 71ft, Reservations accepted, Elev: 820ft/250m, Tel: 641-828-7522, Nearest town: Pella. GPS: 41.400146, -92.994385

10 • C3 | Whitebreast

Total sites: 110, RV sites: 110, Elec sites: 110, Central water, Flush toilet, Free showers, RV dump, Tent & RV camping: $20, 2 group sites: $140-$240, Open Apr-Oct, Max Length: 68ft, Reservations accepted, Elev: 781ft/238m, Tel: 641-828-7522, Nearest town: Knoxville. GPS: 41.386719, -93.027588

11 • C4 | Cottonwood

Total sites: 15, RV sites: 0, Central water, Vault/pit toilet, No showers, No RV dump, Tents only: $14, Walk-to sites, Open May-Sep, Reservations accepted, Elev: 728ft/222m, Tel: 319-338-3543, Nearest town: Coralville. GPS: 41.722824, -91.534738

12 • C4 | Linder Point

Total sites: 26, RV sites: 21, Elec sites: 21, Water at site, Flush toilet, Free showers, RV dump, Tents: $22/RVs: $22-26, 8 full hookups, Generator hours: 0600-2200, Open May-Oct, Max Length: 85ft, Reservations accepted, Elev: 817ft/249m, Tel: 319-338-3543, Nearest town: Iowa City. GPS: 41.725095, -91.541823

13 • C4 | Sandy Beach

Total sites: 58, RV sites: 50, Elec sites: 50, Water at site, Flush toilet, Free showers, RV dump, Tents: $14/RVs: $20-24, 2 full hookups, Open May-Sep, Max Length: 71ft, Reservations accepted, Elev: 745ft/227m, Tel: 319-338-3543, Nearest town: Iowa City. GPS: 41.813477, -91.594971

14 • C4 | Sugar Bottom

Total sites: 249, RV sites: 232, Elec sites: 232, Central water, Flush toilet, Free showers, RV dump, Tents: $14/RVs: $20-24, Open May-Sep, Max Length: 89ft, Reservations accepted, Elev: 764ft/233m, Tel: 319-338-3543, Nearest town: Solon. GPS: 41.760434, -91.562331

15 • C4 | Tailwater East

Total sites: 28, RV sites: 23, Elec sites: 23, Water at site, Flush toilet, Free showers, RV dump, Tents: $14/RVs: $20-24, 1 full hookups, Open Apr-Oct, Max Length: 68ft, Reservations accepted, Elev: 705ft/215m, Tel: 319-338-3543, Nearest town: Iowa City. GPS: 41.720299, -91.528412

16 • C4 | Tailwater West

Total sites: 28, RV sites: 26, Elec sites: 26, Water at site, Flush toilet, Free showers, RV dump, Tents: $14/RVs: $24-26, 8 full hookups, Open May-Oct, Max Length: 69ft, Reservations accepted, Elev: 659ft/201m, Tel: 319-338-3543, Nearest town: Iowa City. GPS: 41.722168, -91.529297

17 • C4 | West Overlook

Total sites: 89, RV sites: 89, Elec sites: 89, Central water, Flush toilet, Free showers, RV dump, Tent & RV camping: $20, Open May-Oct, Max Length: 73ft, Reservations accepted, Elev: 742ft/226m, Tel: 319-338-3543, Nearest town: Iowa City. GPS: 41.726563, -91.535400

18 • C5 | Bulger's Hollow

Total sites: 26, RV sites: 17, Central water, Vault/pit toilet, No showers, RV dump, Tent & RV camping: $12, Free 15 Oct-15 May, Reservations not accepted, Elev: 581ft/177m, Tel: 815-259-3628, Nearest town: Clinton. GPS: 41.935451, -90.180975

19 • C5 | Clark's Ferry

Total sites: 44, RV sites: 44, Elec sites: 44, Central water, Flush toilet, Free showers, RV dump, Tent & RV camping: $20, Open May-Oct, Max Length: 70ft, Reservations accepted, Elev: 568ft/173m, Tel: 563-419-7594, Nearest town: Montpelier. GPS: 41.457764, -90.810303

20 • C5 | Ferry Landing

Total sites: 22, RV sites: 22, No toilets, RV dump, Tent & RV camping: Free, Open all year, Elev: 532ft/162m, Tel: 563-263-7913, Nearest town: Muscatine. GPS: 41.162472, -91.009086

21 • C5 | Shady Creek

Total sites: 53, RV sites: 53, Elec sites: 53, Central water, Flush toilet, Free showers, RV dump, Tent & RV camping: $20, Open May-Oct, Max Length: 92ft, Reservations accepted, Elev: 548ft/167m, Tel: 563-262-8090, Nearest town: Muscatine. GPS: 41.446621, -90.876187

22 • D3 | Bridgeview

Total sites: 103, RV sites: 103, Elec sites: 95, Central water, Flush toilet, Free showers, RV dump, Tents: $14/RVs: $18-20, Open May-Sep, Max Length: 89ft, Reservations accepted, Elev: 945ft/288m, Tel: 641-724-3062, Nearest town: Moravia. GPS: 40.875157, -93.030645

23 • D3 | Buck Creek

Total sites: 42, RV sites: 42, Elec sites: 42, Central water, Flush toilet, Free showers, RV dump, Tent & RV camping: $18-20, Open May-Sep, Max Length: 128ft, Reservations accepted, Elev: 955ft/291m, Tel: 641-724-3206, Nearest town: Centerville. GPS: 40.844323, -92.870972

24 • D3 | Island View

Total sites: 188, RV sites: 188, Elec sites: 188, Central water, Flush toilet, Free showers, RV dump, Tent & RV camping: $18-20, Open May-Sep, Max Length: 119ft, Reservations accepted, Elev: 919ft/280m, Tel: 641-647-2079, Nearest town: Centerville. GPS: 40.836017, -92.915858

25 • D3 | Prairie Ridge

Total sites: 54, RV sites: 54, Elec sites: 54, Central water, Flush toilet, Free showers, RV dump, Tent & RV camping: $18, Group site: $50-$100, Open May-Sep, Max Length: 110ft, Reservations accepted, Elev: 965ft/294m, Tel: 641-724-3103, Nearest town: Moravia. GPS: 40.858596, -92.887478

Kansas

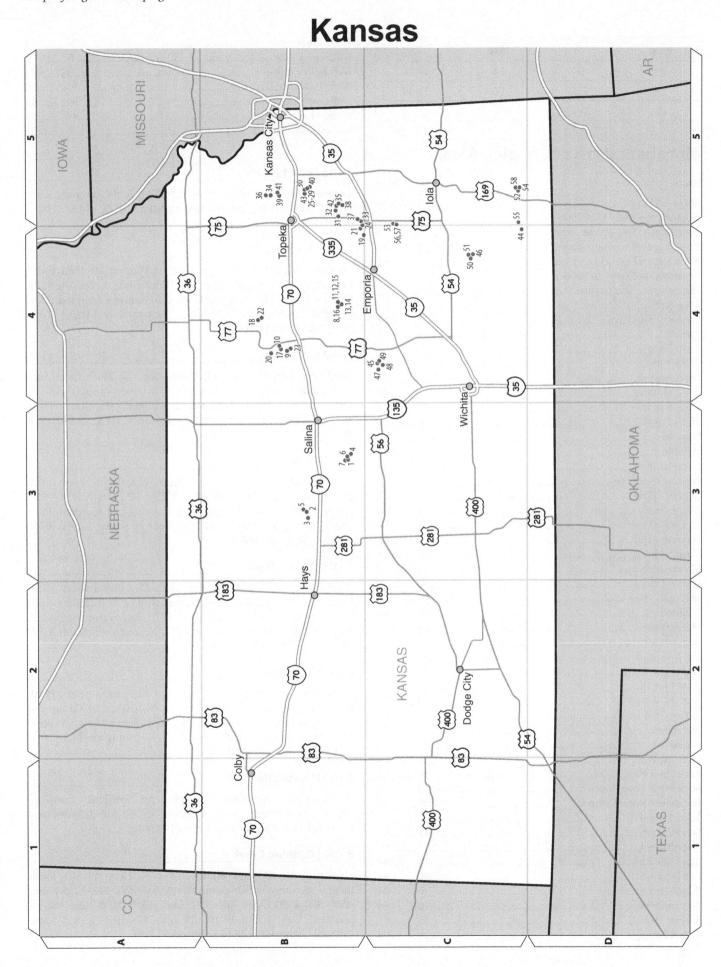

Map	ID	Map	ID
B3	1-7	C4	44-51
B4	8-23	C5	52-58
B5	24-43		

Alphabetical List of Camping Areas

Name	ID	Map
Arrow Rock	24	B5
Bloomington East - Ash Group	25	B5
Bloomington East - Cedar Ridge	26	B5
Bloomington East - Elm Group	27	B5
Bloomington East - Hickory/Walnut	28	B5
Bloomington East - Oak Loop	29	B5
Bloomington West Group	30	B5
Boldt Bluff	1	B3
Canning Creek	8	B4
Carbolyn	31	B5
Card Creek	44	C4
Cedar Park	32	B5
Cherryvale	52	C5
Coeur d'Alene	33	B5
Cottonwood Point	45	C4
Curtis Creek	9	B4
Dam Site	53	C5
Damsite	46	C4
Farnum Creek	10	B4
French Creek Cove	47	C4
Hillsboro Cove	48	C4
Kanza View	11	B4
Kit Carson Cove	12	B4
Longview	34	B5
Lucas Park	2	B3
Marina Cove	13	B4
Marion Cove	49	C4
Michigan Valley	35	B5
Minooka	3	B3
Mound Valley	54	C5
Neosho Park	14	B4
Old Town Park	36	B5
Outlet	37	B5
Outlet Area	38	B5
Outlet Channel	55	C5
Richey Cove	15	B4
Riverside	4	B3
Riverside East	56	C5
Riverside West	57	C5
Rock Creek Park	39	B5
Rock Ridge Cove North	50	C4
Rockhaven Horse Camp	40	B5
Santa Fe Trail	16	B4
School Creek	17	B4
Slough Creek	41	B5
Stockdale Park	18	B4
Sun Dance	19	B4
Sylvan Park	5	B3
Timber Creek	20	B4
Timber Hill	58	C5
Turkey Point	21	B4
Tuttle Creek Cove	22	B4
Venango	6	B3
West Rolling Hills	23	B4
White Hall Bay	51	C4
Wolf Creek	42	B5
Woodridge	43	B5
Yankee Run	7	B3

1 • B3 | Boldt Bluff

Dispersed sites, No water, No toilets, Tent & RV camping: Free, Elev: 1480ft/451m, Nearest town: Salina. GPS: 38.633119, -98.005323

2 • B3 | Lucas Park

Total sites: 92, RV sites: 91, Elec sites: 70, Water at site, Flush toilet, Free showers, RV dump, Tents: $18/RVs: $18-24, Group site $275, Open all year, Max Length: 148ft, Reservations accepted, Elev: 1549ft/472m, Tel: 785-658-2551, Nearest town: Lucas. GPS: 38.951693, -98.514836

3 • B3 | Minooka

Total sites: 145, RV sites: 145, Elec sites: 117, Flush toilet, Free showers, RV dump, Tents: $14/RVs: $18, Group site $200, $8-$10 Oct-Apr, Open all year, Reservations accepted, Elev: 1539ft/469m, Tel: 785-658-2551, Nearest town: Dorrance. GPS: 38.940189, -98.571985

4 • B3 | Riverside

Total sites: 28, RV sites: 28, Elec sites: 16, Water at site, Flush toilet, Free showers, RV dump, Tents: $14/RVs: $20, Oct-Nov: $0-$10, Open May-Sep, Max Length: 60ft, Reservations accepted, Elev: 1437ft/438m, Tel: 785-546-2294, Nearest town: Salina. GPS: 38.610075, -97.957068

5 • B3 | Sylvan Park

Total sites: 25, RV sites: 25, Elec sites: 25, Central water, Flush toilet, Free showers, RV dump, Tents: $18/RVs: $24-26, Group site $150, Open May-Sep, Max Length: 137ft, Reservations accepted, Elev: 1470ft/448m, Tel: 785-658-2551, Nearest town: Lucas. GPS: 38.970092, -98.491471

6 • B3 | Venango

Total sites: 126, RV sites: 126, Elec sites: 88, Central water, Flush toilet, Free showers, RV dump, Tents: $14/RVs: $20, Group site $60, Open May-Sep, Max Length: 64ft, Reservations accepted, Elev: 1529ft/466m, Tel: 785-546-2294, Nearest town: Marquette. GPS: 38.629714, -97.980573

7 • B3 | Yankee Run

Dispersed sites, No water, Vault/pit toilet, Tent & RV camping: Free, Open all year, Elev: 1506ft/459m, Tel: 785-546-2294, Nearest town: Salina. GPS: 38.643798, -98.014438

8 • B4 | Canning Creek

Total sites: 40, RV sites: 40, Elec sites: 37, Central water, Flush toilet, Free showers, RV dump, Tents: $14/RVs: $18-22, 3 group sites - $80-$200, Open Apr-Oct, Max Length: 110ft, Reservations accepted, Elev: 1283ft/391m, Tel: 620-767-5195, Nearest town: Council Grove. GPS: 38.692139, -96.534180

9 • B4 | Curtis Creek

Total sites: 71, RV sites: 68, Elec sites: 61, Water at site, Flush toilet, Free showers, RV dump, Tents: $14/RVs: $14-20, Open Apr-Sep, Max Length: 80ft, Reservations accepted, Elev: 1165ft/355m, Tel: 785-238-5714, Nearest town: Junction City. GPS: 39.092101, -96.953497

10 • B4 | Farnum Creek

Total sites: 59, RV sites: 59, Elec sites: 46, Central water, Flush toilet, Free showers, RV dump, Tents: $14/RVs: $20-21, Open Apr-Sep, Reservations accepted, Elev: 1204ft/367m, Tel: 785-463-5791, Nearest town: Milford. GPS: 39.150253, -96.906788

11 • B4 | Kanza View

Total sites: 5, RV sites: 0, Central water, Vault/pit toilet, No showers, No RV dump, Tents only: $10, Open all year, Reservations not accepted, Elev: 1322ft/403m, Tel: 620-767-5195, Nearest town: Council Grove. GPS: 38.687116, -96.493013

12 • B4 | Kit Carson Cove

Total sites: 15, RV sites: 15, Elec sites: 14, Water at site, Flush toilet, Free showers, No RV dump, Tents: $10/RVs: $17-20, Open Mar-Nov, Reservations not accepted, Elev: 1309ft/399m, Tel: 620-767-5195, Nearest town: Council Grove. GPS: 38.693551, -96.495711

13 • B4 | Marina Cove

Total sites: 4, RV sites: 4, Elec sites: 3, No toilets, No showers, No RV dump, Tent & RV camping: $8-12, Concessionaire, Open all year, Elev: 1286ft/392m, Tel: 620-767-5195, Nearest town: Council Grove. GPS: 38.680403, -96.520171

14 • B4 | Neosho Park

Total sites: 8, RV sites: 8, Elec sites: 8, Water at site, Vault/pit toilet, No showers, No RV dump, Tents: $14/RVs: $14-18, 1 full hookups, Open all year, Reservations not accepted, Elev: 1306ft/398m, Tel: 620-767-5195, Nearest town: Council Grove. GPS: 38.677681, -96.513057

15 • B4 | Richey Cove

Total sites: 39, RV sites: 38, Elec sites: 39, Central water, Flush toilet, Free showers, RV dump, Tent & RV camping: $18-25, Group site $100, Open Apr-Oct, Max Length: 95ft, Reservations accepted, Elev: 1309ft/399m, Tel: 620-767-5195, Nearest town: Council Grove. GPS: 38.701867, -96.498346

16 • B4 | Santa Fe Trail

Total sites: 32, RV sites: 31, Elec sites: 31, Central water, Flush toilet, Free showers, RV dump, Tents: $14/RVs: $18-22, Group site $140, Open Apr-Oct, Max Length: 102ft, Reservations accepted, Elev: 1280ft/390m, Tel: 620-767-5195, Nearest town: Council Grove. GPS: 38.684773, -96.526008

17 • B4 | School Creek

Total sites: 44, RV sites: 44, Central water, Vault/pit toilet, No showers, No RV dump, Tent & RV camping: $10, Free Oct 1-Apr 14 - no services, Open all year, Max Length: 30ft, Reservations not accepted, Elev: 1194ft/364m, Tel: 785-238-5714, Nearest town: Wakefield. GPS: 39.139985, -96.932997

18 • B4 | Stockdale Park

Total sites: 12, RV sites: 12, Elec sites: 12, Flush toilet, Free showers, RV dump, Tent & RV camping: $20, Open May-Oct, Max Length: 135ft, Reservations accepted, Elev: 1174ft/358m, Tel: 785-539-8511, Nearest town: Manhattan. GPS: 39.306527, -96.652791

19 • B4 | Sun Dance

Total sites: 25, RV sites: 25, Central water, Vault/pit toilet, No showers, No RV dump, Tent & RV camping: $10, Stay limit: 14 days, Generator hours: 0600-2200, Reservations not accepted, Elev: 1050ft/320m, Tel: 785-549-3318, Nearest town: Lebo. GPS: 38.479101, -95.859574

20 • B4 | Timber Creek

Total sites: 36, RV sites: 36, Central water, Vault/pit toilet, No showers, No RV dump, Tent & RV camping: $10, Free 1 Oct- 15 Apr, Open all year, Reservations not accepted, Elev: 1191ft/363m, Tel: 785-238-4643, Nearest town: Junction City. GPS: 39.214147, -96.975706

21 • B4 | Turkey Point

Total sites: 47, RV sites: 47, Elec sites: 36, Water at site, Flush toilet, Free showers, RV dump, Tents: $14/RVs: $20-21, 2 group sites $50-$160, Open May-Sep, Max Length: 65ft, Reservations accepted, Elev: 1056ft/322m, Tel: 785-549-3318, Nearest town: Osage City. GPS: 38.497773, -95.789468

22 • B4 | Tuttle Creek Cove

Total sites: 56, RV sites: 56, Elec sites: 39, Central water, Flush toilet, Free showers, RV dump, Tents: $14/RVs: $20, Open May-Oct, Max Length: 140ft, Reservations accepted, Elev: 1129ft/344m, Tel: 785-539-6523, Nearest town: Manhattan. GPS: 39.280363, -96.632384

23 • B4 | West Rolling Hills

Total sites: 65, RV sites: 59, Elec sites: 53, Water at site, Flush toilet, Free showers, RV dump, Tents: $14/RVs: $14-21, Open Apr-Sep, Max Length: 165ft, Reservations accepted, Elev: 1188ft/362m, Tel: 785-238-5714, Nearest town: Junction City. GPS: 39.069060, -96.929020

24 • B5 | Arrow Rock

Total sites: 45, RV sites: 45, Elec sites: 19, Water at site, Flush toilet, Free showers, RV dump, Tent & RV camping: $14-20, Open May-Sep, Max Length: 78ft, Reservations accepted, Elev: 1079ft/329m, Tel: 785-549-3318, Nearest town: Melvern. GPS: 38.490388, -95.761398

25 • B5 | Bloomington East - Ash Group

Total sites: 1, RV sites: 1, Central water, Flush toilet, Free showers, RV dump, Group site: $50, Open May-Sep, Reservations accepted, Elev: 951ft/290m, Tel: 785-843-7665, Nearest town: Lawrence. GPS: 38.903992, -95.387064

26 • B5 | Bloomington East - Cedar Ridge

Total sites: 101, RV sites: 101, Elec sites: 101, Central water, Flush toilet, Free showers, RV dump, Tents: $14/RVs: $14-24, Open May-Oct, Max Length: 60ft, Reservations accepted, Elev: 932ft/284m, Tel: 785-843-7665, Nearest town: Lawrence. GPS: 38.914941, -95.376661

27 • B5 | Bloomington East - Elm Group

Total sites: 1, RV sites: 1, Central water, Vault/pit toilet, No showers, No RV dump, Group site: $50, Open May-Sep, Reservations accepted, Elev: 951ft/290m, Tel: 785-843-7665, Nearest town: Lawrence. GPS: 38.904566, -95.385632

28 • B5 | Bloomington East - Hickory/Walnut

Total sites: 221, RV sites: 221, Elec sites: 94, Central water, Flush toilet, Free showers, RV dump, Tents: $14/RVs: $14-24, Open May-Sep, Max Length: 60ft, Reservations accepted, Elev: 935ft/285m, Tel: 785-843-7665, Nearest town: Lawrence. GPS: 38.907978, -95.375219

29 • B5 | Bloomington East - Oak Loop

Total sites: 20, RV sites: 20, Elec sites: 20, Central water, Flush toilet, Free showers, RV dump, Tents: $14/RVs: $14-24, Open May-Sep, Reservations accepted, Elev: 948ft/289m, Tel: 785-843-7665, Nearest town: Lawrence. GPS: 38.905943, -95.384171

30 • B5 | Bloomington West Group

Total sites: 25, RV sites: 25, Elec sites: 4, Central water, Flush toilet, Free showers, RV dump, Group site: $125, Open Apr-Oct, Elev: 981ft/299m, Tel: 785-843-7665, Nearest town: Lawrence. GPS: 38.923451, -95.400836

31 • B5 | Carbolyn

Total sites: 32, RV sites: 32, Elec sites: 29, Water at site, Flush toilet, Free showers, RV dump, Tent & RV camping: $18, Open May-Sep, Max Length: 55ft, Reservations accepted, Elev: 1037ft/316m, Tel: 785-453-2201, Nearest town: Ottawa. GPS: 38.675316, -95.674886

32 • B5 | Cedar Park

Total sites: 8, RV sites: 8, No water, Vault/pit toilet, Tent & RV camping: Free, Open all year, Reservations not accepted, Elev: 1007ft/307m, Tel: 785-453-2201, Nearest town: Ottawa. GPS: 38.693403, -95.609254

33 • B5 | Coeur d'Alene

Total sites: 59, RV sites: 59, Elec sites: 34, Water at site, Flush toilet, Free showers, RV dump, Tents: $14/RVs: $19-22, 1 full hookups, Open May-Sep, Max Length: 50ft, Reservations accepted, Elev: 1060ft/323m, Tel: 785-549-3318, Nearest town: Melvern. GPS: 38.500634, -95.719094

34 • B5 | Longview

Total sites: 2, RV sites: 2, Elec sites: 1, Central water, Flush toilet, Free showers, RV dump, Group site: $30-$100, Open May-Sep, Reservations accepted, Elev: 1053ft/321m, Tel: 785-597-5144, Nearest town: Oskaloosa. GPS: 39.185579, -95.447043

35 • B5 | Michigan Valley

Total sites: 87, RV sites: 87, Elec sites: 51, Water at site, Flush toilet, Free showers, RV dump, Tents: $14/RVs: $20-24, Open May-Sep, Max Length: 114ft, Reservations accepted, Elev: 1001ft/305m, Tel: 785-453-2201, Nearest town: Michigan Valley. GPS: 38.659745, -95.551545

36 • B5 | Old Town Park

Total sites: 37, RV sites: 33, Elec sites: 33, Central water, Flush toilet, Free showers, RV dump, Tents: $14/RVs: $19, Open Mar-Nov, Max Length: 96ft, Reservations accepted, Elev: 955ft/291m, Tel: 785-597-5144, Nearest town: Oskaloosa. GPS: 39.224768, -95.441114

37 • B5 | Outlet

Total sites: 137, RV sites: 137, Elec sites: 137, Water at site, Flush toilet, Free showers, RV dump, Tents: $20/RVs: $20-24, 89 full hookups, Group site $54, Open Apr-Oct, Max Length: 80ft, Reservations accepted, Elev: 974ft/297m, Tel: 785-549-3318, Nearest town: Melvern. GPS: 38.513987, -95.706245

38 • B5 | Outlet Area

Total sites: 34, RV sites: 34, Elec sites: 34, Water at site, Flush toilet, Free showers, RV dump, Tent & RV camping: $20, Open Apr-Oct, Max Length: 65ft, Reservations accepted, Elev: 955ft/291m, Tel: 785-453-2201, Nearest town: Michigan Valley. GPS: 38.643277, -95.559063

39 • B5 | Rock Creek Park

Total sites: 80, RV sites: 70, Elec sites: 61, Water at site, Flush toilet, Free showers, RV dump, Tents: $14/RVs: $19-20, Open May-Sep, Max Length: 100ft, Reservations accepted, Elev: 902ft/275m, Tel: 785-597-5144, Nearest town: Perry. GPS: 39.121936, -95.450176

40 • B5 | Rockhaven Horse Camp

Total sites: 24, RV sites: 24, Elec sites: 12, Central water, Flush toilet, Free showers, No RV dump, Tent & RV camping: $12-20, 32 sites for equestrian campers only, Corrals and hitching posts, 18 reservable equestrian sites, Open Apr-Nov, Max Length: 66ft, Reservations accepted, Elev: 997ft/304m, Tel: 785-843-7665, Nearest town: Lawrence. GPS: 38.891491, -95.376254

41 • B5 | Slough Creek

Total sites: 215, RV sites: 215, Elec sites: 130, Water at site, Flush toilet, Free showers, RV dump, Tents: $14/RVs: $18-20, Group site: $30, Open Apr-Oct, Max Length: 72ft, Reservations accepted, Elev: 935ft/285m, Tel: 785-597-5144, Nearest town: Perry. GPS: 39.135214, -95.427589

42 • B5 | Wolf Creek

Total sites: 78, RV sites: 78, Elec sites: 45, Central water, Flush toilet, Free showers, RV dump, Tents: $14/RVs: $20, Group site $150, Open May-Sep, Max Length: 55ft, Elev: 1030ft/314m, Tel: 785-453-2201, Nearest town: Michigan Valley. GPS: 38.676514, -95.568359

43 • B5 | Woodridge

Dispersed sites, No water, Vault/pit toilet, Tents only: Free, Open all year - must walk past locked gate in winter, Open all year, Elev: 1034ft/315m, Tel: 785-843-7665, Nearest town: Lawrence. GPS: 38.926414, -95.435695

44 • C4 | Card Creek

Total sites: 19, RV sites: 19, Elec sites: 15, Central water, Flush toilet, Free showers, RV dump, Tent & RV camping: $12-16, Open all year, Reservations not accepted, Elev: 820ft/250m, Tel:

620-336-2741, Nearest town: Independence. GPS: 37.257080, -95.848145

45 • C4 | Cottonwood Point

Total sites: 167, RV sites: 167, Elec sites: 164, Central water, Flush toilet, Free showers, RV dump, Tents: $10/RVs: $18-23, 73 full hookups, Group sites $80-$100, Open Apr-Oct, Max Length: 70ft, Reservations accepted, Elev: 1378ft/420m, Tel: 620-382-2101, Nearest town: Marion. GPS: 38.391828, -97.088847

46 • C4 | Damsite

Total sites: 31, RV sites: 31, Elec sites: 27, Central water, Flush toilet, Free showers, RV dump, Tents: $12/RVs: $17-21, Group site $84, Nov-Mar: $6-$12, Open all year, Max Length: 85ft, Reservations accepted, Elev: 932ft/284m, Tel: 620-658-4445, Nearest town: El Dorado. GPS: 37.645123, -96.069761

47 • C4 | French Creek Cove

Total sites: 17, RV sites: 12, Elec sites: 12, Vault/pit toilet, No showers, No RV dump, Tent & RV camping: $12, Open Mar-Nov, Reservations not accepted, Elev: 1375ft/419m, Tel: 620-382-2101, Nearest town: Marion. GPS: 38.387303, -97.149120

48 • C4 | Hillsboro Cove

Total sites: 52, RV sites: 52, Elec sites: 52, Central water, Flush toilet, Free showers, RV dump, Tent & RV camping: $18-21, 2 group sites - $80, Open Apr-Oct, Max Length: 70ft, Reservations accepted, Elev: 1375ft/419m, Tel: 620-382-2101, Nearest town: Marion. GPS: 38.362656, -97.103112

49 • C4 | Marion Cove

Total sites: 6, RV sites: 2, Central water, Vault/pit toilet, No showers, No RV dump, Tent & RV camping: $10, Open all year, Reservations not accepted, Elev: 1391ft/424m, Tel: 620-382-2101, Nearest town: Marion. GPS: 38.380541, -97.075455

50 • C4 | Rock Ridge Cove North

Total sites: 44, RV sites: 44, Elec sites: 23, Central water, No toilets, No showers, RV dump, Tents: $9/RVs: $9-16, Open Apr-Oct, Reservations not accepted, Elev: 978ft/298m, Tel: 620-658-4445, Nearest town: El Dorado. GPS: 37.661570, -96.105090

51 • C4 | White Hall Bay

Total sites: 20, RV sites: 20, Elec sites: 20, Central water, Flush toilet, Free showers, RV dump, Tents: $13/RVs: $17-21, 4 group sites $50-$84, Open May-Sep, Max Length: 93ft, Reservations accepted, Elev: 1007ft/307m, Tel: 620-658-4445, Nearest town: El Dorado. GPS: 37.669047, -96.072066

52 • C5 | Cherryvale

Total sites: 23, RV sites: 23, Elec sites: 23, Central water, Flush toilet, Free showers, RV dump, Tent & RV camping: $18-24, Group site $200, Open all year, Max Length: 68ft, Reservations accepted, Elev: 919ft/280m, Tel: 620-336-2741, Nearest town: Cherryvale. GPS: 37.279576, -95.472009

53 • C5 | Dam Site

Total sites: 21, RV sites: 21, Central water, Flush toilet, Free showers, RV dump, Group site: $80, Open Apr-Oct, Reservations accepted, Elev: 1079ft/329m, Tel: 620-364-8613, Nearest town: Burlington. GPS: 38.251883, -95.756738

54 • C5 | Mound Valley

Total sites: 82, RV sites: 82, Elec sites: 74, Central water, Flush toilet, Free showers, RV dump, Tents: $14/RVs: $18-24, Group sites $56-$76, Open Mar-Oct, Max Length: 90ft, Reservations accepted, Elev: 919ft/280m, Tel: 620-336-2741, Nearest town: Cherryvale. GPS: 37.272949, -95.455322

55 • C5 | Outlet Channel

Total sites: 16, RV sites: 16, Elec sites: 3, Central water, Vault/pit toilet, No showers, RV dump, Tent & RV camping: $10-14, Open all year, Elev: 781ft/238m, Tel: 620-336-2741, Nearest town: Independence. GPS: 37.280377, -95.782517

56 • C5 | Riverside East

Total sites: 53, RV sites: 53, Elec sites: 53, Water at site, Flush toilet, Free showers, RV dump, Tent & RV camping: $15, Open Apr-Oct, Max Length: 120ft, Reservations accepted, Elev: 1053ft/321m, Tel: 620-364-8613, Nearest town: Burlington. GPS: 38.239695, -95.752725

57 • C5 | Riverside West

Total sites: 40, RV sites: 40, Elec sites: 34, Central water, Vault/pit toilet, No showers, RV dump, Tent & RV camping: $15, Open May-Sep, Max Length: 60ft, Reservations accepted, Elev: 1040ft/317m, Tel: 620-364-8613, Nearest town: Burlington. GPS: 38.235744, -95.757828

58 • C5 | Timber Hill

Total sites: 20, RV sites: 20, Vault/pit toilet, RV dump, Tent & RV camping: $10, Open Apr-Oct, Reservations not accepted, Elev: 942ft/287m, Tel: 620-336-2741, Nearest town: Cherryvale. GPS: 37.293968, -95.451628

Kentucky

Map	ID	Map	ID
B5	1-2	C3	7-27
C1	3-4	C4	28-33
C2	5-6	C5	34-36

Alphabetical List of Camping Areas

Name	ID	Map
Axtel	7	C3
Bailey's Point	8	C3
Barren River Tailwater	9	C3
Beaver Creek	10	C3
Buckhorn	28	C4
Buckhorn Boat-in	29	C4
Cactus Island Boat-in	11	C3
Canal	3	C1
Casey Creek Point	12	C3
Cave Creek	13	C3
Cumberland Point	30	C4
Devils Elbow Ramp	5	C2
Dewey Lake #1	1	B5
Dewey Lake #2	2	B5
Dog Creek	14	C3
Eureka	4	C1
Fall Creek	31	C4
Fishing Creek	32	C4
Grapevine	34	C5
Holmes Bend	15	C3
Huffakre Branch	16	C3
Hurricane Creek	6	C2
Jarvis Point	17	C3
Kendall	18	C3
Laurel Branch	19	C3
Littcarr	35	C5
Moutardier	20	C3
North Fork	21	C3
Pikes Ridge	22	C3
Smith Ridge	23	C3
State Line Point	24	C3
Tailwater	25	C3
The Narrows	26	C3
Trace Branch	36	C5
Waitsboro	33	C4
Wax	27	C3

1 • B5 | Dewey Lake #1

Dispersed sites, No water, No toilets, Tents only: Free, Boat-in, Elev: 673ft/205m, Nearest town: Auxier. GPS: 37.707736, -82.731079

2 • B5 | Dewey Lake #2

Dispersed sites, No water, No toilets, Tents only: Free, Boat-in, Elev: 664ft/202m, Nearest town: Auxier. GPS: 37.726571, -82.737375

3 • C1 | Canal

Total sites: 113, RV sites: 112, Elec sites: 113, Water at site, Flush toilet, Free showers, RV dump, Tents: $18/RVs: $26-34, 17 full hookups, Group site: $240, Open Mar-Oct, Max Length: 99ft, Reservations accepted, Elev: 400ft/122m, Tel: 270-362-4840, Nearest town: Grand Rivers. GPS: 36.995307, -88.215064

4 • C1 | Eureka

Total sites: 26, RV sites: 26, Elec sites: 26, Flush toilet, Free showers, RV dump, Tent & RV camping: $18-26, Open Apr-Sep, Max Length: 65ft, Reservations accepted, Elev: 430ft/131m, Tel: 270-388-9459, Nearest town: Grand Rivers. GPS: 37.023222, -88.197266

5 • C2 | Devils Elbow Ramp

Dispersed sites, No water, Vault/pit toilet, Tent & RV camping: Fee unk, Elev: 373ft/114m, Nearest town: Cadiz. GPS: 36.793157, -87.964372

6 • C2 | Hurricane Creek

Total sites: 51, RV sites: 45, Elec sites: 45, Water at site, Flush toilet, Free showers, RV dump, Tents: $12/RVs: $24-30, Also walk-to sites, 6 walk-to, Open Apr-Oct, Max Length: 78ft, Reservations accepted, Elev: 400ft/122m, Tel: 270-522-8821, Nearest town: Grand Rivers. GPS: 36.919189, -87.977051

7 • C3 | Axtel

Total sites: 139, RV sites: 139, Elec sites: 82, Central water, Flush toilet, Free showers, RV dump, Tents: $18/RVs: $24, Open Apr-Oct, Max Length: 80ft, Reservations accepted, Elev: 558ft/170m, Tel: 270-257-2584, Nearest town: Harned. GPS: 37.623291, -86.455566

8 • C3 | Bailey's Point

Total sites: 201, RV sites: 201, Elec sites: 148, Water at site, Flush toilet, Free showers, RV dump, Tents: $17-18/RVs: $25, Open Apr-Oct, Max Length: 107ft, Reservations accepted, Elev: 587ft/179m, Tel: 270-622-6959, Nearest town: Bowling Green . GPS: 36.889160, -86.095947

9 • C3 | Barren River Tailwater

Total sites: 48, RV sites: 48, Elec sites: 48, Water at site, Flush toilet, Free showers, RV dump, Tent & RV camping: $23, Group site: $50, No services Oct-Apr, Open all year, Max Length: 115ft, Reservations accepted, Elev: 532ft/162m, Nearest town: Scottsville. GPS: 36.894944, -86.132224

10 • C3 | Beaver Creek

Total sites: 12, RV sites: 12, No toilets, Tent & RV camping: $10, Open Apr-Sep, Elev: 591ft/180m, Tel: 207-646-2055, Nearest town: Bowling Green . GPS: 36.928213, -86.029816

11 • C3 | Cactus Island Boat-in

Dispersed sites, No water, Vault/pit toilet, Tents only: $5, Boat-in, Reservations accepted, Elev: 650ft/198m, Tel: 931-243-3136, Nearest town: Burkesville. GPS: 36.631196, -85.291651

12 • C3 | Casey Creek Point

Dispersed sites, No water, Vault/pit toilet, Tents only: $5, Boat-in, Permit required, Reservations accepted, Elev: 674ft/205m, Tel: 931-243-3136. GPS: 36.650803, -85.328727

13 • C3 | Cave Creek

Total sites: 65, RV sites: 65, Elec sites: 36, Central water, No toilets, No showers, RV dump, Tents: $18/RVs: $18-24, Open Apr-Oct, Max Length: 125ft, Reservations accepted, Elev: 577ft/176m, Tel: 270-879-4304, Nearest town: Falls Of Rough. GPS: 37.572449, -86.494214

14 • C3 | Dog Creek

Total sites: 70, RV sites: 70, Elec sites: 50, Central water, Flush toilet, Free showers, RV dump, Tents: $19/RVs: $25, Open May-Oct, Max Length: 105ft, Reservations accepted, Elev: 528ft/161m, Tel: 270-524-5454, Nearest town: Cub Run. GPS: 37.321289, -86.131836

15 • C3 | Holmes Bend

Total sites: 124, RV sites: 124, Elec sites: 101, Central water, Flush toilet, Free showers, RV dump, Tents: $17/RVs: $23-25, Open Apr-Oct, Max Length: 99ft, Reservations accepted, Elev: 876ft/267m, Tel: 270-465-4463, Nearest town: Columbia. GPS: 37.212479, -85.264949

16 • C3 | Huffakre Branch

Dispersed sites, No water, Vault/pit toilet, Tents only: $5, Boat-in, Permit required, Reservations accepted, Elev: 654ft/199m, Tel: 931-243-3136. GPS: 36.635067, -85.259553

17 • C3 | Jarvis Point

Dispersed sites, No water, Vault/pit toilet, Tents only: $5, Boat-in, Permit required, Reservations accepted, Elev: 701ft/214m, Tel: 931-243-3136, Nearest town: Albany. GPS: 36.656828, -85.263947

18 • C3 | Kendall

Total sites: 115, RV sites: 114, Elec sites: 115, Water at site, Flush toilet, Free showers, RV dump, Tents: $16/RVs: $32, Open Apr-Nov, Max Length: 115ft, Reservations accepted, Elev: 591ft/180m, Tel: 270-343-4660, Nearest town: Jamestown. GPS: 36.879728, -85.148194

19 • C3 | Laurel Branch

Total sites: 71, RV sites: 71, Elec sites: 26, Central water, Vault/pit toilet, No showers, RV dump, Tents: $18/RVs: $24, Open Apr-Oct, Max Length: 70ft, Reservations accepted, Elev: 538ft/164m, Tel: 270-257-8839, Nearest town: Mcdaniels. GPS: 37.606689, -86.458984

20 • C3 | Moutardier

Total sites: 167, RV sites: 167, Elec sites: 81, Central water, Flush toilet, Free showers, RV dump, Tents: $15-19/RVs: $25, Open Apr-Oct, Max Length: 95ft, Reservations accepted, Elev: 604ft/184m, Tel: 270-286-4230, Nearest town: Leitchfield. GPS: 37.317546, -86.234977

21 • C3 | North Fork

Total sites: 94, RV sites: 94, Elec sites: 47, Central water, Flush toilet, Free showers, RV dump, Tents: $18/RVs: $24, Open May-Oct, Max Length: 95ft, Reservations accepted, Elev: 522ft/159m, Tel: 270-257-8139, Nearest town: Mcdaniels. GPS: 37.629884, -86.436659

22 • C3 | Pikes Ridge

Total sites: 61, RV sites: 61, Elec sites: 21, Central water, No toilets, No showers, RV dump, Tents: $15/RVs: $21, Open May-Sep, Max Length: 97ft, Reservations accepted, Elev: 663ft/202m, Tel: 270-465-6488, Nearest town: Campbellsville. GPS: 37.284654, -85.293508

23 • C3 | Smith Ridge

Total sites: 80, RV sites: 80, Elec sites: 62, Central water, Flush toilet, Free showers, RV dump, Tents: $17/RVs: $23-25, Open May-Sep, Max Length: 84ft, Reservations accepted, Elev: 755ft/230m, Tel: 270-789-2743, Nearest town: Campbellsville. GPS: 37.294591, -85.292354

24 • C3 | State Line Point

Dispersed sites, No water, Vault/pit toilet, Tents only: $5, Boat-in, Permit required, Reservations accepted, Elev: 655ft/200m, Tel: 931-243-3136, Nearest town: Burkesville. GPS: 36.626864, -85.268911

25 • C3 | Tailwater

Total sites: 45, RV sites: 45, Elec sites: 45, Central water, Flush toilet, Free showers, RV dump, Tent & RV camping: $23, Group site $50, Open May-Sep, Max Length: 115ft, Reservations accepted, Elev: 512ft/156m, Tel: 270-622-7732, Nearest town: Glasgow. GPS: 36.894926, -86.131279

26 • C3 | The Narrows

Total sites: 86, RV sites: 86, Elec sites: 86, Water at site, Flush toilet, Free showers, RV dump, Tent & RV camping: $25, Open May-Sep, Max Length: 111ft, Reservations accepted, Elev: 604ft/184m, Tel: 270-646-3094, Nearest town: Lucas. GPS: 36.904308, -86.070261

27 • C3 | Wax

Total sites: 110, RV sites: 110, Elec sites: 85, Central water, Flush toilet, Free showers, RV dump, Tents: $19/RVs: $25, Open May-Sep, Max Length: 120ft, Reservations accepted, Elev: 535ft/163m, Tel: 270-242-7578, Nearest town: Munfordville. GPS: 37.343926, -86.128045

28 • C4 | Buckhorn

Total sites: 28, RV sites: 24, Elec sites: 24, Central water, Flush toilet, Free showers, RV dump, Tents: $14/RVs: $24-32, Open May-Sep, Max Length: 50ft, Reservations accepted, Elev: 771ft/235m, Tel: 606-398-7220, Nearest town: Buckhorn. GPS: 37.343901, -83.470342

29 • C4 | Buckhorn Boat-in

Dispersed sites, Tents only: $14, Boat-in, Elev: 789ft/240m, Tel: 606-398-7220, Nearest town: Buckhorn. GPS: 37.331894, -83.464743

30 • C4 | Cumberland Point

Total sites: 30, RV sites: 30, Elec sites: 30, Water at site, Flush toilet, Free showers, RV dump, Tents: $22/RVs: $26, Group site $50, Open May-Sep, Max Length: 68ft, Reservations accepted, Elev: 781ft/238m, Tel: 606-871-7886, Nearest town: Nancy. GPS: 36.965922, -84.841877

31 • C4 | Fall Creek

Total sites: 10, RV sites: 10, Elec sites: 10, Central water, Flush toilet, Free showers, RV dump, Tent & RV camping: $26, Open Apr-Oct, Max Length: 61ft, Reservations accepted, Elev: 774ft/236m, Tel: 606-348-6042, Nearest town: Somerset. GPS: 36.922977, -84.847046

32 • C4 | Fishing Creek

Total sites: 46, RV sites: 26, Elec sites: 46, Central water, Flush toilet, Free showers, RV dump, Tents: $22/RVs: $30-36, Open Apr-Oct, Max Length: 73ft, Reservations accepted, Elev: 830ft/253m, Tel: 606-679-5174, Nearest town: Somerset. GPS: 37.072021, -84.689209

33 • C4 | Waitsboro

Total sites: 21, RV sites: 16, Elec sites: 18, Central water, Flush toilet, Free showers, RV dump, Tents: $16/RVs: $23-30, Open Apr-Oct, Max Length: 72ft, Reservations accepted, Elev: 896ft/273m, Tel: 606-561-5513, Nearest town: Somerset. GPS: 37.015704, -84.637102

34 • C5 | Grapevine

Total sites: 28, RV sites: 28, Elec sites: 10, Water at site, Flush toilet, Free showers, RV dump, Tents: $8/RVs: $12, Open May-Sep, Elev: 889ft/271m, Tel: 606-437-7496, Nearest town: Pikeville. GPS: 37.432268, -82.357042

35 • C5 | Littcarr

Total sites: 45, RV sites: 45, Elec sites: 45, Water at site, Flush toilet, Free showers, RV dump, Tent & RV camping: $24-30, 14 full hookups, Open Apr-Oct, Max Length: 54ft, Reservations accepted, Elev: 1106ft/337m, Tel: 606-642-3052, Nearest town: Sassafras. GPS: 37.236385, -82.948308

36 • C5 | Trace Branch

Total sites: 18, RV sites: 18, Elec sites: 18, Water at site, Flush toilet, Free showers, RV dump, Tent & RV camping: $24, Open May-Sep, Max Length: 55ft, Reservations accepted, Elev: 794ft/242m, Tel: 606-672-3670, Nearest town: Hyden. GPS: 37.272377, -83.369806

Louisiana

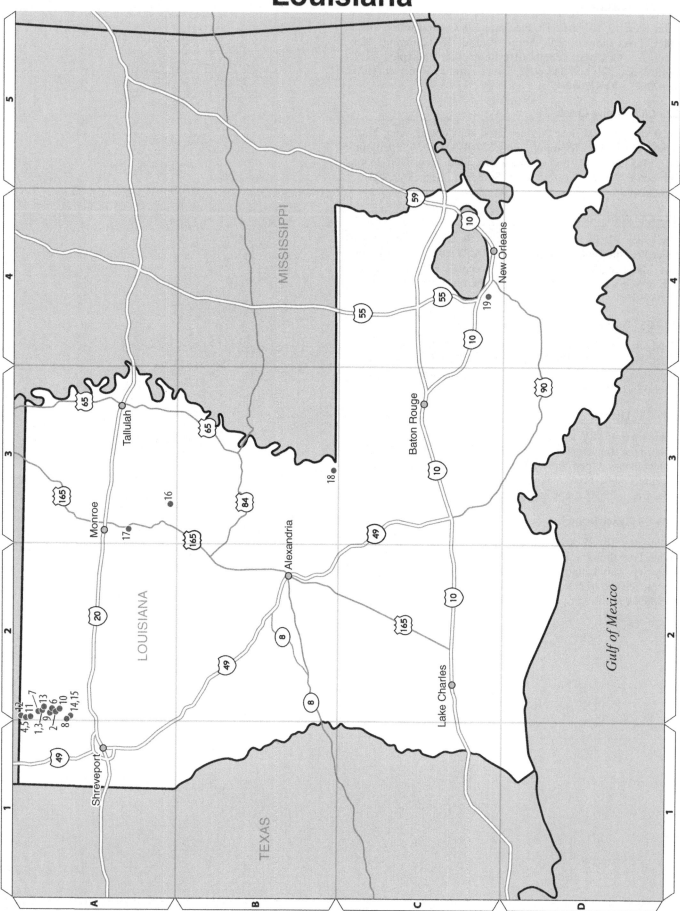

Map	ID	Map	ID
A2	1-15	B3	18
A3	16-17	C4	19

Alphabetical List of Camping Areas

Name	ID	Map
Bodcau WMA - Bodcau Road Dispersed	1	A2
Bodcau WMA - Corner of the Old Field Dispersed	2	A2
Bodcau WMA - Crow Lake	3	A2
Bodcau WMA - Della Field Dispersed	4	A2
Bodcau WMA - Highway 157 Dispersed	5	A2
Bodcau WMA - Highway 160 Dispersed	6	A2
Bodcau WMA - Highway 2 Dispersed	7	A2
Bodcau WMA - Horse Camp	8	A2
Bodcau WMA - Ivan Lake Dispersed	9	A2
Bodcau WMA - Pardee Calloway Dispersed	10	A2
Bodcau WMA - Rainey Wells	11	A2
Bodcau WMA - Teague Lake Dispersed	12	A2
Bodcau WMA - Wenks Landing Dispersed	13	A2
Bonnet Carre Spillway	19	C4
Fort Necessity	16	A3
Old River Lock	18	B3
Prairion Bayou	17	A3
South Abutment East	14	A2
Tom Merrill	15	A2

1 • A2 | Bodcau WMA - Bodcau Road Dispersed

Dispersed sites, No water, No toilets, Tents only: Free, Reservations not accepted, Elev: 222ft/68m, Nearest town: Sarepta. GPS: 32.877074, -93.476436

2 • A2 | Bodcau WMA - Corner of the Old Field Dispersed

Dispersed sites, No water, No toilets, Tent & RV camping: Free, Elev: 173ft/53m, Tel: 318-371-3050, Nearest town: Cotton Valley. GPS: 32.787730, -93.474640

3 • A2 | Bodcau WMA - Crow Lake

Total sites: 2, RV sites: 0, No toilets, Tents only: Free, Reservations not accepted, Elev: 195ft/59m, Tel: 318-949-1804, Nearest town: Sarepta. GPS: 32.880344, -93.464984

4 • A2 | Bodcau WMA - Della Field Dispersed

Dispersed sites, No toilets, Tents only: Free, Elev: 235ft/72m, Nearest town: Spring Hill. GPS: 32.981746, -93.528582

5 • A2 | Bodcau WMA - Highway 157 Dispersed

Total sites: 4, RV sites: 4, No water, Vault/pit toilet, Tent & RV camping: Free, Nothing larger than van/PU, Open all year, Reservations not accepted, Elev: 204ft/62m, Tel: 318-322-6391, Nearest town: Cotton Valley. GPS: 33.005326, -93.518298

6 • A2 | Bodcau WMA - Highway 160 Dispersed

Dispersed sites, No toilets, Tents only: Free, Elev: 181ft/55m, Tel: 318-371-3050, Nearest town: Cotton Valley. GPS: 32.813912, -93.460295

7 • A2 | Bodcau WMA - Highway 2 Dispersed

Dispersed sites, No water, No toilets, Tent & RV camping: Free, Nothing larger than van/PU, Open all year, Reservations not accepted, Elev: 188ft/57m, Tel: 318-371-3050, Nearest town: Cotton Valley. GPS: 32.905116, -93.482726

8 • A2 | Bodcau WMA - Horse Camp

Dispersed sites, No water, No toilets, Tent & RV camping: Free, Reservations not accepted, Elev: 218ft/66m, Tel: 318-371-3050, Nearest town: Bellevue. GPS: 32.718005, -93.527388

9 • A2 | Bodcau WMA - Ivan Lake Dispersed

Total sites: 4, RV sites: 4, No water, Vault/pit toilet, Tent & RV camping: Free, Open all year, Reservations not accepted, Elev: 240ft/73m, Tel: 318-322-6391, Nearest town: Cotton Valley. GPS: 32.831431, -93.493306

10 • A2 | Bodcau WMA - Pardee Calloway Dispersed

Dispersed sites, No water, No toilets, Tents only: Free, Reservations not accepted, Elev: 199ft/61m, Tel: 318-371-3050, Nearest town: Cotton Valley. GPS: 32.773143, -93.462572

11 • A2 | Bodcau WMA - Rainey Wells

Dispersed sites, No toilets, Tents only: Free, Open all year, Reservations not accepted, Elev: 218ft/66m, Tel: 318-322-6391, Nearest town: Bellevue. GPS: 32.958859, -93.519157

12 • A2 | Bodcau WMA - Teague Lake Dispersed

Dispersed sites, No toilets, Tent & RV camping: Free, Elev: 199ft/61m, Nearest town: Springhill. GPS: 33.018774, -93.521408

13 • A2 | Bodcau WMA - Wenks Landing Dispersed

Total sites: 11, RV sites: 0, No toilets, Tents only: Free, Reservations not accepted, Elev: 192ft/59m, Tel: 318-322-6391, Nearest town: Sarepta. GPS: 32.868556, -93.448699

14 • A2 | South Abutment East

Dispersed sites, No water, Vault/pit toilet, Tents only: $6, Reservations not accepted, Elev: 187ft/57m, Tel: 318-322-6391, Nearest town: Bellevue. GPS: 32.701915, -93.508115

15 • A2 | Tom Merrill

Total sites: 20, RV sites: 20, Elec sites: 30, Central water, Flush toilet, Free showers, RV dump, Tent & RV camping: $15, Max Length: 20ft, Reservations not accepted, Elev: 174ft/53m, Tel: 318-322-6391, Nearest town: Bellevue. GPS: 32.699947, -93.512616

16 • A3 | Fort Necessity

Total sites: 10, RV sites: 6, No water, Vault/pit toilet, Tent & RV camping: Fee unk, Reservations not accepted, Elev: 59ft/18m, Tel: 318-322-6391, Nearest town: Monroe. GPS: 32.074044, -91.927618

17 • A3 | Prairion Bayou

Total sites: 8, RV sites: 4, No water, Vault/pit toilet, Tent & RV camping: Fee unk, Open all year, Elev: 79ft/24m, Nearest town: Monroe. GPS: 32.339036, -92.111442

18 • B3 | Old River Lock

Dispersed sites, No water, No toilets, Tent & RV camping: Fee unk, Elev: 31ft/9m, Nearest town: Simmesport. GPS: 31.008313, -91.671768

19 • C4 | Bonnet Carre Spillway

Dispersed sites, No water, Vault/pit toilet, Tent & RV camping: Fee unk, Reservations not accepted, Elev: 10ft/3m, Tel: 985-764-0126, Nearest town: Norco. GPS: 30.021215, -90.408518

Maryland

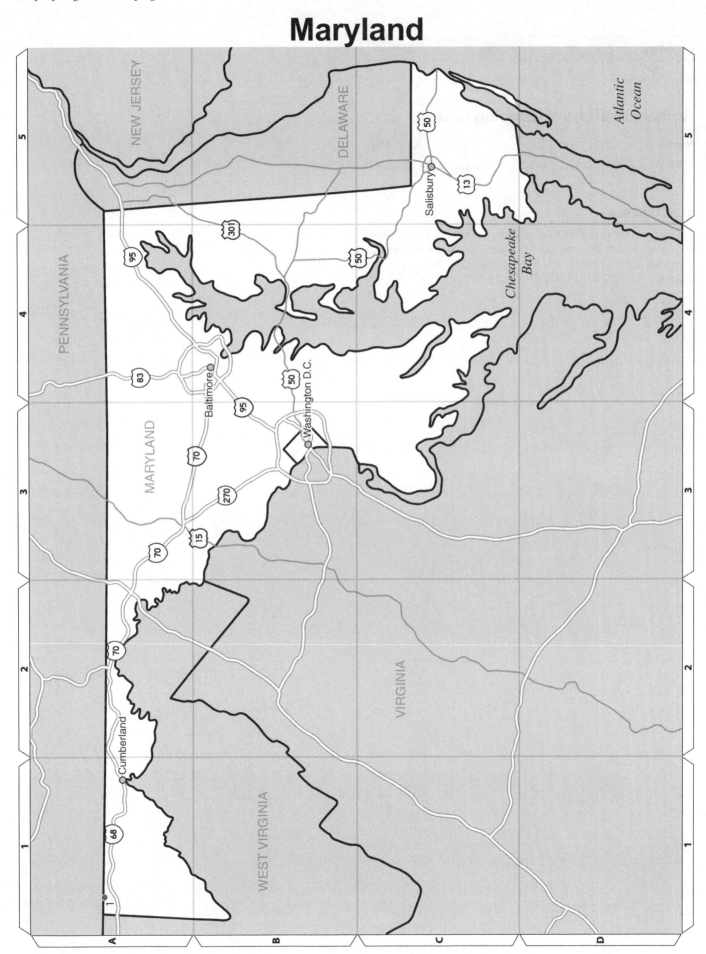

Map	ID	Map	ID
A1	1		

Alphabetical List of Camping Areas

Name   **ID**   **Map**

Mill Run .... 1 .... A1

1 • **A1 | Mill Run**

Total sites: 30, RV sites: 30, Central water, Flush toilet, No showers, RV dump, Tent & RV camping: $15, Open May-Sep, Reservations accepted, Elev: 1519ft/463m, Tel: 814-395-3242, Nearest town: Friendsville. GPS: 39.715543, -79.384979

Massachusetts

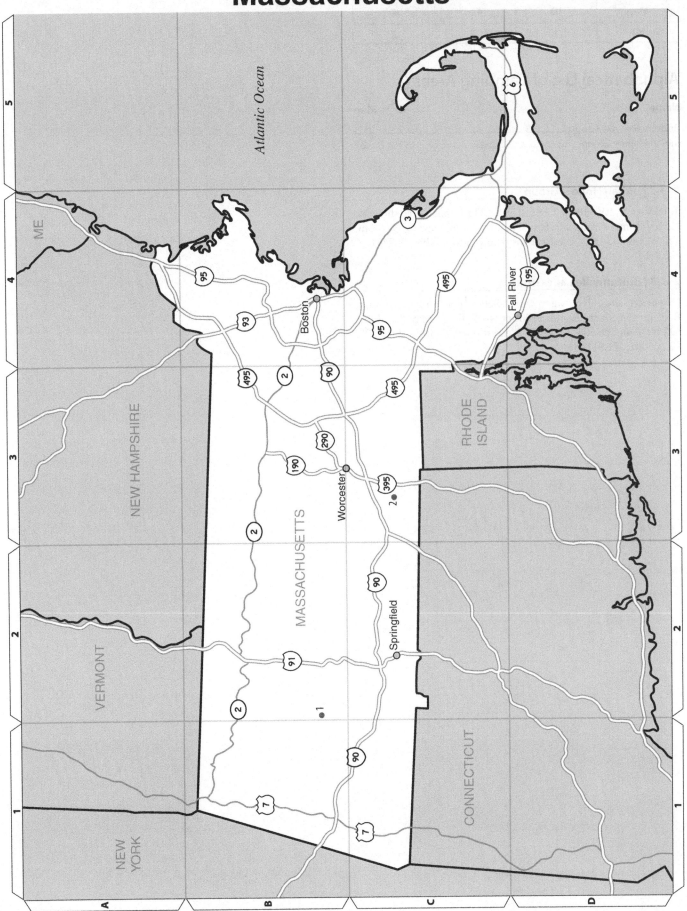

Map	ID	Map	ID
B2	1	C3	2

Alphabetical List of Camping Areas

Name	ID	Map
Buffumville Lake Group	2	C3
Indian Hollow Group	1	B2

1 • B2 | Indian Hollow Group

Total sites: 1, RV sites: 0, Central water, Flush toilet, Free showers, No RV dump, Group site: $90, Open May-Sep, Elev: 673ft/205m, Tel: 413-667-3430, Nearest town: Huntington. GPS: 42.343137, -72.848755

2 • C3 | Buffumville Lake Group

Dispersed sites, No water, No toilets, Tents only: Fee unk, Boat-in, On 3-acre island, $100 for week, Open May-Sep, Elev: 527ft/161m, Tel: 508-248-5697, Nearest town: Southbridge. GPS: 42.105601, -71.911181

Minnesota

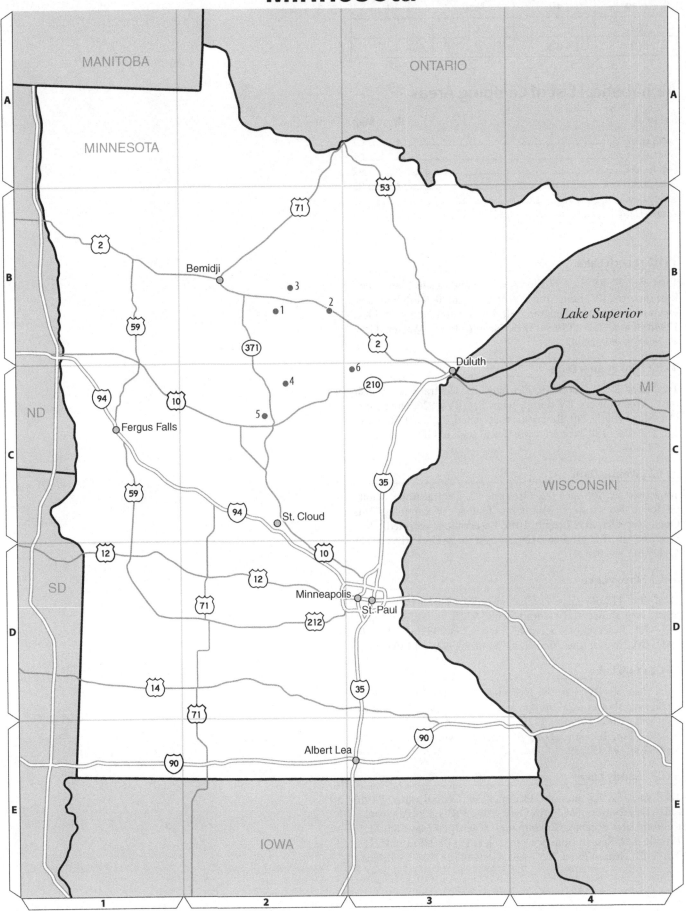

Map	ID	Map	ID
B2	1-3	C3	6
C2	4-5		

Alphabetical List of Camping Areas

Name	ID	Map
Cross Lake	4	C2
Gull Lake	5	C2
Leech Lake	1	B2
Pokegama Dam	2	B2
Sandy Lake	6	C3
Winnie Dam	3	B2

1 • B2 | Leech Lake

Total sites: 77, RV sites: 73, Elec sites: 73, Water at site, Flush toilet, Free showers, RV dump, Tents: $14/RVs: $26-40, 5 full hookups, Open May-Oct, Max Length: 138ft, Reservations accepted, Elev: 1293ft/394m, Tel: 218-654-3145, Nearest town: Walker. GPS: 47.245959, -94.226087

2 • B2 | Pokegama Dam

Total sites: 21, RV sites: 19, Elec sites: 19, Central water, Flush toilet, Free showers, RV dump, Tents: $14/RVs: $26, Open Apr-Oct, Max Length: 79ft, Reservations accepted, Elev: 1312ft/400m, Tel: 218-326-6128, Nearest town: Grand Rapids. GPS: 47.250488, -93.585449

3 • B2 | Winnie Dam

Total sites: 22, RV sites: 22, Elec sites: 22, Central water, Vault/pit toilet, No showers, RV dump, Tent & RV camping: $24, Open May-Oct, Max Length: 104ft, Reservations accepted, Elev: 1339ft/408m, Tel: 218-326-6128, Nearest town: Deer River. GPS: 47.429903, -94.048207

4 • C2 | Cross Lake

Total sites: 118, RV sites: 112, Elec sites: 73, Central water, Flush toilet, Free showers, RV dump, Tents: $22/RVs: $22-36, Open May-Oct, Reservations accepted, Elev: 1253ft/382m, Tel: 651-290-5793, Nearest town: Crosby. GPS: 46.669992, -94.110902

5 • C2 | Gull Lake

Total sites: 39, RV sites: 39, Elec sites: 39, Central water, Flush toilet, Free showers, RV dump, Tent & RV camping: $28, Open May-Oct, Max Length: 122ft, Reservations accepted, Elev: 1220ft/372m, Tel: 218-829-3334, Nearest town: Brainerd. GPS: 46.411133, -94.352539

6 • C3 | Sandy Lake

Total sites: 57, RV sites: 49, Elec sites: 49, Central water, Flush toilet, Free showers, RV dump, Tents: $16-18/RVs: $26, Also walk-to/group sites & cabins, 2 group sites: $60, Open May-Oct, Max Length: 92ft, Reservations accepted, Elev: 1211ft/369m, Tel: 218-426-3482, Nearest town: McGregor. GPS: 46.788187, -93.319564

Mississippi

Map	ID	Map	ID
A2	1-6	B3	19-32
A3	7-14	B4	33-35
A4	15-16	C3	36-37
B2	17-18		

Alphabetical List of Camping Areas

Name	ID	Map
Beach Point	7	A3
Blue Bluff	33	B4
Bryant	19	B3
Bynum Creek	20	B3
Chickasaw Hill	21	B3
Clear Creek	8	A3
DeWayne Hayes	34	B4
Dub Patton	1	A2
Eagle Point	22	B3
Elmer's Hill	9	A3
Ford's Well Horse Camp	23	B3
Gin Creek	36	C3
Gums Crossing	24	B3
Hernando Point	2	A2
Hurricane Landing	10	A3
Kellys Crossing	3	A2
Long Branch	25	B3
North Abutment	26	B3
North Graysport	27	B3
Oak Grove	11	A3
Pat's Bluff	12	A3
Persimmon Hill	17	B2
Piney Grove	15	A4
Pleasant Hill	4	A2
Plum Point	28	B3
Point Pleasant	29	B3
Prophet Bridge	30	B3
Skuna - Turkey Creek	31	B3
Sleepy Bend	13	A3
South Abutment	5	A2
South Outlet Channel	6	A2
Town Creek	35	B4
Twiltley Branch	37	C3
Wallace Creek	18	B2
Water Valley Landing	32	B3
Whitten Park/Fulton	16	A4
Wyatt Crossing	14	A3

1 • A2 | Dub Patton

Total sites: 65, RV sites: 54, Elec sites: 54, Water at site, Flush toilet, Free showers, RV dump, Tent & RV camping: $24, Stay limit: 14 days, Open all year, Max Length: 54ft, Reservations accepted, Elev: 269ft/82m, Tel: 662-562-6261, Nearest town: Hernando. GPS: 34.771744, -90.113014

2 • A2 | Hernando Point

Total sites: 83, RV sites: 83, Elec sites: 83, Water at site, Flush toilet, Free showers, RV dump, Tent & RV camping: $24, Open all year, Max Length: 100ft, Reservations accepted, Elev: 253ft/77m, Tel: 662-562-6261, Nearest town: Hernando. GPS: 34.731741, -90.065417

3 • A2 | Kellys Crossing

Total sites: 24, RV sites: 24, Central water, Vault/pit toilet, No showers, No RV dump, Tent & RV camping: $8, Free Oct-Mar, Stay limit: 14 days, Open all year, Max Length: 20ft, Reservations not accepted, Elev: 299ft/91m, Tel: 662-562-6261, Nearest town: Arkabutla. GPS: 34.726827, -90.106837

4 • A2 | Pleasant Hill

Total sites: 10, RV sites: 10, Central water, Vault/pit toilet, No showers, No RV dump, Tent & RV camping: $8, Free Oct-Mar, Stay limit: 14 days, Open all year, Max Length: 20ft, Reservations not accepted, Elev: 243ft/74m, Tel: 662-562-6261, Nearest town: Hernando. GPS: 34.779171, -90.099823

5 • A2 | South Abutment

Total sites: 80, RV sites: 80, Elec sites: 80, Central water, Flush toilet, Free showers, RV dump, Tent & RV camping: $24, Stay limit: 14 days, Open all year, Max Length: 85ft, Reservations accepted, Elev: 265ft/81m, Tel: 662-562-6261, Nearest town: Arkabutla. GPS: 34.746361, -90.132162

6 • A2 | South Outlet Channel

Dispersed sites, Vault/pit toilet, Tent & RV camping: $10, Stay limit: 14 days, Reservations not accepted, Elev: 212ft/65m, Nearest town: Hernando. GPS: 34.758261, -90.128047

7 • A3 | Beach Point

Total sites: 14, RV sites: 0, Central water, No toilets, No showers, No RV dump, Tents only: $8, Walk-to sites, Free Oct-Mar, Open all year, Max Length: 20ft, Reservations not accepted, Elev: 269ft/82m, Tel: 662-563 4531, Nearest town: Sardis. GPS: 34.418846, -89.810018

8 • A3 | Clear Creek

Total sites: 52, RV sites: 52, Elec sites: 52, Water at site, Flush toilet, Free showers, RV dump, Tent & RV camping: $24, Stay limit: 14 days, Open all year, Max Length: 65ft, Reservations accepted, Elev: 374ft/114m, Tel: 662-563-4531, Nearest town: Oxford. GPS: 34.430747, -89.695667

9 • A3 | Elmer's Hill

Total sites: 5, RV sites: 0, No water, Vault/pit toilet, Tents only: Fee unk, Elev: 279ft/85m, Nearest town: Batesville. GPS: 34.414996, -89.809328

10 • A3 | Hurricane Landing

Total sites: 19, RV sites: 19, Elec sites: 19, Water at site, Flush toilet, Free showers, RV dump, Tent & RV camping: $24, Stay limit: 14 days, Open all year, Max Length: 80ft, Reservations not accepted, Elev: 295ft/90m, Tel: 662-563 4531, Nearest town: Sardis. GPS: 34.493371, -89.585278

11 • A3 | Oak Grove

Total sites: 82, RV sites: 82, Elec sites: 82, Water at site, Flush toilet, Free showers, RV dump, Tent & RV camping: $24, Stay limit: 14 days, Open all year, Max Length: 80ft, Reservations not accepted,

Elev: 221ft/67m, Tel: 662-563 4531, Nearest town: Batesville. GPS: 34.406086, -89.799798

12 • A3 | Pat's Bluff

Total sites: 15, RV sites: 15, Elec sites: 15, Water at site, Vault/pit toilet, No showers, No RV dump, Tent & RV camping: $24, Stay limit: 14 days, Open all year, Max Length: 75ft, Reservations not accepted, Elev: 344ft/105m, Tel: 662-563-4531, Nearest town: Batesville. GPS: 34.420689, -89.732384

13 • A3 | Sleepy Bend

Total sites: 50, RV sites: 50, Central water, No toilets, No showers, No RV dump, Tent & RV camping: $10, Free Oct-Mar, Open Apr-Oct, Max Length: 20ft, Reservations not accepted, Elev: 226ft/69m, Tel: 662-563 4531, Nearest town: Batesville. GPS: 34.410343, -89.814084

14 • A3 | Wyatt Crossing

Total sites: 12, RV sites: 8, Elec sites: 8, Water at site, Flush toilet, Free showers, RV dump, Tents: $9/RVs: $17, Concessionaire, Generator hours: 1000-2200, Elev: 312ft/95m, Tel: 573-579-9958, Nearest town: Oxford. GPS: 34.541487, -89.582646

15 • A4 | Piney Grove

Total sites: 141, RV sites: 141, Elec sites: 141, Water at site, Flush toilet, Free showers, RV dump, Tent & RV camping: $28-30, Open all year, Max Length: 80ft, Reservations accepted, Elev: 459ft/140m, Tel: 662-862-7070, Nearest town: Tishomingo. GPS: 34.564465, -88.327821

16 • A4 | Whitten Park/Fulton

Total sites: 62, RV sites: 62, Elec sites: 62, Water at site, Flush toilet, Free showers, RV dump, Tent & RV camping: $28-30, Open all year, Max Length: 98ft, Reservations accepted, Elev: 341ft/104m, Tel: 662-862-7070, Nearest town: Fulton. GPS: 34.290380, -88.416290

17 • B2 | Persimmon Hill

Total sites: 72, RV sites: 72, Elec sites: 72, Central water, Flush toilet, Free showers, RV dump, Tent & RV camping: $24, Stay limit: 14 days, Open all year, Max Length: 125ft, Reservations accepted, Elev: 302ft/92m, Tel: 662-563-4571, Nearest town: Enid. GPS: 34.136020, -89.902750

18 • B2 | Wallace Creek

Total sites: 101, RV sites: 101, Elec sites: 101, Water at site, Flush toilet, Free showers, RV dump, Tent & RV camping: $24, 99 full hookups, Stay limit: 14 days, Open all year, Max Length: 141ft, Reservations accepted, Elev: 299ft/91m, Tel: 662-563-4571, Nearest town: Enid. GPS: 34.160889, -89.892578

19 • B3 | Bryant

Total sites: 6, RV sites: 3, Water at site, Tents: $6/RVs: $12, Open all year, Reservations not accepted, Elev: 226ft/69m, Tel: 662-226-1679, Nearest town: Grenada. GPS: 33.922582, -89.705505

20 • B3 | Bynum Creek

Total sites: 5, RV sites: 5, Central water, Vault/pit toilet, No showers, No RV dump, Tent & RV camping: Free, Open all year, Max Length: 20ft, Elev: 246ft/75m, Tel: 662-563-4571, Nearest town: Enid. GPS: 34.177727, -89.735574

21 • B3 | Chickasaw Hill

Total sites: 53, RV sites: 44, Elec sites: 44, Water at site, Flush toilet, Free showers, RV dump, Tent & RV camping: $20, Stay limit: 14 days, Open all year, Max Length: 65ft, Reservations accepted, Elev: 338ft/103m, Tel: 662-563-4571, Nearest town: Enid. GPS: 34.165527, -89.823242

22 • B3 | Eagle Point

Total sites: 7, RV sites: 7, Central water, Flush toilet, Free showers, No RV dump, Tent & RV camping: $10, Open all year, Elev: 292ft/89m, Tel: 662-226-5911, Nearest town: Grenada. GPS: 33.802977, -89.762816

23 • B3 | Ford's Well Horse Camp

Total sites: 18, RV sites: 18, Elec sites: 18, Water at site, Vault/pit toilet, No showers, No RV dump, Tent & RV camping: $20, Open all year, Reservations not accepted, Elev: 253ft/77m, Tel: 662-563-4571, Nearest town: Enid. GPS: 34.136908, -89.798161

24 • B3 | Gums Crossing

Total sites: 6, RV sites: 6, Elec sites: 6, Water at site, Flush toilet, Free showers, No RV dump, Tent & RV camping: $14, Open all year, Elev: 234ft/71m, Tel: 662-226-5911, Nearest town: Grenada. GPS: 33.904894, -89.626742

25 • B3 | Long Branch

Total sites: 14, RV sites: 14, Central water, Vault/pit toilet, No showers, No RV dump, Tent & RV camping: $10, Open all year, Max Length: 20ft, Reservations not accepted, Elev: 279ft/85m, Tel: 662-563-4571, Nearest town: Oakland. GPS: 34.126336, -89.845964

26 • B3 | North Abutment

Total sites: 88, RV sites: 88, Elec sites: 88, Water at site, Flush toilet, Free showers, RV dump, Tent & RV camping: $24, Stay limit: 14 days, Open all year, Max Length: 70ft, Reservations accepted, Elev: 243ft/74m, Tel: 662-226-5911, Nearest town: Grenada. GPS: 33.844436, -89.780126

27 • B3 | North Graysport

Total sites: 51, RV sites: 51, Elec sites: 51, Water at site, Flush toilet, Free showers, RV dump, Tent & RV camping: $24, Stay limit: 14 days, Open all year, Max Length: 42ft, Reservations accepted, Elev: 341ft/104m, Tel: 662-226-5911, Nearest town: Grenada. GPS: 33.840675, -89.612364

28 • B3 | Plum Point

Total sites: 10, RV sites: 10, Central water, Vault/pit toilet, No showers, No RV dump, Tent & RV camping: $10, Open all year, Max Length: 20ft, Reservations not accepted, Elev: 361ft/110m, Tel: 662-563-4571, Nearest town: Enid. GPS: 34.162109, -89.854492

29 • B3 | Point Pleasant

Total sites: 3, RV sites: 3, Central water, Vault/pit toilet, No showers, No RV dump, Tent & RV camping: Free, Open all year,

Max Length: 20ft, Reservations not accepted, Elev: 299ft/91m, Tel: 662-563-4571, Nearest town: Enid. GPS: 34.137198, -89.838522

30 • B3 | Prophet Bridge

Total sites: 2, RV sites: 2, No water, No toilets, Tent & RV camping: Free, Reservations not accepted, Elev: 280ft/85m, Tel: 662-563-4571, Nearest town: Enid. GPS: 34.199789, -89.669724

31 • B3 | Skuna - Turkey Creek

Total sites: 6, RV sites: 6, Central water, Vault/pit toilet, No showers, No RV dump, Tent & RV camping: Free, Open all year, Max Length: 20ft, Reservations not accepted, Elev: 207ft/63m, Tel: 662-226-5911, Nearest town: Coffeeville. GPS: 33.878066, -89.689229

32 • B3 | Water Valley Landing

Total sites: 29, RV sites: 29, Elec sites: 29, Water at site, Flush toilet, Free showers, RV dump, Tent & RV camping: $24, 29 full hookups, Stay limit: 14 days, Open all year, Max Length: 105ft, Reservations accepted, Elev: 292ft/89m, Tel: 662-563-4571, Nearest town: Enid. GPS: 34.143516, -89.763582

33 • B4 | Blue Bluff

Total sites: 92, RV sites: 92, Elec sites: 92, Water at site, Flush toilet, Free showers, RV dump, Tents: $26-28/RVs: $26-30, Open all year, Max Length: 105ft, Reservations accepted, Elev: 194ft/59m, Tel: 662-369-2832, Nearest town: Aberdeen. GPS: 33.847037, -88.532817

34 • B4 | DeWayne Hayes

Total sites: 110, RV sites: 100, Elec sites: 100, Water at site, Flush toilet, Free showers, RV dump, Tents: $20/RVs: $26-28, Open all year, Max Length: 120ft, Reservations accepted, Elev: 197ft/60m, Tel: 662-434-6939, Nearest town: Columbus. GPS: 33.594906, -88.477129

35 • B4 | Town Creek

Total sites: 110, RV sites: 100, Elec sites: 100, Water at site, Flush toilet, Free showers, RV dump, Tents: $20/RVs: $26-28, Open Feb-Nov, Max Length: 120ft, Reservations accepted, Elev: 190ft/58m, Tel: 662-494-4885, Nearest town: West Point. GPS: 33.613583, -88.495609

36 • C3 | Gin Creek

Total sites: 7, RV sites: 7, Central water, Vault/pit toilet, No showers, No RV dump, Tent & RV camping: $10, Open all year, Elev: 354ft/108m, Tel: 601-626-8431, Nearest town: Meridian. GPS: 32.521365, -88.809394

37 • C3 | Twiltley Branch

Total sites: 61, RV sites: 61, Elec sites: 49, Water at site, Flush toilet, Free showers, RV dump, Tents: $14/RVs: $18-20, 2 group sites: $30-$60, Coordinates for gatehouse: 33.500216,-88.811990, Open all year, Max Length: 120ft, Reservations accepted, Elev: 354ft/108m, Tel: 601-626-8068, Nearest town: Collinsville. GPS: 32.495559, -88.810559

Missouri

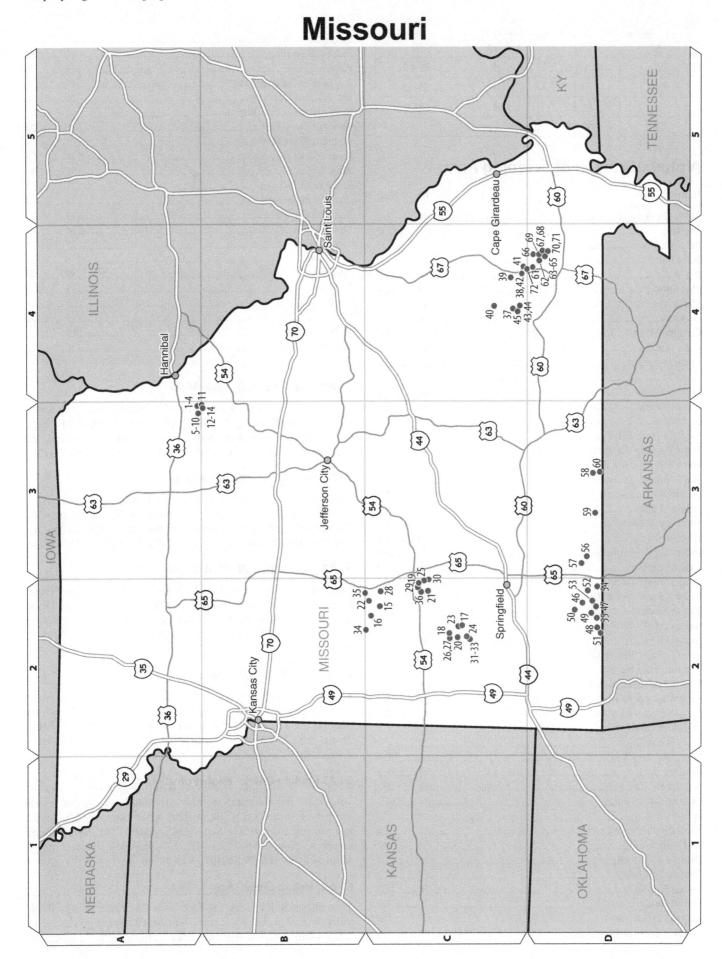

Map	ID	Map	ID
A3	1-13	D2	46-55
B3	14	D3	56-60
C2	15-36	D4	61-72
C4	37-45		

Alphabetical List of Camping Areas

Name	ID	Map
Aunts Creek	46	D2
Baxter	47	D2
Beaver Creek	56	D3
Berry Bend	15	C2
Big M	48	D2
Blue Springs	61	D4
Bluff View	37	C4
Bucksaw	16	C2
Campbell Point	49	D2
Cape Fair	50	D2
Cedar Ridge	17	C2
Chaonia	62	D4
Crabtree Cove	18	C2
Damsite Park	19	C2
Eagle Rock	51	D2
Frank Russell - Clear View	1	A3
Frank Russell - Equestrian	2	A3
Frank Russell - Flint Ridge	3	A3
Frank Russell - Joanna	4	A3
Greenville	38	C4
Hawker Point	20	C2
Highway 34 Bridge	39	C4
Highway K	40	C4
Indian Creek - Eagle Point	5	A3
Indian Creek - Fox	6	A3
Indian Creek - Group	7	A3
Indian Creek - Night Hawk	8	A3
Indian Creek - Sentry Ridge	9	A3
Indian Creek - Walk-to	10	A3
Indian Point	52	D2
John C. "Jack" Briscoe Group	11	A3
Johnson Tract Natural Area	41	C4
Lake Wappapello Islands Camp Site 6	63	D4
Lake Wappapello Islands Camp Sites 1-3	64	D4
Lake Wappapello Islands Camp Sites 4-5	65	D4
Lightfoot Landing	21	C2
Long Shoal	22	C2
Lost Creek Landing	66	D4
Masters	23	C2
Mill Creek	53	D2
Mutton Creek Group	24	C2
Nemo Landing	25	C2
Northern Primitive Camping Zone Dispersed	42	C4
Old Highway 86	54	D2
Orleans Trail North	26	C2
Orleans Trail South	27	C2
Osage Bluff Park	28	C2
Outlet Park	29	C2
Peoples Creek Lower	67	D4
Peoples Creek Upper	68	D4
Piedmont Park	43	C4
Pittsburg Landing	30	C2
Possum Creek	69	D4
Ray Behrens - Cedar Ridge	12	A3
Ray Behrens - Deer Run	14	B3
Ray Behrens - Little Bluestem	13	A3
Redman Creek East	70	D4
Redman Creek West	71	D4
River Road	44	C4
River Run	57	D3
Ruark Bluff East	31	C2
Ruark Bluff Group	32	C2
Ruark Bluff West	33	C2
Sparrowfoot	34	C2
Sulphur Springs	72	D4
Tecumseh	58	D3
Theodosia	59	D3
Thibaut Point	35	C2
Udall Park	60	D3
Viola	55	D2
Webb Creek	45	C4
Wheatland Park	36	C2

1 • A3 | Frank Russell - Clear View

Total sites: 9, RV sites: 9, Elec sites: 9, Central water, Flush toilet, Free showers, RV dump, Tent & RV camping: $20, Open May-Sep, Max Length: 76ft, Reservations accepted, Elev: 695ft/212m, Tel: 573-735-4097, Nearest town: Perry. GPS: 39.531143, -91.651136

2 • A3 | Frank Russell - Equestrian

Total sites: 7, RV sites: 7, Elec sites: 7, Central water, Flush toilet, Free showers, RV dump, Tent & RV camping: $20, Open Apr-Oct, Max Length: 70ft, Reservations accepted, Elev: 713ft/217m, Tel: 573-735-4097, Nearest town: Perry. GPS: 39.535781, -91.651686

3 • A3 | Frank Russell - Flint Ridge

Total sites: 34, RV sites: 34, Elec sites: 34, Central water, Flush toilet, Free showers, RV dump, Tent & RV camping: $20, Open Apr-Oct, Max Length: 85ft, Reservations accepted, Elev: 684ft/208m, Tel: 573-735-4097, Nearest town: Perry. GPS: 39.529518, -91.650958

4 • A3 | Frank Russell - Joanna

Total sites: 22, RV sites: 22, Elec sites: 22, Central water, Flush toilet, Free showers, RV dump, Tent & RV camping: $20, Open May-Sep, Max Length: 81ft, Reservations accepted, Elev: 704ft/215m, Tel: 573-735-4097, Nearest town: Perry. GPS: 39.534464, -91.651526

5 • A3 | Indian Creek - Eagle Point

Total sites: 56, RV sites: 56, Elec sites: 56, Water at site, Flush toilet, Free showers, RV dump, Tent & RV camping: $20-26, 17 full hookups, Open Apr-Sep, Max Length: 120ft, Reservations accepted, Elev: 738ft/225m, Tel: 573-565-2112, Nearest town: Monroe City. GPS: 39.529197, -91.699746

6 • A3 | Indian Creek - Fox

Total sites: 28, RV sites: 28, Elec sites: 28, Water at site, Flush toilet, Free showers, RV dump, Tent & RV camping: $20-26, 14 full hookups, Open Apr-Sep, Max Length: 83ft, Reservations accepted, Elev: 715ft/218m, Tel: 573-565-2112, Nearest town: Monroe City. GPS: 39.527981, -91.703153

7 • A3 | Indian Creek - Group
Total sites: 25, RV sites: 25, Elec sites: 25, Central water, Flush toilet, Free showers, RV dump, Group site: $125, Open Apr-Sep, Reservations accepted, Elev: 682ft/208m, Tel: 573-565-2112, Nearest town: Monroe City. GPS: 39.526341, -91.734599

8 • A3 | Indian Creek - Night Hawk
Total sites: 33, RV sites: 33, Elec sites: 33, Water at site, Flush toilet, Free showers, RV dump, Tent & RV camping: $20-26, 8 full hookups, Open Apr-Sep, Max Length: 91ft, Reservations accepted, Elev: 682ft/208m, Tel: 573-565-2112, Nearest town: Monroe City. GPS: 39.519387, -91.711979

9 • A3 | Indian Creek - Sentry Ridge
Total sites: 66, RV sites: 66, Elec sites: 66, Water at site, Flush toilet, Free showers, RV dump, Tent & RV camping: $20-26, 27 full hookups, Open Apr-Sep, Max Length: 87ft, Reservations accepted, Elev: 705ft/215m, Tel: 573-565-2112, Nearest town: Monroe City. GPS: 39.517398, -91.714972

10 • A3 | Indian Creek - Walk-to
Total sites: 20, RV sites: 0, Central water, Vault/pit toilet, Tents only: $8, Walk-to sites, Open Apr-Sep, Reservations accepted, Elev: 715ft/218m, Tel: 573-565-2112, Nearest town: Monroe City. GPS: 39.534797, -91.691893

11 • A3 | John C. "Jack" Briscoe Group
Total sites: 6, RV sites: 6, Central water, Vault/pit toilet, No showers, No RV dump, Group site: $30-$40, Open Apr-Sep, Max Length: 60ft, Reservations not accepted, Elev: 709ft/216m, Tel: 573-735-4097, Nearest town: Monroe City. GPS: 39.517915, -91.644663

12 • A3 | Ray Behrens - Cedar Ridge
Total sites: 41, RV sites: 41, Elec sites: 41, Central water, Flush toilet, Free showers, RV dump, Tent & RV camping: $20, Open Apr-Nov, Max Length: 107ft, Reservations accepted, Elev: 630ft/192m, Tel: 573-735-4097, Nearest town: Hannibal. GPS: 39.522698, -91.658659

13 • A3 | Ray Behrens - Little Bluestem
Total sites: 69, RV sites: 69, Elec sites: 69, Water at site, Flush toilet, Free showers, RV dump, Tent & RV camping: $20-26, 28 full hookups, Open Apr-Nov, Max Length: 96ft, Reservations accepted, Elev: 699ft/213m, Tel: 573-735-4097, Nearest town: Hannibal. GPS: 39.519308, -91.659149

14 • B3 | Ray Behrens - Deer Run
Total sites: 53, RV sites: 53, Elec sites: 53, Water at site, Flush toilet, Free showers, RV dump, Tent & RV camping: $20-26, 28 full hookups, Open Apr-Nov, Max Length: 104ft, Reservations accepted, Elev: 692ft/211m, Tel: 573-735-4097, Nearest town: Hannibal. GPS: 39.510763, -91.663224

15 • C2 | Berry Bend
Total sites: 101, RV sites: 101, Elec sites: 101, Water at site, Flush toilet, Free showers, RV dump, Tents: $15/RVs: $20-30, 8 full hookups, Limited utilities shoulder season, Open Mar-Nov, Max Length: 75ft, Reservations accepted, Elev: 807ft/246m, Tel: 660-438-3872, Nearest town: Warsaw. GPS: 38.191774, -93.511397

16 • C2 | Bucksaw
Total sites: 148, RV sites: 148, Elec sites: 131, Water at site, Flush toilet, Free showers, RV dump, Tents: $15/RVs: $20-30, Lmited services shoulder season, Open Mar-Nov, Max Length: 83ft, Reservations accepted, Elev: 748ft/228m, Tel: 660-447-3402, Nearest town: Tightwad. GPS: 38.253245, -93.599176

17 • C2 | Cedar Ridge
Total sites: 54, RV sites: 42, Elec sites: 30, Central water, Flush toilet, Free showers, RV dump, Tents: $14-16/RVs: $18-24, 1 Dec-14 Mar: Free/limited services, Open all year, Max Length: 60ft, Reservations accepted, Elev: 902ft/275m, Tel: 417-995-2045, Nearest town: Stockton. GPS: 37.577766, -93.682047

18 • C2 | Crabtree Cove
Total sites: 59, RV sites: 59, Elec sites: 32, Central water, Flush toilet, Free showers, RV dump, Tents: $14-16/RVs: $18-20, 1 Dec-14 Mar: Free/limited services, Open all year, Max Length: 50ft, Reservations accepted, Elev: 873ft/266m, Tel: 417-276-3113, Nearest town: Stockton. GPS: 37.668231, -93.757689

19 • C2 | Damsite Park
Total sites: 88, RV sites: 88, Elec sites: 80, Water at site, Flush toilet, Free showers, RV dump, Tents: $14-16/RVs: $22, 1 full hookups, Oct-Nov and 15 Mar-15 Apr: $10/Reduced services 1 Nov-15 Mar: Free, Open all year, Max Length: 45ft, Reservations accepted, Elev: 919ft/280m, Tel: 417-745-2244, Nearest town: Hermitage. GPS: 37.903262, -93.307976

20 • C2 | Hawker Point
Total sites: 52, RV sites: 52, Elec sites: 25, Central water, Flush toilet, Free showers, RV dump, Tents: $14-16/RVs: $18-20, 1 Dec-14 Mar: Free/limited services, Open all year, Max Length: 65ft, Reservations accepted, Elev: 879ft/268m, Tel: 417-276-7266, Nearest town: Stockton. GPS: 37.611766, -93.784859

21 • C2 | Lightfoot Landing
Total sites: 36, RV sites: 35, Elec sites: 35, Water at site, Flush toilet, Free showers, RV dump, Tents: $14/RVs: $16-22, Oct-Nov and 15 Mar-15 Apr: $10, Reduced services 1 Nov-15 Mar: Free, Open all year, Max Length: 45ft, Reservations accepted, Elev: 882ft/269m, Tel: 417-282-6890, Nearest town: Wheatland. GPS: 37.831463, -93.363768

22 • C2 | Long Shoal
Total sites: 89, RV sites: 89, Elec sites: 77, Water at site, Flush toilet, Free showers, RV dump, Tents: $15/RVs: $20-30, 1 full hookups, No utilities Oct-Apr - $10, Open Mar-Nov, Max Length: 103ft, Reservations accepted, Elev: 764ft/233m, Tel: 660-438-2342, Nearest town: Warsaw. GPS: 38.269849, -93.468494

23 • C2 | Masters
Total sites: 66, RV sites: 66, Central water, Flush toilet, Free showers, RV dump, Tent & RV camping: $14, Reduced amenities in winter, Open all year, Max Length: 60ft, Elev: 938ft/286m,

Tel: 417-276-6847, Nearest town: Stockton. GPS: 37.594878, -93.685241

24 • C2 | Mutton Creek Group

Total sites: 12, RV sites: 12, Elec sites: 12, Central water, Flush toilet, Free showers, RV dump, Group site: Fee unk, Elev: 915ft/279m, Tel: 417-995-3355, Nearest town: Stockton. GPS: 37.541827, -93.780871

25 • C2 | Nemo Landing

Total sites: 117, RV sites: 114, Elec sites: 53, Water at site, Flush toilet, Free showers, RV dump, Tents: $14-16/RVs: $20-22, Group site: $200, Reduced services Oct-Nov and 15 Mar-15 Apr: $10/1 Nov-15 Mar: Free, Open all year, Max Length: 45ft, Reservations accepted, Elev: 945ft/288m, Tel: 417-993-5529, Nearest town: Hermitage. GPS: 37.864080, -93.274220

26 • C2 | Orleans Trail North

Total sites: 75, RV sites: 75, Elec sites: 18, Central water, Flush toilet, Free showers, RV dump, Tents: $14/RVs: $22-24, No fee Sep-May, Open all year, Max Length: 50ft, Elev: 951ft/290m, Tel: 417-276-6948, Nearest town: Stockton. GPS: 37.669226, -93.787306

27 • C2 | Orleans Trail South

Total sites: 42, RV sites: 42, Central water, Flush toilet, Free showers, RV dump, Tent & RV camping: $14, Group site: $160, No fee Sep-May, Open all year, Max Length: 35ft, Elev: 932ft/284m, Tel: 417-276-6948, Nearest town: Stockton. GPS: 37.659938, -93.792224

28 • C2 | Osage Bluff Park

Total sites: 61, RV sites: 61, Elec sites: 41, Central water, Flush toilet, Free showers, RV dump, Tents: $15/RVs: $20, Open Apr-Sep, Max Length: 80ft, Elev: 747ft/228m, Tel: 660-438-7317, Nearest town: Warsaw. GPS: 38.184547, -93.377871

29 • C2 | Outlet Park

Total sites: 21, RV sites: 21, Elec sites: 19, Central water, Flush toilet, Free showers, No RV dump, Tents: $14/RVs: $22, Group site: $40, Reduced services Oct-Nov and 15 Mar-15 Apr: $10/1 Nov-15 Mar: Free, Open all year, Max Length: 40ft, Reservations accepted, Elev: 810ft/247m, Tel: 417-745-2290, Nearest town: Hermitage. GPS: 37.904977, -93.327388

30 • C2 | Pittsburg Landing

Total sites: 25, RV sites: 13, Central water, Vault/pit toilet, No showers, No RV dump, Tent & RV camping: $10, Open all year, Reservations not accepted, Elev: 889ft/271m, Tel: 417-745-6411, Nearest town: Pittsburgh. GPS: 37.836949, -93.261612

31 • C2 | Ruark Bluff East

Total sites: 73, RV sites: 73, Elec sites: 24, Central water, Flush toilet, Free showers, RV dump, Tents: $14-16/RVs: $18-20, 1 Dec-14 Mar: Free/limited services, Open all year, Max Length: 80ft, Reservations accepted, Elev: 892ft/272m, Tel: 417-637-5303, Nearest town: Stockton. GPS: 37.523031, -93.795644

32 • C2 | Ruark Bluff Group

Total sites: 1, RV sites: 1, Central water, Flush toilet, Free showers, No RV dump, Group site: $160, Open Apr-Sep, Reservations accepted, Elev: 898ft/274m, Tel: 417-637-5279, Nearest town: Stockton. GPS: 37.529984, -93.808282

33 • C2 | Ruark Bluff West

Total sites: 67, RV sites: 67, Elec sites: 41, Central water, Flush toilet, Free showers, RV dump, Tents: $14-16/RVs: $18-20, Open Apr-Sep, Max Length: 55ft, Elev: 876ft/267m, Tel: 417-637-5279, Nearest town: Stockton. GPS: 37.523151, -93.816894

34 • C2 | Sparrowfoot

Total sites: 83, RV sites: 83, Elec sites: 83, Central water, Flush toilet, Free showers, RV dump, Tent & RV camping: $20-25, Open Apr-Sep, Max Length: 91ft, Reservations accepted, Elev: 732ft/223m, Tel: 660-438-7317, Nearest town: Clinton. GPS: 38.292066, -93.733656

35 • C2 | Thibaut Point

Total sites: 44, RV sites: 44, Elec sites: 39, Central water, Flush toilet, Free showers, RV dump, Tents: $15/RVs: $20, Group sites: $50-$100, Open Apr-Sep, Max Length: 65ft, Reservations accepted, Elev: 794ft/242m, Tel: 660-438-2767, Nearest town: Warsaw. GPS: 38.297119, -93.394043

36 • C2 | Wheatland Park

Total sites: 68, RV sites: 68, Elec sites: 65, Water at site, Flush toilet, Free showers, RV dump, Tents: $14-16/RVs: $18-22, Reduced services Oct-Nov and 15 Mar-15 Apr: $10/1 Nov-15 Mar: Free, Open all year, Max Length: 45ft, Reservations accepted, Elev: 925ft/282m, Tel: 417-282-5267, Nearest town: Hermitage. GPS: 37.879395, -93.373779

37 • C4 | Bluff View

Total sites: 55, RV sites: 55, Elec sites: 41, Water at site, Flush toilet, Free showers, RV dump, Tents: $14/RVs: $16-20, Open May-Sep, Max Length: 210ft, Elev: 594ft/181m, Tel: 573-233-7777, Nearest town: Piedmont. GPS: 37.183815, -90.790445

38 • C4 | Greenville

Total sites: 103, RV sites: 98, Elec sites: 98, Water at site, Flush toilet, Free showers, RV dump, Tents: $16/RVs: $24, 4 full hookups, Stay limit: 14 days, Open Mar-Nov, Max Length: 115ft, Reservations accepted, Elev: 390ft/119m, Tel: 573-224-3884, Nearest town: Greenville. GPS: 37.102539, -90.458740

39 • C4 | Highway 34 Bridge

Dispersed sites, No water, No toilets, Tent & RV camping: Fee unk, Reservations not accepted, Elev: 404ft/123m, Tel: 573-222-8562, Nearest town: Greenville. GPS: 37.194532, -90.502131

40 • C4 | Highway K

Total sites: 80, RV sites: 80, Elec sites: 55, Water at site, Flush toilet, Free showers, RV dump, Tents: $14/RVs: $16-20, Open Mar-Oct, Max Length: 96ft, Elev: 581ft/177m, Tel: 573-233-7777, Nearest town: Annapolis. GPS: 37.324875, -90.767749

41 • C4 | Johnson Tract Natural Area

Total sites: 2, RV sites: 0, No water, No toilets, Tents only: Free, Hike-in, Open all year, Reservations not accepted, Elev: 584ft/178m, Tel: 573-222-8562, Nearest town: Greenville. GPS: 37.092489, -90.421018

42 • C4 | Northern Primitive Camping Zone Dispersed

Dispersed sites, No water, No toilets, Tents only: Free, Elev: 390ft/119m, Tel: 573-222-8562, Nearest town: Poplar Bluff. GPS: 37.117211, -90.468997

43 • C4 | Piedmont Park

Total sites: 97, RV sites: 97, Elec sites: 85, Water at site, Flush toilet, Free showers, RV dump, Tents: $14/RVs: $16-20, Group site: $40, Open Apr-Oct, Max Length: 120ft, Reservations accepted, Elev: 604ft/184m, Tel: 573-233-7777, Nearest town: Piedmont. GPS: 37.142281, -90.769442

44 • C4 | River Road

Total sites: 107, RV sites: 107, Elec sites: 107, Central water, Flush toilet, Free showers, RV dump, Tents: $14/RVs: $16-20, No services 1 Nov-14 Mar, Open all year, Max Length: 120ft, Reservations accepted, Elev: 469ft/143m, Tel: 573-223-4424, Nearest town: Piedmont. GPS: 37.133545, -90.768311

45 • C4 | Webb Creek

Total sites: 35, RV sites: 35, Elec sites: 25, Central water, Flush toilet, Free showers, RV dump, Tents: $14/RVs: $16-20, Open May-Sep, Max Length: 40ft, Reservations accepted, Elev: 597ft/182m, Tel: 573-233-7777, Nearest town: Ellington. GPS: 37.150024, -90.809364

46 • D2 | Aunts Creek

Total sites: 55, RV sites: 55, Elec sites: 52, Central water, Flush toilet, Free showers, RV dump, Tents: $16/RVs: $20-21, Open May-Sep, Max Length: 75ft, Elev: 984ft/300m, Tel: 417-739-2792, Nearest town: Kimberling City. GPS: 36.671729, -93.461336

47 • D2 | Baxter

Total sites: 54, RV sites: 54, Elec sites: 49, Central water, Flush toilet, Free showers, RV dump, Tents: $16/RVs: $21, Open May-Sep, Max Length: 102ft, Reservations accepted, Elev: 945ft/288m, Tel: 417-779-5370, Nearest town: Lampe. GPS: 36.567871, -93.499268

48 • D2 | Big M

Total sites: 61, RV sites: 61, Elec sites: 23, Water at site, Flush toilet, Free showers, RV dump, Tents: $16/RVs: $21-23, 14 full hookups, Open May-Sep, Max Length: 85ft, Reservations accepted, Elev: 948ft/289m, Tel: 417-271-3190, Nearest town: Cassville. GPS: 36.556655, -93.680022

49 • D2 | Campbell Point

Total sites: 72, RV sites: 72, Elec sites: 64, Central water, Flush toilet, Free showers, RV dump, Tents: $16/RVs: $20-23, Open Apr-Oct, Max Length: 80ft, Reservations accepted, Elev: 961ft/293m, Tel: 417-858-3903, Nearest town: Shell Knob. GPS: 36.597168, -93.552246

50 • D2 | Cape Fair

Total sites: 47, RV sites: 47, Elec sites: 47, Water at site, Flush toilet, Free showers, RV dump, Tents: $16/RVs: $20-21, Open Apr-Oct, Max Length: 72ft, Reservations accepted, Elev: 955ft/291m, Tel: 417-538-2220, Nearest town: Cape Fair. GPS: 36.722656, -93.529053

51 • D2 | Eagle Rock

Total sites: 57, RV sites: 57, Elec sites: 26, Central water, Flush toilet, Free showers, RV dump, Tents: $16/RVs: $21, Open May-Oct, Max Length: 92ft, Reservations accepted, Elev: 988ft/301m, Tel: 417-271-3215, Nearest town: Eagle Rock. GPS: 36.527344, -93.728271

52 • D2 | Indian Point

Total sites: 83, RV sites: 83, Elec sites: 82, Water at site, Flush toilet, Free showers, RV dump, Tents: $16-20/RVs: $16-21, Group site: $50, Open Apr-Oct, Max Length: 60ft, Reservations accepted, Elev: 971ft/296m, Tel: 417-338-2121, Nearest town: Monroe City. GPS: 36.630287, -93.351129

53 • D2 | Mill Creek

Total sites: 67, RV sites: 67, Elec sites: 67, Water at site, Flush toilet, Free showers, RV dump, Tent & RV camping: $21, Open Apr-Oct, Max Length: 70ft, Reservations accepted, Elev: 955ft/291m, Tel: 417-779-5378, Nearest town: Kimberling City. GPS: 36.593884, -93.441021

54 • D2 | Old Highway 86

Total sites: 77, RV sites: 77, Elec sites: 77, Water at site, Flush toilet, Free showers, RV dump, Tent & RV camping: $21, Open Apr-Oct, Max Length: 70ft, Reservations accepted, Elev: 942ft/287m, Tel: 417-779-5376, Nearest town: Branson. GPS: 36.560059, -93.317871

55 • D2 | Viola

Total sites: 51, RV sites: 50, Elec sites: 37, Water at site, Flush toilet, Free showers, RV dump, Tents: $16/RVs: $20-28, Open May-Sep, Max Length: 84ft, Reservations accepted, Elev: 981ft/299m, Tel: 417-858-3904, Nearest town: Viola. GPS: 36.561931, -93.595653

56 • D3 | Beaver Creek

Total sites: 33, RV sites: 33, Elec sites: 33, Central water, Flush toilet, Free showers, RV dump, Tent & RV camping: $20-21, Open Apr-Sep, Max Length: 42ft, Reservations accepted, Elev: 696ft/212m, Tel: 870-546-3708, Nearest town: Forsyth. GPS: 36.640356, -93.045991

57 • D3 | River Run

Total sites: 32, RV sites: 32, Elec sites: 32, Central water, Flush toilet, Free showers, RV dump, Tent & RV camping: $18, Open Apr-Sep, Max Length: 40ft, Reservations not accepted, Elev: 686ft/209m, Tel: 870-546-3646, Nearest town: Forsyth. GPS: 36.679932, -93.101074

58 • D3 | Tecumseh

Total sites: 7, RV sites: 7, Central water, Vault/pit toilet, No showers, No RV dump, Tent & RV camping: $11, Open May-Sep, Reservations not accepted, Elev: 610ft/186m, Tel: 501-425-2760, Nearest town: Gainesville. GPS: 36.586587, -92.286826

59 • D3 | Theodosia

Total sites: 31, RV sites: 31, Elec sites: 27, Central water, Flush toilet, Free showers, RV dump, Tents: $16/RVs: $20-22, Open May-Sep, Max Length: 46ft, Reservations accepted, Elev: 686ft/209m, Tel: 870-273-4626, Nearest town: Theodosia. GPS: 36.576660, -92.651611

60 • D3 | Udall Park

Total sites: 7, RV sites: 7, Central water, Vault/pit toilet, No showers, No RV dump, Tent & RV camping: $12, Open May-Sep, Reservations not accepted, Elev: 538ft/164m, Tel: 501-425-2760, Nearest town: Bakersfield. GPS: 36.544592, -92.285376

61 • D4 | Blue Springs

Total sites: 2, RV sites: 2, No water, No toilets, Tent & RV camping: Free, 2 sites in parking lot, Reservations not accepted, Elev: 387ft/118m, Tel: 573-222-8562, Nearest town: Poplar Bluff. GPS: 37.028829, -90.416247

62 • D4 | Chaonia

Total sites: 9, RV sites: 9, Central water, Vault/pit toilet, No showers, No RV dump, Tent & RV camping: $10, Stay limit: 14 days, Open all year, Reservations not accepted, Elev: 374ft/114m, Tel: 573-222-8562, Nearest town: Poplar Bluff. GPS: 36.972268, -90.360134

63 • D4 | Lake Wappapello Islands Camp Site 6

Total sites: 1, RV sites: 0, No water, Vault/pit toilet, Tents only: $10, Boat-in, Stay limit: 14 days, Reservations accepted, Elev: 365ft/111m, Tel: 573-222-8562, Nearest town: Poplar Bluff. GPS: 36.929386, -90.312587

64 • D4 | Lake Wappapello Islands Camp Sites 1-3

Total sites: 3, RV sites: 0, No water, Vault/pit toilet, Tents only: $10, Boat-in, Stay limit: 14 days, Reservations accepted, Elev: 359ft/109m, Tel: 573-222-8562, Nearest town: Poplar Bluff. GPS: 36.929095, -90.309819

65 • D4 | Lake Wappapello Islands Camp Sites 4-5

Total sites: 2, RV sites: 0, No water, Vault/pit toilet, Tents only: $10, Boat-in, Stay limit: 14 days, Reservations accepted, Elev: 364ft/111m, Tel: 573-222-8562, Nearest town: Poplar Bluff. GPS: 36.933986, -90.313294

66 • D4 | Lost Creek Landing

Total sites: 3, RV sites: 3, No water, No toilets, Tent & RV camping: Free, 3 sites in parking lot, Open all year, Reservations not accepted, Elev: 364ft/111m, Tel: 573-222-8562, Nearest town: Poplar Bluff. GPS: 37.017312, -90.299396

67 • D4 | Peoples Creek Lower

Total sites: 38, RV sites: 38, Elec sites: 38, Water at site, Flush toilet, Free showers, No RV dump, Tents: $16/RVs: $20, Stay limit: 14 days, Open all year, Max Length: 59ft, Reservations accepted, Elev: 366ft/112m, Tel: 573-222-8562, Nearest town: Wappapello. GPS: 36.950931, -90.280404

68 • D4 | Peoples Creek Upper

Total sites: 19, RV sites: 19, Elec sites: 19, Water at site, Flush toilet, Free showers, No RV dump, Tent & RV camping: $24, 19 full hookups, Stay limit: 14 days, Open all year, Reservations accepted, Elev: 442ft/135m, Tel: 573-222-8562, Nearest town: Wappapello. GPS: 36.944251, -90.275001

69 • D4 | Possum Creek

Total sites: 2, RV sites: 2, No water, Vault/pit toilet, Tent & RV camping: Free, Open all year, Reservations not accepted, Elev: 440ft/134m, Tel: 573-222-8562, Nearest town: Poplar Bluff. GPS: 36.963968, -90.302329

70 • D4 | Redman Creek East

Total sites: 69, RV sites: 69, Elec sites: 69, Water at site, Flush toilet, Free showers, RV dump, Tent & RV camping: $24, Stay limit: 14 days, Open all year, Reservations accepted, Elev: 449ft/137m, Tel: 573-222-8233, Nearest town: Wappapello. GPS: 36.921677, -90.280921

71 • D4 | Redman Creek West

Total sites: 40, RV sites: 40, Elec sites: 40, Water at site, Flush toilet, Free showers, RV dump, Tent & RV camping: $24, Stay limit: 14 days, Open all year, Reservations accepted, Elev: 473ft/144m, Tel: 573-222-8233, Nearest town: Wappapello. GPS: 36.918813, -90.286798

72 • D4 | Sulphur Springs

Total sites: 4, RV sites: 4, No water, Vault/pit toilet, Tent & RV camping: Free, Open all year, Reservations not accepted, Elev: 486ft/148m, Tel: 573-222-8562, Nearest town: Greenville. GPS: 37.069825, -90.426586

Montana

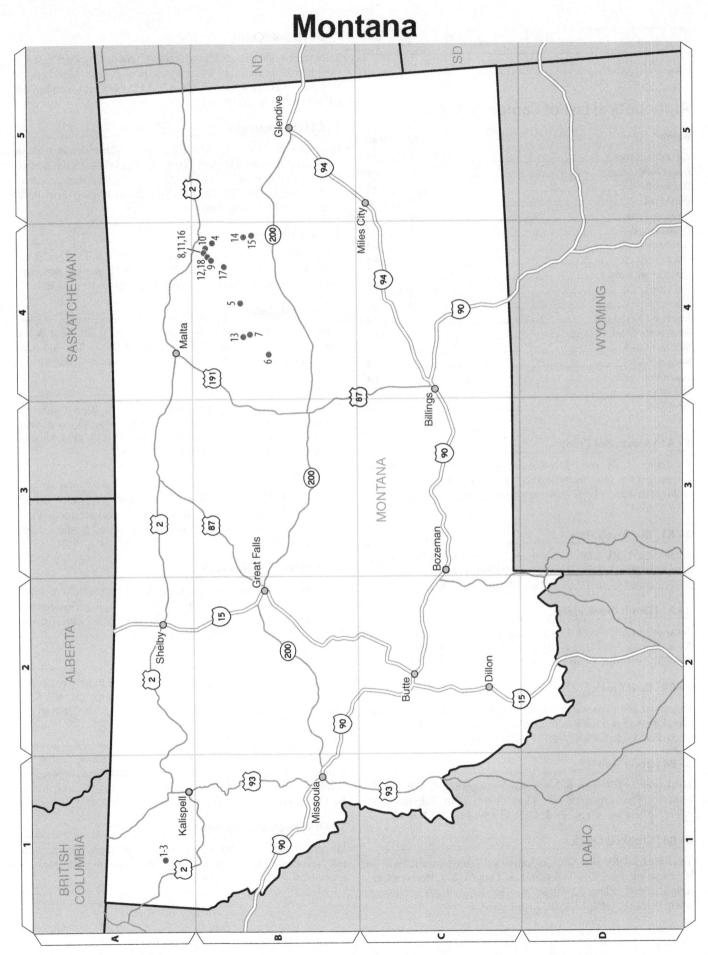

Map	ID	Map	ID
A1	1-3	B4	4-18

Alphabetical List of Camping Areas

Name	ID	Map
Alexander Creek	1	A1
Bear Creek	4	B4
Blackwell Flats	2	A1
Bone Trail	5	B4
Crooked Creek	6	B4
Devils Creek	7	B4
Downstream	8	B4
Duck Creek	9	B4
Dunn Creek Flats	3	A1
Flat Lake	10	B4
Floodplain	11	B4
Fort Peck West	12	B4
Fourchette Creek	13	B4
McGuire Creek	14	B4
Nelson Creek	15	B4
Roundhouse Point	16	B4
The Pines	17	B4
West End	18	B4

1 • A1 | Alexander Creek

Total sites: 2, RV sites: 2, No water, Vault/pit toilet, Tent & RV camping: Free, Stay limit: 14 days, Open May-Oct, Elev: 2162ft/659m, Tel: 406-293-5577, Nearest town: Libby. GPS: 48.392478, -115.328601

2 • A1 | Blackwell Flats

Total sites: 7, RV sites: 7, No water, Vault/pit toilet, Tent & RV camping: Free, Open all year, Elev: 2129ft/649m, Tel: 406-293-5577, Nearest town: Libby. GPS: 48.369101, -115.321618

3 • A1 | Dunn Creek Flats

Total sites: 13, RV sites: 13, Central water, Vault/pit toilet, Tent & RV camping: Free, Open May-Oct, Elev: 2136ft/651m, Tel: 406-293-5577, Nearest town: Libby. GPS: 48.380386, -115.319961

4 • B4 | Bear Creek

Dispersed sites, No water, Vault/pit toilet, Tent & RV camping: Free, Open all year, Elev: 2260ft/689m, Tel: 406-526-3411, Nearest town: Fort Peck. GPS: 47.947777, -106.301073

5 • B4 | Bone Trail

Total sites: 6, RV sites: 6, No water, Vault/pit toilet, Tent & RV camping: Free, Open all year, Elev: 2306ft/703m, Tel: 406-526-3411, Nearest town: Fort Peck. GPS: 47.689641, -107.176118

6 • B4 | Crooked Creek

Total sites: 20, RV sites: 20, Central water, Vault/pit toilet, Tent & RV camping: Free, Open all year, Max Length: 25ft, Reservations not accepted, Elev: 2254ft/687m, Tel: 406-429-2999, Nearest town: Winnett. GPS: 47.431933, -107.937325

7 • B4 | Devils Creek

Total sites: 6, RV sites: 6, Vault/pit toilet, Tent & RV camping: Free, Rough road impassable when wet, Open all year, Max Length: 16ft, Elev: 2241ft/683m, Tel: 406-526-3411, Nearest town: Jordan. GPS: 47.618009, -107.653362

8 • B4 | Downstream

Total sites: 86, RV sites: 80, Elec sites: 71, Central water, Flush toilet, Free showers, RV dump, Tents: $14/RVs: $14-25, Group site: $184, Open May-Sep, Max Length: 75ft, Reservations accepted, Elev: 2057ft/627m, Tel: 406-526-3411, Nearest town: Fort Peck. GPS: 48.008347, -106.428618

9 • B4 | Duck Creek

Total sites: 15, RV sites: 15, No water, Vault/pit toilet, Tent & RV camping: Free, Open all year, Elev: 2241ft/683m, Tel: 406-526-3411, Nearest town: Fort Peck. GPS: 47.970014, -106.540356

10 • B4 | Flat Lake

Total sites: 3, RV sites: 3, No water, Vault/pit toilet, Tent & RV camping: Free, Open all year, Elev: 2231ft/680m, Tel: 406-526-3411, Nearest town: Fort Peck. GPS: 48.017373, -106.372261

11 • B4 | Floodplain

Total sites: 5, RV sites: 5, Central water, Vault/pit toilet, No showers, No RV dump, Tent & RV camping: Free, Open all year, Max Length: 50ft, Elev: 2034ft/620m, Tel: 406-526-3224, Nearest town: Fort Peck. GPS: 48.033816, -106.428542

12 • B4 | Fort Peck West

Total sites: 3, RV sites: 3, No toilets, No showers, No RV dump, Tent & RV camping: Free, Reservations not accepted, Elev: 2259ft/689m, Tel: 406-526-3493, Nearest town: Nashua. GPS: 47.996509, -106.484597

13 • B4 | Fourchette Creek

Total sites: 44, RV sites: 44, No water, Vault/pit toilet, Tent & RV camping: Free, Open all year, Max Length: 25ft, Reservations not accepted, Elev: 2247ft/685m, Tel: 406-526-3224, Nearest town: Malta. GPS: 47.668995, -107.669112

14 • B4 | McGuire Creek

Total sites: 12, RV sites: 12, No water, Vault/pit toilet, Tent & RV camping: Free, Open all year, Elev: 2234ft/681m, Tel: 406-526-3411, Nearest town: Fort Peck. GPS: 47.627081, -106.230709

15 • B4 | Nelson Creek

Total sites: 25, RV sites: 25, No water, Vault/pit toilet, Tent & RV camping: Free, Open all year, Max Length: 40ft, Reservations not accepted, Elev: 2298ft/700m, Tel: 406-526-3411, Nearest town: Fort Peck. GPS: 47.562681, -106.223866

16 • B4 | Roundhouse Point

Dispersed sites, No water, Tent & RV camping: Free, Reservations not accepted, Elev: 2060ft/628m, Tel: 406-526-3493, Nearest town: Nashua. GPS: 48.024691, -106.443038

17 • B4 | The Pines

Total sites: 30, RV sites: 30, Central water, Vault/pit toilet, No showers, No RV dump, Tent & RV camping: Free, Open all year, Max Length: 30ft, Reservations not accepted, Elev: 2251ft/686m, Tel: 406-526-3411, Nearest town: Fort Peck. GPS: 47.839275, -106.632371

18 • B4 | West End

Total sites: 20, RV sites: 13, Elec sites: 13, Central water, Flush toilet, Free showers, RV dump, Tents: $15/RVs: $25, Reservations are only allowed on the day of arrival, Open May-Sep, Max Length: 35ft, Reservations accepted, Elev: 2300ft/701m, Tel: 406-526-3411, Nearest town: Fort Peck. GPS: 47.993953, -106.497111

Nebraska

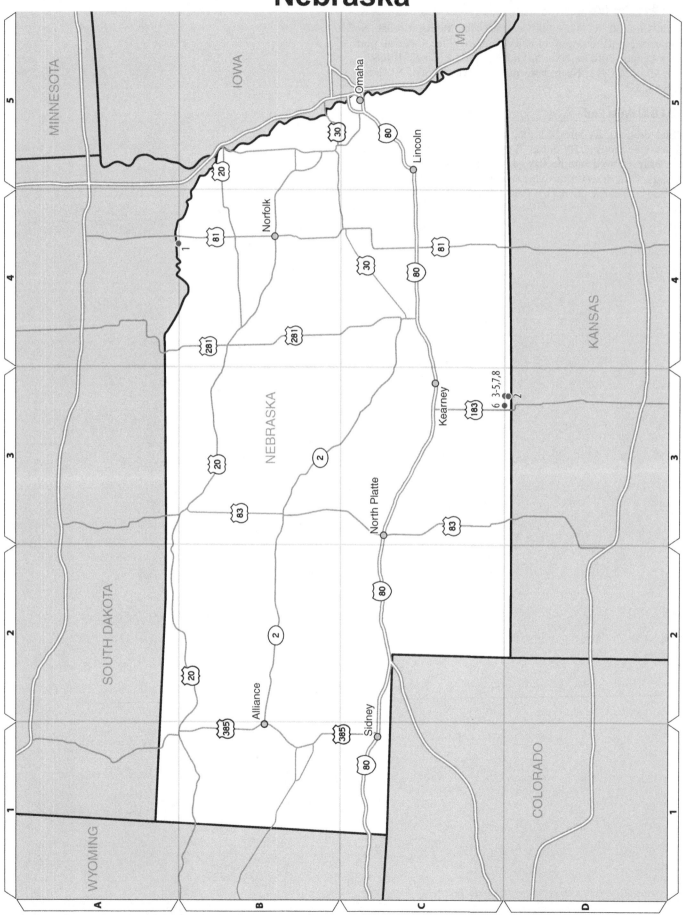

Map	ID	Map	ID
B4	1	C3	2-8

Alphabetical List of Camping Areas

Name	ID	Map
Cedar Point	2	C3
East Gremlin Cove	3	C3
Gremlin Cove	4	C3
Hunter Cove	5	C3
Methodist Cove	6	C3
Nebraska Tailwaters	1	B4
North Outlet	7	C3
South Outlet	8	C3

1 • B4 | Nebraska Tailwaters

Total sites: 42, RV sites: 31, Elec sites: 31, Central water, Flush toilet, Free showers, RV dump, Tents: $14/RVs: $16, Group site: $30, Open May-Oct, Max Length: 84ft, Reservations accepted, Elev: 1175ft/358m, Tel: 402-667-7873, Nearest town: Yankton SD. GPS: 42.848161, -97.466121

2 • C3 | Cedar Point

Dispersed sites, No water, Vault/pit toilet, Tents only: $12, Reservations not accepted, Elev: 2031ft/619m, Nearest town: Republican City. GPS: 40.049221, -99.215077

3 • C3 | East Gremlin Cove

Dispersed sites, No water, Vault/pit toilet, Tent & RV camping: $12, Reservations not accepted, Elev: 1951ft/595m, Nearest town: Republican City. GPS: 40.085237, -99.209826

4 • C3 | Gremlin Cove

Total sites: 70, RV sites: 70, Vault/pit toilet, Tent & RV camping: $14, Open all year, Reservations not accepted, Elev: 1998ft/609m, Tel: 308-799-2105, Nearest town: Republican City. GPS: 40.085187, -99.214764

5 • C3 | Hunter Cove

Total sites: 151, RV sites: 131, Elec sites: 84, Central water, Flush toilet, Free showers, RV dump, Tents: $18/RVs: $22-24, Oct/Nov/Apr: $16, Open Apr-Nov, Max Length: 85ft, Reservations accepted, Elev: 2014ft/614m, Tel: 308-799-2105, Nearest town: Republican City. GPS: 40.083625, -99.228373

6 • C3 | Methodist Cove

Total sites: 133, RV sites: 133, Elec sites: 62, Water at site, Flush toilet, Free showers, RV dump, Tents: $18/RVs: $24-28, 32 full hookups, Open May-Sep, Max Length: 120ft, Reservations accepted, Elev: 1982ft/604m, Tel: 308-799-2105, Nearest town: Alma. GPS: 40.084385, -99.323462

7 • C3 | North Outlet

Total sites: 30, RV sites: 30, Central water, Vault/pit toilet, No showers, No RV dump, Tent & RV camping: $12, Open all year, Reservations not accepted, Elev: 1932ft/589m, Tel: 308-799-2105, Nearest town: Republican City. GPS: 40.072998, -99.210205

8 • C3 | South Outlet

Total sites: 30, RV sites: 30, Central water, Vault/pit toilet, No showers, No RV dump, Tent & RV camping: $12, Open all year, Reservations not accepted, Elev: 1886ft/575m, Tel: 308-799-2105, Nearest town: Republican City. GPS: 40.070313, -99.208984

New Mexico

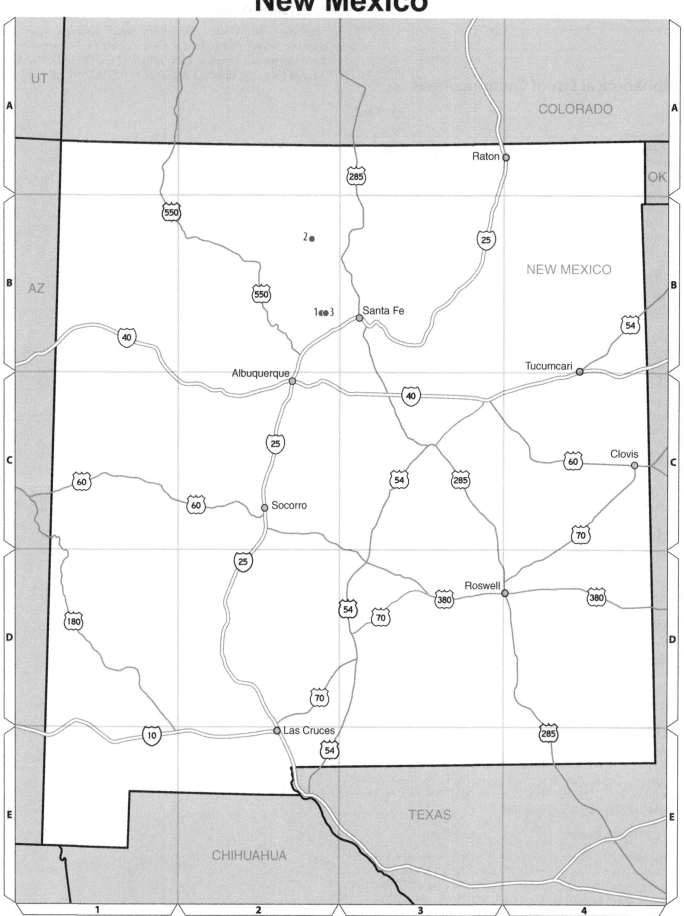

Map	ID	Map	ID
B2	1-3		

Alphabetical List of Camping Areas

Name	ID	Map
Cochiti Lake	1	B2
Riana	2	B2
Tetilla Peak	3	B2

1 • B2 | Cochiti Lake

Total sites: 80, RV sites: 80, Elec sites: 48, Central water, Flush toilet, Free showers, RV dump, Tents: $12/RVs: $12-20, Open all year, Max Length: 34ft, Reservations accepted, Elev: 5472ft/1668m, Tel: 505-465-0307, Nearest town: Santa Fe. GPS: 35.642917, -106.325718

2 • B2 | Riana

Total sites: 52, RV sites: 37, Elec sites: 13, Water at site, Flush toilet, Free showers, RV dump, Tents: $8-12/RVs: $12-16, Open Apr-Oct, Max Length: 80ft, Reservations accepted, Elev: 6378ft/1944m, Tel: 505-685-4371, Nearest town: Abiquiu. GPS: 36.246676, -106.431336

3 • B2 | Tetilla Peak

Total sites: 46, RV sites: 46, Elec sites: 36, Central water, Flush toilet, Free showers, RV dump, Tents: $12/RVs: $12-20, Open Apr-Oct, Max Length: 50ft, Reservations accepted, Elev: 5554ft/1693m, Tel: 505-465-0307, Nearest town: Albuquerque. GPS: 35.646578, -106.308021

North Carolina

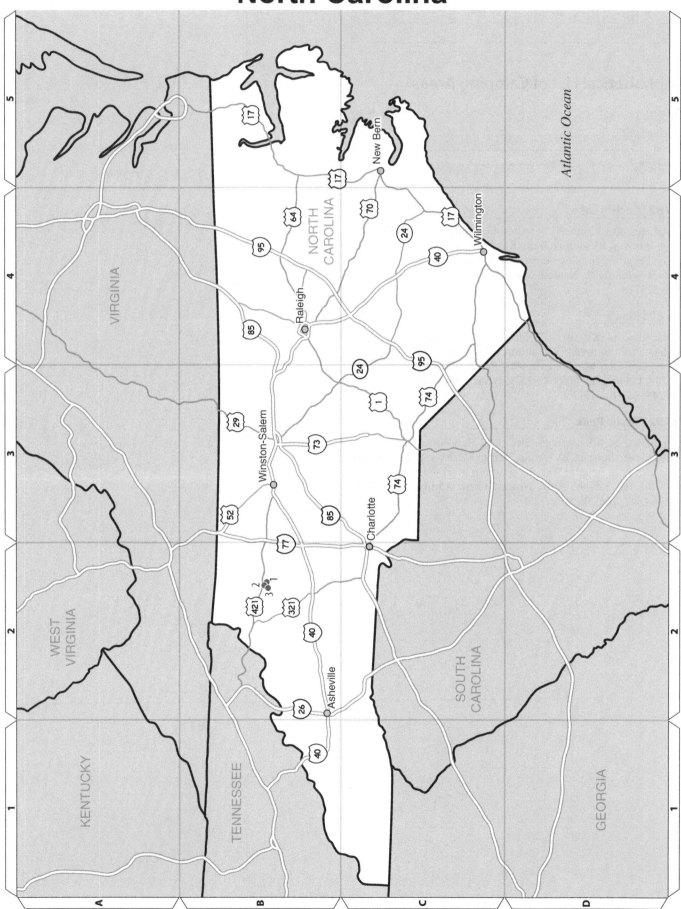

Map	ID	Map	ID
B2	1-3		

Alphabetical List of Camping Areas

Name	ID	Map
Bandit's Roost	1	B2
Fort Hamby Park	2	B2
Warrior Creek	3	B2

1 • B2 | Bandit's Roost

Total sites: 102, RV sites: 85, Elec sites: 85, Water at site, Flush toilet, Free showers, RV dump, Tents: $18/RVs: $28, Open Apr-Oct, Max Length: 148ft, Reservations accepted, Elev: 1096ft/334m, Tel: 336-921-3190, Nearest town: Wilkesboro. GPS: 36.123293, -81.246545

2 • B2 | Fort Hamby Park

Total sites: 32, RV sites: 32, Elec sites: 32, Central water, Flush toilet, Free showers, RV dump, Tent & RV camping: $28, Group site: $125, Open Apr-Oct, Max Length: 143ft, Elev: 1207ft/368m, Tel: 336-973-0104, Nearest town: Wilkesboro. GPS: 36.130410, -81.270060

3 • B2 | Warrior Creek

Total sites: 61, RV sites: 55, Elec sites: 55, Water at site, Flush toilet, Free showers, RV dump, Tents: $20/RVs: $24, Open Apr-Oct, Max Length: 120ft, Reservations accepted, Elev: 1174ft/358m, Tel: 336-921-2177, Nearest town: Wilkesboro. GPS: 36.108763, -81.291488

North Dakota

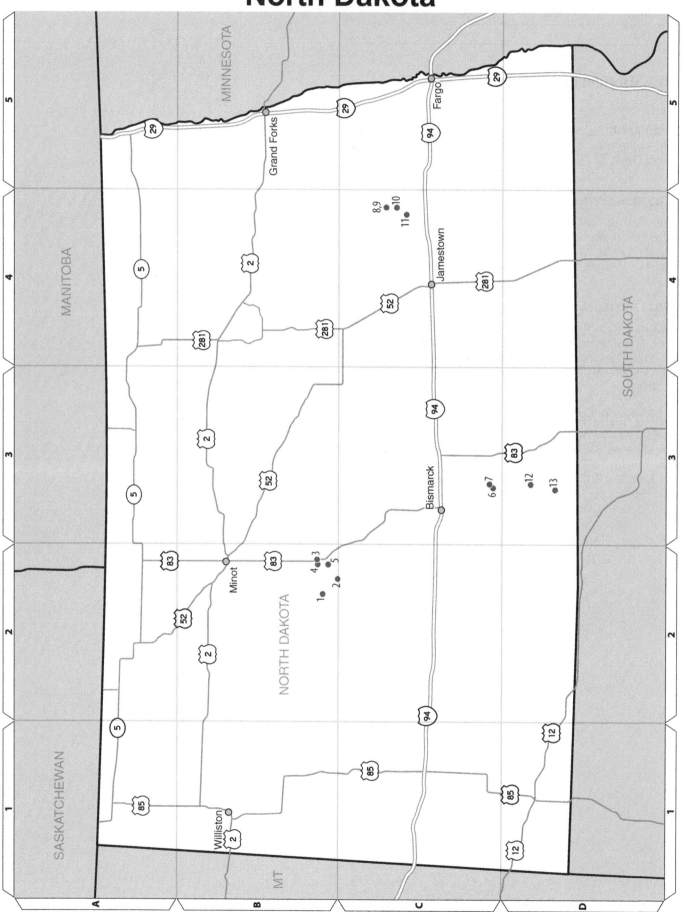

Map	ID	Map	ID
B2	1-5	C4	8-11
C3	6-7	D3	12-13

Alphabetical List of Camping Areas

Name	ID	Map
Ashtabula Crossing East	8	C4
Ashtabula Crossing West	9	C4
Badger Bay Dispersed	6	C3
Beaver Creek	12	D3
Cattail Bay	13	D3
Douglas Creek	1	B2
Downstream	2	B2
East Totten	3	B2
Eggerts Landing	10	C4
Hazelton	7	C3
Mel Rieman	11	C4
Totten Trail	4	B2
Wolf Creek	5	B2

1 • B2 | Douglas Creek

Total sites: 19, RV sites: 19, Central water, Vault/pit toilet, No showers, No RV dump, Tent & RV camping: Free, Generator hours: 0600-2200, Reservations not accepted, Elev: 1864ft/568m, Tel: 701-654-7411, x247, Nearest town: Garrison. GPS: 47.578241, -101.574642

2 • B2 | Downstream

Total sites: 114, RV sites: 98, Elec sites: 98, Central water, Flush toilet, Free showers, RV dump, Tents: $14/RVs: $24, Open May-Sep, Max Length: 79ft, Reservations accepted, Elev: 1696ft/517m, Tel: 701-654-7411, Nearest town: Pick City. GPS: 47.480957, -101.427246

3 • B2 | East Totten

Total sites: 40, RV sites: 40, Elec sites: 30, Central water, Vault/pit toilet, No showers, RV dump, Tents: $12/RVs: $20, Open May-Sep, Max Length: 25ft, Reservations accepted, Elev: 1841ft/561m, Tel: 701-654-7411, Nearest town: Coleharbor. GPS: 47.617912, -101.262039

4 • B2 | Totten Trail

Total sites: 40, RV sites: 40, Elec sites: 30, Central water, No toilets, No showers, RV dump, Tents: $12/RVs: $20, Open May-Sep, Reservations accepted, Elev: 1857ft/566m, Tel: 701-654-7411, Nearest town: Coleharbor. GPS: 47.615726, -101.287275

5 • B2 | Wolf Creek

Total sites: 67, RV sites: 67, Central water, Vault/pit toilet, No showers, RV dump, Tent & RV camping: $12, Open May-Sep, Reservations accepted, Elev: 1827ft/557m, Tel: 701-654-7411, Nearest town: Riverdale. GPS: 47.546875, -101.298584

6 • C3 | Badger Bay Dispersed

Dispersed sites, No water, No toilets, Tent & RV camping: Free, Reservations not accepted, Elev: 1646ft/502m, Nearest town: Hazelton. GPS: 46.492356, -100.572073

7 • C3 | Hazelton

Total sites: 30, RV sites: 30, Elec sites: 12, No water, Vault/pit toilet, Tents: $12/RVs: $16, Open May-Sep, Reservations accepted, Elev: 1657ft/505m, Tel: 701-255-0015, Nearest town: Hazelton. GPS: 46.519962, -100.544233

8 • C4 | Ashtabula Crossing East

Total sites: 38, RV sites: 32, Elec sites: 32, Central water, Flush toilet, Free showers, RV dump, Tents: $20/RVs: $26, Open May-Sep, Max Length: 84ft, Reservations accepted, Elev: 1276ft/389m, Tel: 701-845-2970, Nearest town: Valley City. GPS: 47.158180, -98.003810

9 • C4 | Ashtabula Crossing West

Total sites: 38, RV sites: 26, Elec sites: 26, Central water, Flush toilet, No showers, RV dump, Tents: $20/RVs: $26, Open May-Sep, Max Length: 60ft, Reservations accepted, Elev: 1302ft/397m, Tel: 701-845-2970, Nearest town: Valley City. GPS: 47.162449, -98.006587

10 • C4 | Eggerts Landing

Total sites: 41, RV sites: 37, Elec sites: 37, Water at site, Flush toilet, Free showers, RV dump, Tents: $20/RVs: $26, Open May-Sep, Max Length: 80ft, Reservations accepted, Elev: 1283ft/391m, Tel: 701-444-6777, Nearest town: Valley City. GPS: 47.095474, -98.010614

11 • C4 | Mel Rieman

Total sites: 27, RV sites: 15, Elec sites: 15, Water at site, Flush toilet, Free showers, No RV dump, Tents: $20/RVs: $26, Open May-Sep, Max Length: 80ft, Reservations accepted, Elev: 1345ft/410m, Tel: 701-845-2970, Nearest town: Valley City. GPS: 47.033144, -98.071673

12 • D3 | Beaver Creek

Total sites: 51, RV sites: 51, Elec sites: 37, Central water, Flush toilet, Free showers, RV dump, Tents: $16/RVs: $16-20, Open May-Sep, Reservations accepted, Elev: 1657ft/505m, Tel: 701-255-0015, Nearest town: Linton. GPS: 46.252776, -100.540771

13 • D3 | Cattail Bay

Total sites: 13, RV sites: 13, Central water, Vault/pit toilet, No showers, No RV dump, Tent & RV camping: Free, Elev: 1608ft/490m, Tel: 701-255-0015, Nearest town: Strasburg. GPS: 46.094604, -100.591974

Ohio

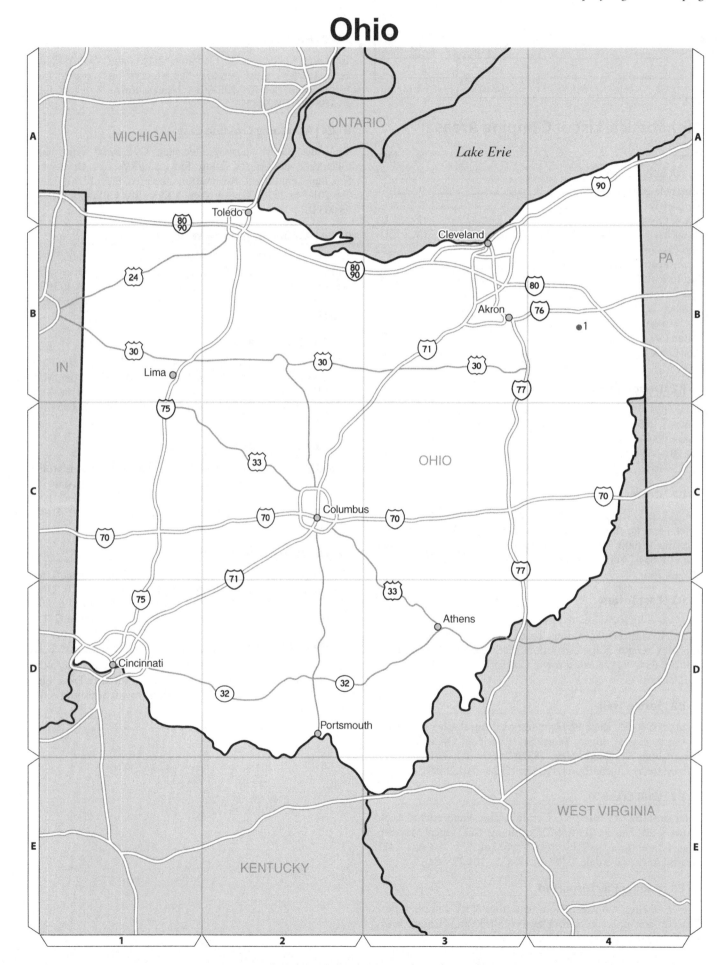

Map	ID	Map	ID
B4	1		

Alphabetical List of Camping Areas

Name   **ID**   **Map**

Mill Creek .... 1 .... B4

1 • B4 | Mill Creek

Total sites: 314, RV sites: 314, Elec sites: 107, Central water, Flush toilet, Free showers, RV dump, Tents: $16-20/RVs: $24-30, Open May-Sep, Max Length: 81ft, Reservations required, Elev: 1037ft/316m, Tel: 330-547-8180, Nearest town: Berlin Center. GPS: 41.008726, -80.999144

Oklahoma

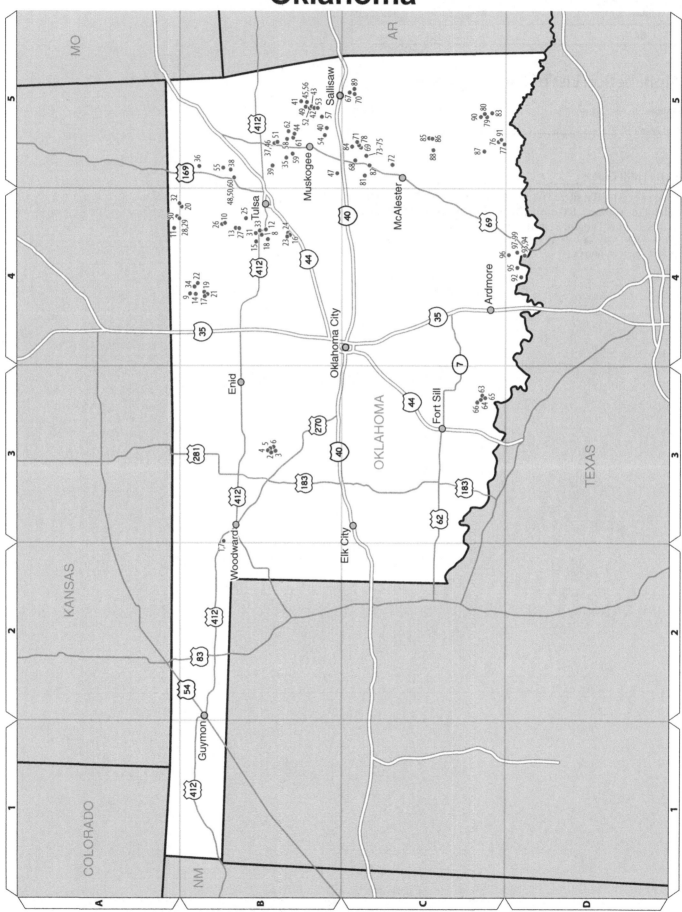

Map	ID	Map	ID
B3	1-7	C3	63-66
B4	8-34	C5	67-91
B5	35-62	D4	92-99

Alphabetical List of Camping Areas

Name	ID	Map
Afton Landing	35	B5
Appalachia Bay	8	B4
Applegate Cove	67	C5
Bear Creek Cove	9	B4
Beaver Point	1	B3
Belle Starr	68	C5
Big Bend	2	B3
Big Creek Ramp	36	B5
Birch Cove	10	B4
Blue Bill Point	37	B5
Blue Creek	38	B5
Bluff Landing	39	B5
Boulanger Landing	11	B4
Brewers Bend	40	B5
Brooken Cove	69	C5
Brush Creek	12	B4
Bull Creek Peninsula	13	B4
Buncombe Creek	92	D4
Burns Run East	93	D4
Burns Run West	94	D4
Canadian	3	B3
Caney Creek	95	D4
Carters Landing	41	B5
Chicken Creek	42	B5
Chisolm Trail Ridge	63	C3
Cookson Bend	43	B5
Coon Creek	14	B4
Cowlington Point	70	C5
Cowskin Bay South	15	B4
Dam Site East	71	C5
Damsite	44	B5
Elk Creek Landing	45	B5
Elm Point	72	C5
Fairview Group	4	B3
Flatrock Creek	46	B5
Gentry Creek	47	B5
Hawthorn Bluff	48	B5
Heyburn Park	16	B4
Highway 9 Landing East Loop	73	C5
Highway 9 Landing North Loop	74	C5
Highway 9 Landing South Loop	75	C5
Hugo Lake Group Camp	76	C5
Johnson Creek	96	D4
Kiamichi Park	77	C5
Kiowa 1	64	C3
Ladybird Landing	78	C5
Lakeside	97	D4
Little River Park	79	C5
Longdale	5	B3
Lost Rapids	80	C5
McFadden Cove	17	B4
Mill Creek Bay	81	C5
Moneka Park	65	C3
New Mannford Ramp	18	B4
Oak Ridge	82	C5
Osage Cove	19	B4
Pettit Bay	49	B5
Pine Creek Cove	83	C5
Platter Flats Equestrian	98	D4
Platter Flats Family	99	D4
Porum Landing	84	C5
Post Oak Park	20	B4
Potato Hills Central	85	C5
Potato Hills South	86	C5
Rattan Landing	87	C5
Redbud Bay	50	B5
Rocky Point	51	B5
Sandy Cove	6	B3
Sandy Park	21	B4
Sardis Cove	88	C5
Sarge Creek	22	B4
Sheppard Point	23	B4
Short Mountain Cove	89	C5
Sizemore Landing	52	B5
Snake Creek Cove	53	B5
Spaniard Creek	54	B5
Spencer Creek	55	B5
Standing Rock	56	B5
Strayhorn Landing	57	B5
Sunset Bay	24	B4
Supply Park	7	B3
Tall Chief Cove	25	B4
Taylor Ferry	58	B5
Tullahasse Loop	59	B5
Turkey Creek	90	C5
Twin Cove	26	B4
Twin Points	27	B4
Verdigris River Park	60	B5
Virgil Point	91	C5
Wah-Sha-She Park - Below Dam	28	B4
Wah-Sha-She Park - Lakeview	29	B4
Wah-Sha-She Park - Quarry Cove	30	B4
Wahoo Bay	61	B5
Walnut Creek	31	B4
Washington Cove	32	B4
Washington Irving South	33	B4
Washunga Bay	34	B4
Wichita Ridge	66	C3
Wildwood	62	B5

1 • B3 | Beaver Point

Total sites: 16, RV sites: 16, No water, Vault/pit toilet, Tent & RV camping: $9, Open all year, Elev: 2037ft/621m, Tel: 580-766-2701, Nearest town: Woodward. GPS: 36.549564, -99.574598

2 • B3 | Big Bend

Total sites: 114, RV sites: 114, Elec sites: 102, Water at site, Flush toilet, Free showers, RV dump, Tents: $17/RVs: $22-24, Open Apr-Oct, Max Length: 38ft, Reservations accepted, Elev: 1657ft/505m, Tel: 580-886-3576, Nearest town: Canton. GPS: 36.120729, -98.615761

3 • B3 | Canadian

Total sites: 130, RV sites: 130, Elec sites: 130, Central water, Flush toilet, Free showers, RV dump, Tent & RV camping: $22-24, Open Apr-Sep, Max Length: 45ft, Reservations accepted, Elev: 1676ft/511m, Tel: 580-886-3454, Nearest town: Canton. GPS: 36.089394, -98.607004

4 • B3 | Fairview Group

Total sites: 1, RV sites: 1, Central water, Vault/pit toilet, No showers, No RV dump, Group site: $50, Open Apr-Sep, Reservations accepted, Elev: 1654ft/504m, Tel: 580-886-3454, Nearest town: Longdale. GPS: 36.143762, -98.594604

5 • B3 | Longdale

Total sites: 35, RV sites: 35, Central water, Vault/pit toilet, No showers, No RV dump, Tent & RV camping: $14, Open Apr-Sep, Max Length: 40ft, Reservations accepted, Elev: 1663ft/507m, Tel: 580-274-3454, Nearest town: Longdale. GPS: 36.129150, -98.581787

6 • B3 | Sandy Cove

Total sites: 35, RV sites: 35, Elec sites: 35, Central water, Flush toilet, Free showers, No RV dump, Tent & RV camping: $21, Open Apr-Oct, Max Length: 40ft, Reservations accepted, Elev: 1663ft/507m, Tel: 580-274-3576, Nearest town: Longdale. GPS: 36.105322, -98.569122

7 • B3 | Supply Park

Total sites: 112, RV sites: 112, Elec sites: 96, Central water, Flush toilet, Free showers, RV dump, Tents: $17/RVs: $22-24, Group site $176, Open Apr-Oct, Max Length: 113ft, Reservations accepted, Elev: 2021ft/616m, Tel: 580-766-2001, Nearest town: Woodward. GPS: 36.541216, -99.579185

8 • B4 | Appalachia Bay

Total sites: 28, RV sites: 28, Water at site, Vault/pit toilet, No showers, No RV dump, Tent & RV camping: $10, Stay limit: 14 days, Open all year, Reservations not accepted, Elev: 761ft/232m, Tel: 918-865-2621, Nearest town: Sand Springs. GPS: 36.184717, -96.296108

9 • B4 | Bear Creek Cove

Total sites: 22, RV sites: 22, Elec sites: 22, Central water, Flush toilet, Free showers, RV dump, Tent & RV camping: $16, Open Apr-Oct, Max Length: 40ft, Reservations accepted, Elev: 1070ft/326m, Tel: 580-762-5611, Nearest town: Newkirk. GPS: 36.840084, -96.911168

10 • B4 | Birch Cove

Total sites: 85, RV sites: 85, Elec sites: 85, Central water, Flush toilet, Free showers, RV dump, Tent & RV camping: $20, 2 group sites: $80-$100, Open Apr-Oct, Max Length: 132ft, Elev: 830ft/253m, Tel: 918-396-3170, Nearest town: Barnsdall. GPS: 36.522100, -96.165800

11 • B4 | Boulanger Landing

Dispersed sites, No water, Vault/pit toilet, Tent & RV camping: Fee unk, Elev: 759ft/231m, Nearest town: Bowring. GPS: 36.970107, -96.200141

12 • B4 | Brush Creek

Total sites: 20, RV sites: 20, Elec sites: 20, Water at site, No toilets, No showers, No RV dump, Tent & RV camping: $15-20, Elev: 702ft/214m, Tel: 918-865-2621, Nearest town: Sand Springs. GPS: 36.149599, -96.246946

13 • B4 | Bull Creek Peninsula

Total sites: 41, RV sites: 41, No water, Vault/pit toilet, Tent & RV camping: $8, Open all year, Reservations not accepted, Elev: 755ft/230m, Tel: 918-396-3170, Nearest town: Skiatook. GPS: 36.414626, -96.220594

14 • B4 | Coon Creek

Total sites: 54, RV sites: 54, Elec sites: 54, Central water, Flush toilet, Free showers, RV dump, Tent & RV camping: $20, Open Mar-Oct, Max Length: 55ft, Reservations accepted, Elev: 1034ft/315m, Tel: 580-762-5611, Nearest town: Ponca City. GPS: 36.788330, -96.918457

15 • B4 | Cowskin Bay South

Total sites: 30, RV sites: 30, Vault/pit toilet, Tent & RV camping: Free, Open May-Sep, Elev: 774ft/236m, Tel: 918-865-2621, Nearest town: Cleveland. GPS: 36.231445, -96.364258

16 • B4 | Heyburn Park

Total sites: 45, RV sites: 45, Elec sites: 45, Water at site, Flush toilet, Free showers, RV dump, Tent & RV camping: $25, Group fee: $100, Open all year, Max Length: 120ft, Reservations accepted, Elev: 797ft/243m, Tel: 918-247-6601, Nearest town: Kellyville. GPS: 35.949220, -96.307710

17 • B4 | McFadden Cove

Total sites: 15, RV sites: 15, Elec sites: 15, Central water, Vault/pit toilet, No showers, No RV dump, Tent & RV camping: $14, Open Mar-Nov, Reservations not accepted, Elev: 1034ft/315m, Tel: 580-762-7323, Nearest town: Ponca City. GPS: 36.703502, -96.934476

18 • B4 | New Mannford Ramp

Total sites: 47, RV sites: 44, Elec sites: 44, Central water, Flush toilet, Free showers, RV dump, Tent & RV camping: $15, Near RR, Open Apr-Oct, Reservations not accepted, Elev: 755ft/230m, Tel: 918-865-2621, Nearest town: Mannford. GPS: 36.133301, -96.343994

19 • B4 | Osage Cove

Total sites: 94, RV sites: 94, Elec sites: 94, Central water, Flush toilet, Free showers, RV dump, Tent & RV camping: $20, 3 group sites $100, Open Mar-Oct, Max Length: 60ft, Reservations accepted, Elev: 1066ft/325m, Tel: 580-762-5611, Nearest town: Ponca City. GPS: 36.714854, -96.901545

20 • B4 | Post Oak Park

Total sites: 17, RV sites: 17, Elec sites: 17, Central water, Flush toilet, Free showers, RV dump, Tent & RV camping: $22-24, Open Apr-Oct, Max Length: 83ft, Reservations accepted, Elev: 748ft/228m, Tel: 918-532-4334, Nearest town: Copan. GPS: 36.899717, -95.968468

21 • B4 | Sandy Park

Total sites: 12, RV sites: 12, Elec sites: 12, Central water, Vault/pit toilet, No showers, No RV dump, Tent & RV camping: $16, Open Apr-Sep, Reservations not accepted, Elev: 978ft/298m, Tel: 580-762-7323, Nearest town: Ponca City. GPS: 36.694439, -96.923559

22 • B4 | Sarge Creek

Total sites: 52, RV sites: 52, Elec sites: 52, Central water, Flush toilet, Free showers, RV dump, Tent & RV camping: $20, Group site $100, Open Mar-Oct, Max Length: 60ft, Reservations accepted, Elev: 1060ft/323m, Tel: 580-762-5611, Nearest town: Ponca City. GPS: 36.765869, -96.808350

23 • B4 | Sheppard Point

Total sites: 38, RV sites: 21, Elec sites: 21, Central water, Flush toilet, Free showers, RV dump, Tents: $15/RVs: $25, Open all year, Max Length: 84ft, Reservations accepted, Elev: 781ft/238m, Tel: 918-247-4551, Nearest town: Salpupa. GPS: 35.952399, -96.313219

24 • B4 | Sunset Bay

Total sites: 12, RV sites: 8, Central water, Vault/pit toilet, No showers, RV dump, Tent & RV camping: $7, Open all year, Elev: 791ft/241m, Tel: 918-247-6391, Nearest town: Kellyville. GPS: 35.951646, -96.292304

25 • B4 | Tall Chief Cove

Total sites: 50, RV sites: 50, Elec sites: 50, Central water, Flush toilet, Free showers, RV dump, Tent & RV camping: $20-30, Open Apr-Oct, Max Length: 90ft, Reservations accepted, Elev: 735ft/224m, Tel: 918-288-6820, Nearest town: Skiatook. GPS: 36.321641, -96.116259

26 • B4 | Twin Cove

Total sites: 11, RV sites: 11, Central water, Vault/pit toilet, No showers, No RV dump, Tent & RV camping: $10, Open Apr-Sep, Elev: 876ft/267m, Tel: 918-396-3170, Nearest town: Barnsdall. GPS: 36.537919, -96.171583

27 • B4 | Twin Points

Total sites: 49, RV sites: 49, Elec sites: 49, Central water, Flush toilet, Free showers, RV dump, Tent & RV camping: $20, Open Apr-Oct, Max Length: 96ft, Reservations accepted, Elev: 771ft/235m, Tel: 918-396-1376, Nearest town: Skiatook. GPS: 36.389902, -96.219313

28 • B4 | Wah-Sha-She Park - Below Dam

Dispersed sites, No water, No toilets, Tents: $12/RVs: $18, Elev: 723ft/220m, Tel: 918-336-4141, Nearest town: Chautaugua. GPS: 36.927259, -96.085135

29 • B4 | Wah-Sha-She Park - Lakeview

Total sites: 47, RV sites: 47, No water, Flush toilet, Tents: $12/RVs: $18, Elev: 760ft/232m, Tel: 918-336-4141, Nearest town: Chautaugua. GPS: 36.928074, -96.099761

30 • B4 | Wah-Sha-She Park - Quarry Cove

Dispersed sites, Tents: $12/RVs: $18, Elev: 781ft/238m, Tel: 918-532-4627, Nearest town: Copan. GPS: 36.936899, -96.076419

31 • B4 | Walnut Creek

Total sites: 70, RV sites: 63, Elec sites: 63, Water at site, Flush toilet, Free showers, RV dump, Tents: $14/RVs: $20, Includes 32 equestrian sites, Stay limit: 14 days, Open Apr-Oct, Elev: 771ft/235m, Tel: 918-865-2621, Nearest town: Prue. GPS: 36.238287, -96.280876

32 • B4 | Washington Cove

Total sites: 101, RV sites: 101, Elec sites: 101, Central water, Flush toilet, Free showers, RV dump, Tents: $16/RVs: $22, Open Apr-Oct, Max Length: 75ft, Reservations accepted, Elev: 764ft/233m, Tel: 918-532-4129, Nearest town: Copan. GPS: 36.910411, -95.939713

33 • B4 | Washington Irving South

Total sites: 40, RV sites: 40, Elec sites: 38, Central water, Flush toilet, Free showers, RV dump, Tents: $15/RVs: $25, Open Jan-Oct, Max Length: 62ft, Reservations accepted, Elev: 748ft/228m, Tel: 918-865-2621, Nearest town: Tulsa. GPS: 36.198063, -96.258612

34 • B4 | Washunga Bay

Total sites: 24, RV sites: 24, Elec sites: 24, Central water, Flush toilet, Free showers, RV dump, Tents: $20/RVs: $20-24, Open Mar-Oct, Max Length: 60ft, Reservations accepted, Elev: 1027ft/313m, Tel: 580-762-5611, Nearest town: Ponca City. GPS: 36.791474, -96.837663

35 • B5 | Afton Landing

Total sites: 42, RV sites: 20, Elec sites: 20, Central water, Flush toilet, Free showers, RV dump, Tents: $15/RVs: $22, Open May-Sep, Elev: 561ft/171m, Tel: 918-489-5541, Nearest town: Wagoner. GPS: 35.946289, -95.486816

36 • B5 | Big Creek Ramp

Total sites: 12, RV sites: 12, No water, Vault/pit toilet, Tent & RV camping: Free, Open all year, Elev: 666ft/203m, Tel: 918-443-2250, Nearest town: Nowata. GPS: 36.729714, -95.541055

37 • B5 | Blue Bill Point

Total sites: 43, RV sites: 43, Elec sites: 40, Central water, Flush toilet, Free showers, RV dump, Tents: $14/RVs: $18-20, Open Apr-Nov, Max Length: 50ft, Reservations accepted, Elev: 597ft/182m, Tel: 918-476-6638, Nearest town: Wagoner. GPS: 36.041369, -95.335555

38 • B5 | Blue Creek

Total sites: 61, RV sites: 60, Elec sites: 24, Central water, Flush toilet, Free showers, RV dump, Tents: $16/RVs: $20, Open Apr-Oct, Max Length: 100ft, Reservations accepted, Elev: 686ft/209m, Tel: 918-341-4244, Nearest town: Foyil. GPS: 36.452356, -95.593989

39 • B5 | Bluff Landing

Total sites: 21, RV sites: 21, Elec sites: 21, Water at site, Flush toilet, Free showers, RV dump, Tent & RV camping: $15, Open May-Sep, Elev: 554ft/169m, Tel: 918-489-5541, Nearest town: Broken Arrow. GPS: 36.069257, -95.560655

40 • B5 | Brewers Bend

Total sites: 42, RV sites: 32, Elec sites: 32, Water at site, Flush toilet, Free showers, RV dump, Tent & RV camping: $15, Open May-Sep, Reservations not accepted, Elev: 532ft/162m, Tel: 918-487-9512, Nearest town: Webbers Falls. GPS: 35.576249, -95.183694

41 • B5 | Carters Landing

Total sites: 25, RV sites: 10, Elec sites: 10, Water at site, Vault/pit toilet, No showers, No RV dump, Tents: $7/RVs: $16, Open all year, Reservations not accepted, Elev: 617ft/188m, Tel: 918-487-5252, Nearest town: Tahlequah. GPS: 35.798032, -94.892641

42 • B5 | Chicken Creek

Total sites: 101, RV sites: 101, Elec sites: 101, Central water, Flush toilet, Free showers, RV dump, Tent & RV camping: $16-19, Open Apr-Nov, Max Length: 146ft, Reservations accepted, Elev: 696ft/212m, Tel: 918-487-5252, Nearest town: Vian. GPS: 35.682315, -94.963283

43 • B5 | Cookson Bend

Total sites: 129, RV sites: 129, Elec sites: 64, Central water, Flush toilet, Free showers, RV dump, Tents: $12-14/RVs: $16-19, Open all year, Max Length: 160ft, Reservations accepted, Elev: 712ft/217m, Tel: 918-487-5252, Nearest town: Cookson. GPS: 35.708033, -94.959944

44 • B5 | Damsite

Total sites: 23, RV sites: 23, No water, Vault/pit toilet, No showers, No RV dump, Tent & RV camping: Free, Open Mar-Oct, Reservations accepted, Elev: 515ft/157m, Tel: 918-683-6618, Nearest town: Okay. GPS: 35.866943, -95.232422

45 • B5 | Elk Creek Landing

Total sites: 41, RV sites: 41, Elec sites: 18, Central water, Flush toilet, Free showers, RV dump, Tents: $12-14/RVs: $16-18, Open Mar-Nov, Max Length: 84ft, Reservations accepted, Elev: 774ft/236m, Tel: 918-487-5252, Nearest town: Cookson. GPS: 35.751465, -94.902832

46 • B5 | Flatrock Creek

Total sites: 32, RV sites: 32, Elec sites: 30, Central water, Flush toilet, Free showers, RV dump, Tents: $14/RVs: $18-20, Open all year, Max Length: 38ft, Reservations accepted, Elev: 604ft/184m, Tel: 918-476-6766, Nearest town: Wagoner. GPS: 36.044298, -95.328549

47 • B5 | Gentry Creek

Total sites: 37, RV sites: 36, Elec sites: 19, Central water, Flush toilet, Free showers, RV dump, Tents: $14/RVs: $20, Open Mar-Oct, Max Length: 50ft, Reservations accepted, Elev: 620ft/189m, Tel: 918-799-5843, Nearest town: Checotah. GPS: 35.495891, -95.667203

48 • B5 | Hawthorn Bluff

Total sites: 56, RV sites: 56, Elec sites: 41, Central water, Flush toilet, Free showers, RV dump, Tents: $16/RVs: $16-20, Open Apr-Oct, Max Length: 105ft, Reservations accepted, Elev: 666ft/203m, Tel: 918-443-2319, Nearest town: Oologah. GPS: 36.430344, -95.679139

49 • B5 | Pettit Bay

Total sites: 86, RV sites: 86, Elec sites: 74, Water at site, Flush toilet, Free showers, RV dump, Tents: $14/RVs: $18-20, 2 full hookups, Open all year, Max Length: 98ft, Reservations accepted, Elev: 718ft/219m, Tel: 918-487-5252, Nearest town: Keys. GPS: 35.754865, -94.946468

50 • B5 | Redbud Bay

Total sites: 12, RV sites: 12, No toilets, No showers, No RV dump, Tent & RV camping: $16, Reservations not accepted, Elev: 666ft/203m, Tel: 918-443-2250, Nearest town: Oologah. GPS: 36.420853, -95.671598

51 • B5 | Rocky Point

Total sites: 65, RV sites: 65, Elec sites: 62, Water at site, Flush toilet, Free showers, RV dump, Tents: $14/RVs: $18-22, 2 full hookups, Open all year, Max Length: 123ft, Reservations accepted, Elev: 597ft/182m, Tel: 918-462-2042, Nearest town: Wagoner. GPS: 36.032628, -95.316762

52 • B5 | Sizemore Landing

Total sites: 32, RV sites: 32, Vault/pit toilet, Tent & RV camping: $5, Open all year, Max Length: 32ft, Reservations not accepted, Elev: 761ft/232m, Tel: 918-487-5252, Nearest town: Keys. GPS: 35.718882, -94.963812

53 • B5 | Snake Creek Cove

Total sites: 111, RV sites: 111, Elec sites: 111, Water at site, Flush toilet, Free showers, RV dump, Tent & RV camping: $18-20, 4 full hookups, Open Mar-Nov, Max Length: 118ft, Reservations accepted, Elev: 689ft/210m, Tel: 918-487-5252, Nearest town: Vian. GPS: 35.649835, -94.972129

54 • B5 | Spaniard Creek

Total sites: 36, RV sites: 36, Elec sites: 36, Water at site, Flush toilet, Free showers, RV dump, Tent & RV camping: $14-18, Open May-Sep, Reservations not accepted, Elev: 492ft/150m, Tel: 918-489-5541, Nearest town: Muskogee. GPS: 35.599762, -95.264596

55 • B5 | Spencer Creek

Total sites: 51, RV sites: 51, Elec sites: 29, Central water, Flush toilet, Free showers, RV dump, Tents: $16/RVs: $20, Open Apr-Oct, Max Length: 75ft, Reservations accepted, Elev: 679ft/207m, Tel: 918-341-3690, Nearest town: Foyil. GPS: 36.515625, -95.565918

56 • B5 | Standing Rock

Dispersed sites, No water, Vault/pit toilet, Tents only: Free, Open all year, Reservations not accepted, Elev: 712ft/217m, Nearest town: Cookson. GPS: 35.749268, -94.921631

57 • B5 | Strayhorn Landing

Total sites: 40, RV sites: 40, Elec sites: 40, Central water, Flush toilet, Free showers, RV dump, Tent & RV camping: $18-20, Oct-Nov/Mar: $16-$18, Open Apr-Nov, Max Length: 125ft, Reservations accepted, Elev: 633ft/193m, Tel: 918-487-5252, Nearest town: Gore. GPS: 35.616275, -95.058681

58 • B5 | Taylor Ferry

Total sites: 91, RV sites: 91, Elec sites: 85, Central water, Flush toilet, Free showers, RV dump, Tents: $14/RVs: $18-20, Open all year, Max Length: 45ft, Reservations accepted, Elev: 584ft/178m, Tel: 918-485-4792, Nearest town: Wagoner. GPS: 35.933039, -95.281604

59 • B5 | Tullahasse Loop

Total sites: 6, RV sites: 6, No water, Vault/pit toilet, Tent & RV camping: Free, Reservations not accepted, Elev: 520ft/158m, Tel: 918-682-4314, Nearest town: Porter. GPS: 35.890397, -95.447786

60 • B5 | Verdigris River Park

Total sites: 8, RV sites: 8, Central water, Vault/pit toilet, No showers, No RV dump, Tent & RV camping: $12, Open all year, Elev: 607ft/185m, Tel: 918-443-2250, Nearest town: Oologah. GPS: 36.421791, -95.683478

61 • B5 | Wahoo Bay

Total sites: 14, RV sites: 0, Central water, Vault/pit toilet, Tents only: Free, Reservations not accepted, Elev: 571ft/174m, Tel: 918-682-4314, Nearest town: Muskogee. GPS: 35.878848, -95.272823

62 • B5 | Wildwood

Total sites: 30, RV sites: 30, Elec sites: 30, Central water, Flush toilet, Free showers, RV dump, Tent & RV camping: $16-20, Open all year, Reservations accepted, Elev: 554ft/169m, Tel: 918-682-4314, Nearest town: Wagoner. GPS: 35.918785, -95.210491

63 • C3 | Chisolm Trail Ridge

Total sites: 95, RV sites: 95, Elec sites: 95, Central water, Flush toilet, Free showers, RV dump, Tent & RV camping: $16-20, Open May-Sep, Max Length: 60ft, Reservations accepted, Elev: 978ft/298m, Tel: 580-439-8040, Nearest town: Waurika. GPS: 34.249500, -98.035080

64 • C3 | Kiowa 1

Total sites: 164, RV sites: 164, Elec sites: 164, Water at site, Flush toilet, Free showers, RV dump, Tent & RV camping: $16-20, 2 group sites - $100, Open Mar-Oct, Max Length: 60ft, Reservations accepted, Elev: 994ft/303m, Tel: 580-963-9031, Nearest town: Waurika. GPS: 34.260254, -98.076660

65 • C3 | Moneka Park

Total sites: 38, RV sites: 38, Central water, Vault/pit toilet, No showers, No RV dump, Tent & RV camping: $14-18, Open Mar-Oct, Reservations not accepted, Elev: 919ft/280m, Tel: 580-963-2111, Nearest town: Waurika. GPS: 34.227081, -98.052314

66 • C3 | Wichita Ridge

Total sites: 27, RV sites: 27, Elec sites: 10, Central water, No toilets, No showers, RV dump, Tents: $14/RVs: $18, Open all year, Reservations not accepted, Elev: 978ft/298m, Tel: 580-963-2111, Nearest town: Hastings. GPS: 34.291504, -98.105957

67 • C5 | Applegate Cove

Total sites: 27, RV sites: 27, Elec sites: 27, Water at site, Flush toilet, Free showers, RV dump, Tent & RV camping: $15, 1 group site, Open Apr-Sep, Elev: 502ft/153m, Tel: 918-775-4475, Nearest town: Sallisaw. GPS: 35.360994, -94.825311

68 • C5 | Belle Starr

Total sites: 111, RV sites: 111, Elec sites: 111, Central water, Flush toilet, Free showers, RV dump, Tent & RV camping: $20-22, Dec-Mar: $12 (no water/electric), Open all year, Max Length: 60ft, Reservations accepted, Elev: 620ft/189m, Tel: 918-799-5843, Nearest town: Eufaula. GPS: 35.330832, -95.539239

69 • C5 | Brooken Cove

Total sites: 73, RV sites: 73, Elec sites: 73, Central water, Flush toilet, Free showers, RV dump, Tent & RV camping: $20-24, Open Apr-Oct, Max Length: 75ft, Reservations accepted, Elev: 636ft/194m, Tel: 918-799-5843, Nearest town: Eufaula. GPS: 35.286408, -95.394044

70 • C5 | Cowlington Point

Total sites: 35, RV sites: 35, Elec sites: 32, Water at site, Flush toilet, Free showers, RV dump, Tent & RV camping: $10-15, 15A only, Open Apr-Sep, Elev: 489ft/149m, Tel: 918-775-4475, Nearest town: Sallisaw. GPS: 35.317139, -94.828125

71 • C5 | Dam Site East

Total sites: 65, RV sites: 60, Elec sites: 44, Central water, Flush toilet, Free showers, No RV dump, Tents: $11/RVs: $11-16, Open Apr-Oct, Elev: 548ft/167m, Tel: 918-484-5135, Nearest town: Eufaula. GPS: 35.305363, -95.353406

72 • C5 | Elm Point

Total sites: 17, RV sites: 14, Elec sites: 14, Central water, No toilets, No showers, RV dump, Tents: $7/RVs: $11, Open Mar-Oct, Reservations not accepted, Elev: 604ft/184m, Tel: 918-484-5135, Nearest town: McAlester. GPS: 35.013526, -95.599439

73 • C5 | Highway 9 Landing East Loop

Total sites: 6, RV sites: 6, Elec sites: 5, Water available, Flush toilet, Free showers, RV dump, Tents: $12-14/RVs: $16-20, Open Mar-Oct, Max Length: 50ft, Reservations accepted, Elev: 610ft/186m, Tel: 918-799-5843, Nearest town: Eufaula. GPS: 35.238007, -95.486689

74 • C5 | Highway 9 Landing North Loop

Total sites: 36, RV sites: 36, Elec sites: 27, Water available, Flush toilet, Free showers, RV dump, Tents: $12-14/RVs: $16-20, Open Mar-Oct, Max Length: 50ft, Reservations accepted, Elev: 620ft/189m, Tel: 918-799-5843, Nearest town: Eufaula. GPS: 35.242676, -95.491455

75 • C5 | Highway 9 Landing South Loop

Total sites: 31, RV sites: 31, Elec sites: 30, Water available, Flush toilet, Free showers, RV dump, Tents: $12-14/RVs: $16-20, Open Mar-Oct, Max Length: 48ft, Reservations accepted, Elev: 633ft/193m, Tel: 918-799-5843, Nearest town: Eufaula. GPS: 35.237849, -95.494679

76 • C5 | Hugo Lake Group Camp

Total sites: 4, RV sites: 4, Elec sites: 4, Central water, No toilets, No showers, No RV dump, Group site: $75, Open Apr-Sep, Elev: 472ft/144m, Tel: 580-326-3345, Nearest town: Sawyer. GPS: 34.054389, -95.386037

77 • C5 | Kiamichi Park

Total sites: 86, RV sites: 86, Elec sites: 84, Central water, Flush toilet, Free showers, RV dump, Tents: $14-16/RVs: $18-22, Open all year, Max Length: 44ft, Reservations accepted, Elev: 456ft/139m, Tel: 580-326-3345, Nearest town: Hugo. GPS: 34.019485, -95.419895

78 • C5 | Ladybird Landing

Total sites: 57, RV sites: 52, Elec sites: 44, Central water, Flush toilet, Free showers, RV dump, Tents: $14/RVs: $20-24, Dec-Feb: $10, Stay limit: 14 days, Generator hours: 0600-2200, Open Mar-Nov, Max Length: 50ft, Reservations accepted, Elev: 655ft/200m, Tel: 918-799-5843, Nearest town: Eufaula. GPS: 35.299419, -95.370202

79 • C5 | Little River Park

Total sites: 55, RV sites: 55, Elec sites: 30, Water at site, Flush toilet, Free showers, RV dump, Tents: $14/RVs: $19-23, Group fee: $65, Open Mar-Oct, Max Length: 100ft, Reservations accepted, Elev: 515ft/157m, Tel: 580-876-3720, Nearest town: New Ringold. GPS: 34.163818, -95.120850

80 • C5 | Lost Rapids

Total sites: 30, RV sites: 30, Elec sites: 17, Central water, No toilets, No showers, RV dump, Tents: $12/RVs: $17, Group site $65, Open all year, Max Length: 81ft, Reservations accepted, Elev: 476ft/145m, Tel: 580-876-3720, Nearest town: New Ringold. GPS: 34.177183, -95.104655

81 • C5 | Mill Creek Bay

Total sites: 12, RV sites: 12, Central water, Vault/pit toilet, No showers, No RV dump, Tent & RV camping: $7, Open Mar-Oct, Elev: 633ft/193m, Tel: 918-484-5135, Nearest town: Eufaula. GPS: 35.256871, -95.701795

82 • C5 | Oak Ridge

Total sites: 13, RV sites: 13, Elec sites: 8, Central water, Vault/pit toilet, No showers, No RV dump, Tents: $7/RVs: $11, Open Mar-Oct, Elev: 620ft/189m, Tel: 918-484-5135, Nearest town: Eufaula. GPS: 35.216094, -95.601531

83 • C5 | Pine Creek Cove

Total sites: 41, RV sites: 41, Elec sites: 40, Water at site, Flush toilet, Free showers, RV dump, Tents: $14/RVs: $19-23, Open all year, Max Length: 105ft, Reservations accepted, Elev: 482ft/147m, Tel: 580-933-4215, Nearest town: Valliant. GPS: 34.112182, -95.089056

84 • C5 | Porum Landing

Total sites: 49, RV sites: 49, Elec sites: 45, Central water, Flush toilet, Free showers, RV dump, Tents: $14/RVs: $14-20, Open all year, Max Length: 45ft, Reservations accepted, Elev: 617ft/188m, Tel: 918-799-5843, Nearest town: Porum. GPS: 35.356955, -95.391587

85 • C5 | Potato Hills Central

Total sites: 82, RV sites: 82, Elec sites: 82, Central water, Flush toilet, Free showers, RV dump, Tent & RV camping: $18, 2 group sites: $150, Open all year, Max Length: 96ft, Reservations accepted, Elev: 640ft/195m, Tel: 918-569-4131, Nearest town: Clayton. GPS: 34.672548, -95.327024

86 • C5 | Potato Hills South

Total sites: 18, RV sites: 18, Central water, No toilets, No showers, RV dump, Tent & RV camping: $12, Open Apr-Oct, Max Length: 84ft, Reservations accepted, Elev: 636ft/194m, Tel: 918-569-4131, Nearest town: Clayton. GPS: 34.662777, -95.329626

87 • C5 | Rattan Landing

Total sites: 13, RV sites: 13, Elec sites: 13, Water at site, No toilets, No showers, No RV dump, Tent & RV camping: $14, Generator hours: 0600-2200, Open all year, Elev: 456ft/139m, Tel: 580-326-3345, Nearest town: Rattan. GPS: 34.197085, -95.483022

88 • C5 | Sardis Cove

Total sites: 45, RV sites: 45, Elec sites: 22, Central water, No toilets, No showers, RV dump, Tent & RV camping: $10-15, Open Apr-Oct, Reservations not accepted, Elev: 640ft/195m, Tel: 918-569-4131, Nearest town: Clayton. GPS: 34.649462, -95.451124

89 • C5 | Short Mountain Cove

Total sites: 32, RV sites: 32, Elec sites: 26, Water at site, Flush toilet, Free showers, RV dump, Tent & RV camping: $15, Open May-Sep, Reservations not accepted, Elev: 515ft/157m, Tel: 918-775-4475, Nearest town: Sallisaw. GPS: 35.322266, -94.783691

90 • C5 | Turkey Creek

Total sites: 30, RV sites: 30, Elec sites: 8, Water at site, No toilets, No showers, RV dump, Tents: $12/RVs: $17, Open Mar-Oct, Max Length: 100ft, Reservations accepted, Elev: 446ft/136m, Tel: 580-876-3720, Nearest town: Wright City. GPS: 34.214938, -95.124157

91 • C5 | Virgil Point

Total sites: 52, RV sites: 52, Elec sites: 52, Central water, Flush toilet, Free showers, RV dump, Tent & RV camping: $18-22, Open all year, Reservations accepted, Elev: 479ft/146m, Tel: 580-326-3345, Nearest town: Hugo. GPS: 34.049316, -95.378906

92 • D4 | Buncombe Creek

Total sites: 54, RV sites: 54, Elec sites: 54, Water at site, Flush toilet, Free showers, RV dump, Tent & RV camping: $24, Open Apr-Sep, Max Length: 45ft, Reservations accepted, Elev: 669ft/204m, Tel: 580-564-2901, Nearest town: Madill. GPS: 33.896484, -96.809570

93 • D4 | Burns Run East

Total sites: 53, RV sites: 44, Elec sites: 44, Water at site, Flush toilet, Free showers, RV dump, Tents: $16/RVs: $26-28, Open all year, Max Length: 95ft, Reservations accepted, Elev: 643ft/196m, Tel: 580-965-4660, Nearest town: Cartwright. GPS: 33.848355, -96.581575

94 • D4 | Burns Run West

Total sites: 117, RV sites: 105, Elec sites: 105, Water at site, Flush toilet, Free showers, RV dump, Tents: $16/RVs: $22-26, 4 group sites: $110, Open Apr-Sep, Max Length: 150ft, Reservations accepted, Elev: 673ft/205m, Tel: 580-965-4922, Nearest town: Cartwright. GPS: 33.853567, -96.593111

95 • D4 | Caney Creek

Total sites: 51, RV sites: 41, Elec sites: 41, Water at site, Flush toilet, Free showers, RV dump, Tents: $16/RVs: $24-26, Open all year, Max Length: 80ft, Reservations accepted, Elev: 679ft/207m, Tel: 580-564-2632, Nearest town: Kingston. GPS: 33.929956, -96.705331

96 • D4 | Johnson Creek

Total sites: 54, RV sites: 54, Elec sites: 54, Water at site, Flush toilet, Free showers, RV dump, Tent & RV camping: $24-26, Open all year, Max Length: 80ft, Reservations accepted, Elev: 663ft/202m, Tel: 580-924-7316, Nearest town: Kingston. GPS: 34.001301, -96.570109

97 • D4 | Lakeside

Total sites: 137, RV sites: 133, Elec sites: 133, Water at site, Flush toilet, Free showers, RV dump, Tents: $16/RVs: $24-26, Reduced services Dec-Mar: $14-$16, Open May-Sep, Max Length: 90ft, Reservations accepted, Elev: 646ft/197m, Tel: 580-920-0176, Nearest town: Durant. GPS: 33.935723, -96.548683

98 • D4 | Platter Flats Equestrian

Total sites: 57, RV sites: 57, Elec sites: 37, Water at site, Flush toilet, Free showers, RV dump, Tents: $16/RVs: $24-26, Open all year, Max Length: 65ft, Reservations accepted, Elev: 646ft/197m, Tel: 580-434-5864, Nearest town: Platter. GPS: 33.922287, -96.544596

99 • D4 | Platter Flats Family

Total sites: 26, RV sites: 26, Elec sites: 26, Water at site, Flush toilet, Free showers, RV dump, Tent & RV camping: $24-26, Open all year, Max Length: 65ft, Reservations accepted, Elev: 659ft/201m, Tel: 580-434-5864, Nearest town: Platter. GPS: 33.924042, -96.547187

Oregon

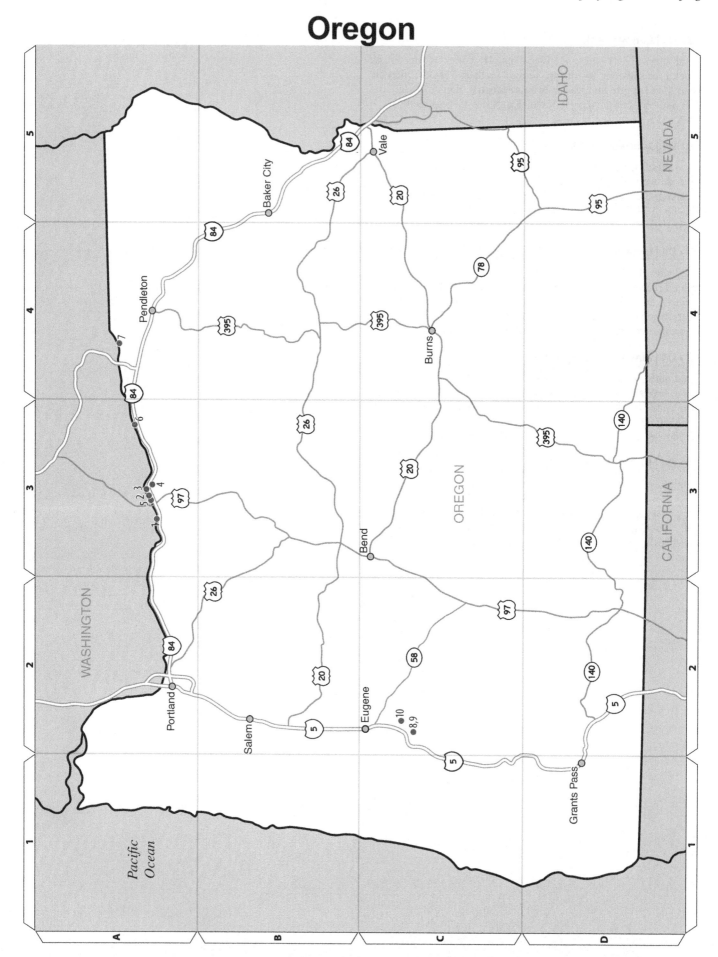

Map	ID	Map	ID
A3	1-6	C2	8-10
A4	7		

Alphabetical List of Camping Areas

Name	ID	Map
Celilo Park	1	A3
Giles French	2	A3
LePage Park	3	A3
Philippi	4	A3
Pine Meadows Main	8	C2
Primitive	9	C2
Rufus Landing	5	A3
Sand Station	7	A4
Schwarz Park	10	C2
Threemile Canyon/Quesnel	6	A3

1 • A3 | Celilo Park

Dispersed sites, Vault/pit toilet, Tent & RV camping: Free, Tent Camping Friday-Saturday-Sunday evenings only, Beside RR, Stay limit: 7 days, Open Apr-Oct, Reservations not accepted, Elev: 167ft/51m, Tel: 541-506-7819, Nearest town: The Dalles. GPS: 45.650442, -120.961022

2 • A3 | Giles French

Dispersed sites, Flush toilet, Tent & RV camping: Free, Near RR, Stay limit: 7 days, Open Apr-Oct, Reservations not accepted, Elev: 190ft/58m, Tel: 541-506-7819, Nearest town: The Dalles. GPS: 45.708258, -120.700583

3 • A3 | LePage Park

Total sites: 42, RV sites: 22, Elec sites: 22, Central water, Flush toilet, Free showers, RV dump, Tents: $15/RVs: $30-35, Stay limit: 14 days, Open Apr-Oct, Max Length: 56ft, Reservations accepted, Elev: 276ft/84m, Tel: 541-739-2713, Nearest town: Rufus. GPS: 45.726312, -120.649176

4 • A3 | Philippi

Dispersed sites, Flush toilet, Free showers, Tents only: Free, Boat-in, Stay limit: 7 days, Open May-Sep, Reservations not accepted, Elev: 302ft/92m, Nearest town: Rufus. GPS: 45.705495, -120.599329

5 • A3 | Rufus Landing

Dispersed sites, No water, Vault/pit toilet, Tent & RV camping: Free, Stay limit: 7 days, Open Apr-Oct, Reservations not accepted, Elev: 179ft/55m, Tel: 541-506-7819, Nearest town: Rufus. GPS: 45.693131, -120.755837

6 • A3 | Threemile Canyon/Quesnel

Dispersed sites, No water, Vault/pit toilet, Tent & RV camping: Free, 7 campsites behind locked gate are for tribal members only., Stay limit: 7 days, Open Apr-Oct, Reservations not accepted, Elev: 275ft/84m, Tel: 541-506-7819, Nearest town: Boardman. GPS: 45.811293, -119.970087

7 • A4 | Sand Station

Total sites: 1, No water, Vault/pit toilet, Group site: Fee unk, Open May-Sep, Reservations required, Elev: 351ft/107m, Tel: 541-922-2268, Nearest town: Umatilla. GPS: 45.922027, -119.119752

8 • C2 | Pine Meadows Main

Total sites: 107, RV sites: 92, Central water, Flush toilet, Free showers, RV dump, Tents: $16/RVs: $24, Open May-Sep, Max Length: 105ft, Reservations accepted, Elev: 804ft/245m, Tel: 541-942-5631, Nearest town: Cottage Grove. GPS: 43.700402, -123.056876

9 • C2 | Primitive

Total sites: 15, RV sites: 15, Vault/pit toilet, Tent & RV camping: $12, Elev: 833ft/254m, Tel: 541-942-5631, Nearest town: Cottage Grove. GPS: 43.695677, -123.065108

10 • C2 | Schwarz Park

Total sites: 72, RV sites: 72, Central water, Flush toilet, Free showers, RV dump, Tent & RV camping: $22, 6 group sites: $150, Open Apr-Sep, Max Length: 114ft, Reservations accepted, Elev: 761ft/232m, Tel: 541-942-1418, Nearest town: Cottage Grove. GPS: 43.786042, -122.960717

Pennsylvania

Map	ID	Map	ID
A3	1	C1	10
B1	2	C2	11-12
B2	3-6	C3	13-21
B3	7-9	D2	22

Alphabetical List of Camping Areas

Name	ID	Map
Branch Camp	13	C3
Bush	11	C2
Crooked Creek	10	C1
East Branch Lake	3	B2
Ives Run - Main CG	7	B3
Ives Run - Overflow	8	B3
Ives Run - Pine Camp	9	B3
Kellettville CG	4	B2
Kiski Group Camp Area	12	C2
Nancy's Boat-to-Shore Camp	14	C3
Outflow	22	D2
Seven Points - Bay Camp	15	C3
Seven Points - Big Meadows	16	C3
Seven Points - Point	17	C3
Seven Points - Ridge Camp	18	C3
Seven Points - Senoia	19	C3
Seven Points - Valley Camp	20	C3
Shenango	2	B1
Susquehannock	21	C3
Tionesta Rec Area - Loops 1-3	5	B2
Tionesta Rec Area - Loops 4	6	B2
Tompkins	1	A3

1 • A3 | Tompkins

Total sites: 123, RV sites: 83, Elec sites: 83, Central water, Flush toilet, Free showers, RV dump, Tents: $20/RVs: $20-40, Stay limit: 14 days, Open May-Sep, Reservations accepted, Elev: 1171ft/357m, Tel: 570-827-2109, Nearest town: Tioga. GPS: 41.981201, -77.188965

2 • B1 | Shenango

Total sites: 327, RV sites: 322, Elec sites: 107, Central water, Flush toilet, Free showers, RV dump, Tents: $20/RVs: $20-34, Open May-Sep, Max Length: 199ft, Reservations accepted, Elev: 925ft/282m, Tel: 724-646-1124, Nearest town: Sharpville. GPS: 41.295032, -80.436134

3 • B2 | East Branch Lake

Total sites: 32, RV sites: 32, Elec sites: 25, Central water, Flush toilet, Free showers, RV dump, Tent & RV camping: $15-20, Open Apr-Oct, Max Length: 40ft, Reservations accepted, Elev: 1765ft/538m, Tel: 814-965-2065, Nearest town: Wilcox. GPS: 41.564209, -78.594727

4 • B2 | Kellettville CG

Total sites: 20, RV sites: 20, No water, Flush toilet, RV dump, Tent & RV camping: $15, Open Apr-Oct, Max Length: 60ft, Reservations accepted, Elev: 1165ft/355m, Tel: 814-755-3512, Nearest town: Kelletville. GPS: 41.543363, -79.257532

5 • B2 | Tionesta Rec Area - Loops 1-3

Total sites: 87, RV sites: 87, Elec sites: 87, Water at site, Flush toilet, Free showers, RV dump, Tent & RV camping: $40, 87 full hookups, Open May-Sep, Max Length: 75ft, Reservations accepted, Elev: 1070ft/326m, Tel: 814-755-3512, Nearest town: Tionesta. GPS: 41.482677, -79.445994

6 • B2 | Tionesta Rec Area - Loops 4

Total sites: 37, RV sites: 37, Elec sites: 37, Water at site, Flush toilet, Free showers, RV dump, Tent & RV camping: $40, 37 full hookups, Open May-Sep, Max Length: 65ft, Reservations accepted, Elev: 1076ft/328m, Tel: 814-755-3512, Nearest town: Tionesta. GPS: 41.477661, -79.445071

7 • B3 | Ives Run - Main CG

Total sites: 188, RV sites: 188, Elec sites: 131, Water at site, Flush toilet, Free showers, RV dump, Tents: $20/RVs: $36-40, 76 full hookups, Open May-Oct, Max Length: 108ft, Reservations accepted, Elev: 1122ft/342m, Tel: 570-835-5281, Nearest town: Tioga. GPS: 41.889455, -77.177287

8 • B3 | Ives Run - Overflow

Total sites: 24, RV sites: 24, Tent & RV camping: $20, Elev: 1099ft/335m, Tel: 570-835-5281, Nearest town: Tioga. GPS: 41.881646, -77.188793

9 • B3 | Ives Run - Pine Camp

Total sites: 32, RV sites: 32, No toilets, Tent & RV camping: $20, Reservations accepted, Elev: 1089ft/332m, Tel: 570-835-5281, Nearest town: Tioga. GPS: 41.892571, -77.159999

10 • C1 | Crooked Creek

Total sites: 12, RV sites: 12, Central water, Vault/pit toilet, No showers, No RV dump, Tent & RV camping: $15, Open May-Sep, Reservations accepted, Elev: 1001ft/305m, Tel: 724-763-3161, Nearest town: Ford City. GPS: 40.709439, -79.514787

11 • C2 | Bush

Total sites: 44, RV sites: 44, Elec sites: 12, Flush toilet, Pay showers, RV dump, Tents: $20/RVs: $24-26, Reservations not accepted, Elev: 981ft/299m, Tel: 724-639-9013, Nearest town: Saltsburg. GPS: 40.437334, -79.436723

12 • C2 | Kiski Group Camp Area

Total sites: 1, RV sites: 0, No toilets, Group site: Free, Reservations not accepted, Elev: 1125ft/343m, Tel: 724-639-9013, Nearest town: New Alexandria. GPS: 40.442863, -79.434705

13 • C3 | Branch Camp

Total sites: 27, RV sites: 27, Elec sites: 27, Central water, Free showers, Tent & RV camping: Fee unk, Outdoor showers, Leased, Elev: 599ft/183m, Tel: 814-695-2249, Nearest town: Ardenheim. GPS: 40.441219, -77.974023

14 • C3 | Nancy's Boat-to-Shore Camp

Total sites: 50, RV sites: 0, No water, Vault/pit toilet, Tents only: $15, Boat-in, Nov-Mar: Free, Generator hours: 0800-2200,

Reservations required, Elev: 792ft/241m, Tel: 814-658-3405, Nearest town: Hesston. GPS: 40.344644, -78.142878

15 • C3 | Seven Points - Bay Camp

Total sites: 19, RV sites: 13, Elec sites: 13, Central water, Flush toilet, No showers, RV dump, Tents: $24/RVs: $30, Also walk-to & group sites, Stay limit: 14 days, Open Apr-Oct, Max Length: 50ft, Reservations accepted, Elev: 876ft/267m, Tel: 814-658-3405, Nearest town: Huntingdon. GPS: 40.385089, -78.070519

16 • C3 | Seven Points - Big Meadows

Total sites: 43, RV sites: 43, Elec sites: 43, Central water, Flush toilet, Free showers, RV dump, Tent & RV camping: $26-30, Stay limit: 14 days, Open Apr-Oct, Max Length: 45ft, Reservations accepted, Elev: 1063ft/324m, Tel: 814-658-3405, Nearest town: Huntingdon. GPS: 40.386895, -78.076261

17 • C3 | Seven Points - Point

Total sites: 43, RV sites: 43, Elec sites: 43, Central water, Flush toilet, Free showers, RV dump, Tent & RV camping: $30-36, Stay limit: 14 days, Open Apr-Oct, Max Length: 80ft, Reservations accepted, Elev: 820ft/250m, Tel: 814-658-3405, Nearest town: Huntingdon. GPS: 40.371756, -78.080939

18 • C3 | Seven Points - Ridge Camp

Total sites: 43, RV sites: 43, Elec sites: 43, Central water, Flush toilet, Free showers, RV dump, Tent & RV camping: $30, Stay limit: 14 days, Open Apr-Oct, Max Length: 60ft, Reservations accepted, Elev: 1089ft/332m, Tel: 814-658-3405, Nearest town: Huntingdon. GPS: 40.385131, -78.081417

19 • C3 | Seven Points - Senoia

Total sites: 90, RV sites: 90, Elec sites: 90, Central water, Flush toilet, Free showers, RV dump, Tent & RV camping: $30-36, Stay limit: 14 days, Open Apr-Oct, Max Length: 140ft, Reservations accepted, Elev: 810ft/247m, Tel: 814-658-3405, Nearest town: Huntingdon. GPS: 40.383287, -78.065815

20 • C3 | Seven Points - Valley Camp

Total sites: 25, RV sites: 25, Elec sites: 25, Central water, No toilets, No showers, RV dump, Tent & RV camping: $30, Stay limit: 14 days, Open Apr-Oct, Max Length: 40ft, Reservations accepted, Elev: 909ft/277m, Tel: 814-658-3405, Nearest town: Huntingdon. GPS: 40.378613, -78.081031

21 • C3 | Susquehannock

Total sites: 61, RV sites: 37, Central water, Vault/pit toilet, No showers, No RV dump, Tent & RV camping: $16-25, Open May-Sep, Max Length: 70ft, Reservations accepted, Elev: 810ft/247m, Tel: 814-658-6806, Nearest town: Huntingdon. GPS: 40.387237, -78.049497

22 • D2 | Outflow

Total sites: 61, RV sites: 51, Elec sites: 36, Water at site, Flush toilet, Free showers, RV dump, Tents: $14-25/RVs: $25-48, 4 full hookups, No water/limited services in winter, Open Apr-Oct, Max Length: 64ft, Reservations accepted, Elev: 1316ft/401m, Tel: 814-395-3242, Nearest town: Confluence. GPS: 39.804469, -79.366961

South Carolina

Map	ID	Map	ID
A1	1-3	B2	6-8
B1	4-5		

Alphabetical List of Camping Areas

Name	ID	Map
Coneross	1	A1
Crescent Group	4	B1
Hawe Creek	6	B2
Leroys Ferry	7	B2
Modoc	8	B2
Oconee Point	2	A1
Springfield	5	B1
Twin Lakes	3	A1

1 • A1 | Coneross

Total sites: 105, RV sites: 105, Elec sites: 93, Water at site, Flush toilet, Free showers, RV dump, Tents: $20/RVs: $26-32, Open May-Sep, Max Length: 56ft, Reservations accepted, Elev: 732ft/223m, Tel: 888-893-0678, Nearest town: Townville. GPS: 34.593949, -82.891641

2 • A1 | Oconee Point

Total sites: 70, RV sites: 70, Elec sites: 70, Water at site, Flush toilet, Free showers, RV dump, Tent & RV camping: $28-34, Open May-Oct, Max Length: 50ft, Reservations accepted, Elev: 673ft/205m, Tel: 888-893-0678, Nearest town: Townville. GPS: 34.601326, -82.870085

3 • A1 | Twin Lakes

Total sites: 99, RV sites: 99, Elec sites: 99, Water at site, Flush toilet, Free showers, RV dump, Tent & RV camping: $26-32, Open all year, Max Length: 62ft, Reservations accepted, Elev: 761ft/232m, Tel: 888-893-0678, Nearest town: Clemson. GPS: 34.627738, -82.850794

4 • B1 | Crescent Group

Total sites: 2, RV sites: 2, Elec sites: 2, Central water, Flush toilet, Free showers, RV dump, Group site: $140-$308, Open Apr-Oct, Max Length: 40ft, Reservations accepted, Elev: 669ft/204m, Tel: 888-893-0678, Nearest town: Anderson. GPS: 34.381095, -82.816589

5 • B1 | Springfield

Total sites: 79, RV sites: 79, Elec sites: 79, Water at site, Flush toilet, Free showers, RV dump, Tent & RV camping: $28, Open Apr-Oct, Max Length: 60ft, Reservations accepted, Elev: 748ft/228m, Tel: 888-893-0678, Nearest town: Anderson. GPS: 34.443211, -82.820924

6 • B2 | Hawe Creek

Total sites: 34, RV sites: 34, Elec sites: 34, Central water, Flush toilet, Free showers, RV dump, Tent & RV camping: $26-28, Open Mar-Sep, Max Length: 45ft, Reservations accepted, Elev: 394ft/120m, Tel: 864-443-5441, Nearest town: McCormick. GPS: 33.836182, -82.338379

7 • B2 | Leroys Ferry

Total sites: 10, RV sites: 10, Central water, Vault/pit toilet, No showers, No RV dump, Tent & RV camping: $10, Open all year, Reservations accepted, Elev: 400ft/122m, Tel: 864-333-1100, Nearest town: Willington. GPS: 33.921143, -82.489746

8 • B2 | Modoc

Total sites: 69, RV sites: 69, Elec sites: 68, Central water, Flush toilet, Free showers, RV dump, Tents: $18/RVs: $24-28, Open Mar-Sep, Max Length: 48ft, Reservations accepted, Elev: 344ft/105m, Tel: 864-333-2272, Nearest town: Modoc. GPS: 33.719482, -82.224121

South Dakota

Map	ID	Map	ID
C1	1-2	D5	7
C3	3-6		

Alphabetical List of Camping Areas

Name	ID	Map
Cold Brook	1	C1
Cottonwood	7	D5
Cottonwood Springs	2	C1
Left Tailrace	3	C3
North Shore	4	C3
Old Fort Thompson	5	C3
Right Tailrace	6	C3

1 • C1 | Cold Brook

Total sites: 13, RV sites: 13, Central water, Vault/pit toilet, No showers, No RV dump, Tent & RV camping: $18, Not big-rig friendly, Generator hours: 0600-2200, Open May-Sep, Max Length: 36ft, Reservations accepted, Elev: 3594ft/1095m, Tel: 605-745-5476, Nearest town: Hot Springs. GPS: 43.462275, -103.491976

2 • C1 | Cottonwood Springs

Total sites: 13, RV sites: 13, Central water, Vault/pit toilet, No showers, No RV dump, Tent & RV camping: $10, Max Length: 30ft, Reservations not accepted, Elev: 4012ft/1223m, Nearest town: Hot Springs. GPS: 43.439572, -103.571568

3 • C3 | Left Tailrace

Total sites: 90, RV sites: 78, Elec sites: 78, Central water, Flush toilet, Free showers, RV dump, Tents: $16/RVs: $22, Open May-Sep, Max Length: 89ft, Reservations accepted, Elev: 1368ft/417m, Tel: 605-245-2255, Nearest town: Fort Thompson. GPS: 44.041016, -99.440186

4 • C3 | North Shore

Total sites: 24, RV sites: 24, Central water, Vault/pit toilet, No showers, No RV dump, Tent & RV camping: Free, Open all year, Elev: 1457ft/444m, Tel: 605-245-2255, Nearest town: Fort Thompson. GPS: 44.065188, -99.475442

5 • C3 | Old Fort Thompson

Total sites: 13, RV sites: 13, Central water, Flush toilet, Free showers, RV dump, Tent & RV camping: Free, Open all year, Elev: 1358ft/414m, Tel: 605-245-2255, Nearest town: Fort Thompson. GPS: 44.059442, -99.445538

6 • C3 | Right Tailrace

Dispersed sites, Central water, Flush toilet, Tent & RV camping: Free, Reservations not accepted, Elev: 1374ft/419m, Nearest town: Fort Thompson. GPS: 44.036311, -99.439985

7 • D5 | Cottonwood

Total sites: 77, RV sites: 77, Elec sites: 77, Water available, Flush toilet, Free showers, RV dump, Tent & RV camping: $20-22, Open Apr-Oct, Max Length: 125ft, Reservations accepted, Elev: 1214ft/370m, Tel: 402-667-7873, Nearest town: Yankton. GPS: 42.859350, -97.483080

Tennessee

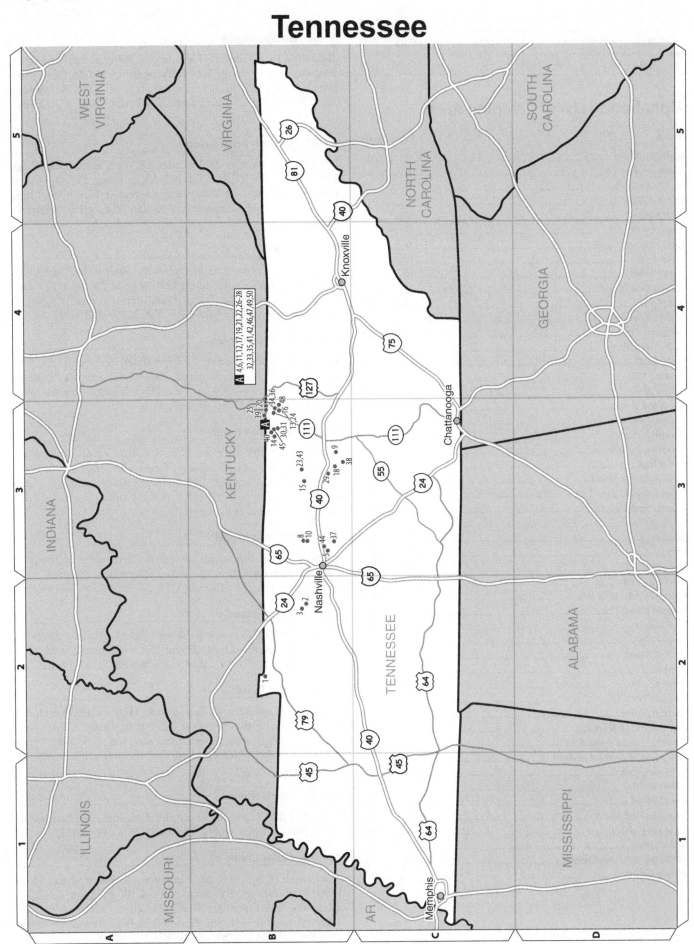

Map	ID	Map	ID
B2	1-3	B3	4-50

Alphabetical List of Camping Areas

Name	ID	Map
Anderson Point	4	B3
Anderson Road	5	B3
Big Goat Island	6	B3
Bumpus Mills	1	B2
Cactus Island	7	B3
Cages Bend	8	B3
Cane Hollow	9	B3
Cedar Creek	10	B3
Clark Island	11	B3
County Line Island	12	B3
Cove Creek	13	B3
Dale Hollow Dam	14	B3
Defeated Creek	15	B3
Eagle Creek Ferry	16	B3
First Island	17	B3
Floating Mill	18	B3
Geiger Island	19	B3
Gunnels Camp	20	B3
Harpeth River Bridge	2	B2
Hendrick's Creek	21	B3
Hendrick's Creek	22	B3
Horse Trail	23	B3
Jackson Creek Island	24	B3
Jones Chapel	25	B3
Jouett Creek Point	26	B3
Kemper Flats	27	B3
Lillydale	28	B3
Lock A	3	B2
Long Branch	29	B3
Mitchell Creek	30	B3
Mitchell Creek Boat-in	31	B3
Moore Hollow Point	32	B3
Noel Island	33	B3
Obey River	34	B3
Phillips Island	35	B3
Plankyard	36	B3
Poole Knobs	37	B3
Ragland Bottom	38	B3
Rayburn Point	39	B3
Red Oak Ridge A TH	40	B3
Roberts Hollow Point Boat-in	41	B3
Roberts Hollow Point Boat-in	42	B3
Salt Lick Creek	43	B3
Seven Points	44	B3
Sewell Bend	45	B3
Sherman Hollow	46	B3
State Line Island	47	B3
Taylors Ford	48	B3
West Fork Ashburn Creek	49	B3
Willow Grove	50	B3

1 • B2 | Bumpus Mills

Total sites: 15, RV sites: 15, Elec sites: 15, Water at site, Flush toilet, Free showers, RV dump, Tent & RV camping: $24-26, Open May-Sep, Max Length: 65ft, Reservations accepted, Elev: 505ft/154m, Tel: 270-362-4236, Nearest town: Clarksville. GPS: 36.622560, -87.878900

2 • B2 | Harpeth River Bridge

Total sites: 15, RV sites: 15, Elec sites: 15, Water at site, Flush toilet, Free showers, No RV dump, Tent & RV camping: $22, Open Apr-Oct, Max Length: 50ft, Reservations accepted, Elev: 394ft/120m, Tel: 615-792-4195, Nearest town: Ashland City. GPS: 36.284180, -87.144531

3 • B2 | Lock A

Total sites: 45, RV sites: 38, Elec sites: 45, Water at site, Flush toilet, Free showers, RV dump, Tents: $24/RVs: $24-28, Open Apr-Oct, Reservations accepted, Elev: 479ft/146m, Tel: 615-792-3715, Nearest town: Ashland City. GPS: 36.315675, -87.190212

4 • B3 | Anderson Point

Dispersed sites, No water, Vault/pit toilet, Tents only: $5, Also boat-in sites, Permit required, Open all year, Reservations accepted, Elev: 664ft/202m, Tel: 931-243-3136, Nearest town: Celina. GPS: 36.611781, -85.366928

5 • B3 | Anderson Road

Total sites: 36, RV sites: 36, Elec sites: 10, Central water, Flush toilet, Free showers, RV dump, Tents: $20-22/RVs: $30, Open May-Sep, Max Length: 215ft, Reservations accepted, Elev: 495ft/151m, Tel: 615-361-1980, Nearest town: Nashville. GPS: 36.108079, -86.607884

6 • B3 | Big Goat Island

Dispersed sites, No water, No toilets, Tents only: $5, Boat-in, Permit required, Open all year, Reservations accepted, Elev: 654ft/199m, Tel: 931-243-3136. GPS: 36.599378, -85.348105

7 • B3 | Cactus Island

Dispersed sites, No water, Vault/pit toilet, Tents only: $5, Boat-in, Permit required, Open all year, Reservations accepted, Elev: 654ft/199m, Tel: 931-243-3136. GPS: 36.630879, -85.291162

8 • B3 | Cages Bend

Total sites: 42, RV sites: 42, Elec sites: 42, Water at site, Flush toilet, Free showers, RV dump, Tent & RV camping: $30-35, Open Apr-Oct, Max Length: 45ft, Reservations accepted, Elev: 469ft/143m, Tel: 615-824-4989, Nearest town: Old Hickory. GPS: 36.303989, -86.514766

9 • B3 | Cane Hollow

Dispersed sites, No water, Tent & RV camping: Free, Elev: 646ft/197m, Nearest town: Sparta. GPS: 36.032511, -85.620322

10 • B3 | Cedar Creek

Total sites: 58, RV sites: 58, Elec sites: 58, Water at site, Flush toilet, Free showers, RV dump, Tent & RV camping: $30-35, 1 group site: $35, Open Apr-Oct, Max Length: 97ft, Reservations accepted, Elev: 453ft/138m, Tel: 615-754-4947, Nearest town: Old Hickory. GPS: 36.278289, -86.510379

11 • B3 | Clark Island
Dispersed sites, No water, Tents only: $5, Boat-in, Open all year, Reservations accepted, Elev: 657ft/200m, Tel: 931-243-3136, Nearest town: Celina. GPS: 36.585747, -85.368331

12 • B3 | County Line Island
Dispersed sites, No water, Vault/pit toilet, Tents only: $5, Boat-in, Open all year, Reservations accepted, Elev: 654ft/199m, Tel: 931-243-3136, Nearest town: Celina. GPS: 36.585094, -85.278483

13 • B3 | Cove Creek
Dispersed sites, Vault/pit toilet, Tents only: $5, Open all year, Reservations accepted, Elev: 758ft/231m, Tel: 931-243-3136, Nearest town: Celina. GPS: 36.547119, -85.212402

14 • B3 | Dale Hollow Dam
Total sites: 78, RV sites: 78, Elec sites: 78, Central water, Flush toilet, Free showers, RV dump, Tent & RV camping: $32, Open Apr-Oct, Reservations accepted, Elev: 581ft/177m, Tel: 931-243-3554, Nearest town: Celina. GPS: 36.538445, -85.458775

15 • B3 | Defeated Creek
Total sites: 155, RV sites: 155, Elec sites: 155, Central water, Flush toilet, Free showers, RV dump, Tent & RV camping: $25-30, Open Mar-Oct, Max Length: 150ft, Reservations accepted, Elev: 525ft/160m, Tel: 615-774-3141, Nearest town: Carthage. GPS: 36.298584, -85.909668

16 • B3 | Eagle Creek Ferry
Dispersed sites, No water, Vault/pit toilet, Tents only: $5, Walk-to/boat-in sites, Open all year, Reservations accepted, Elev: 643ft/196m, Tel: 931-243-3136. GPS: 36.505228, -85.196458

17 • B3 | First Island
Dispersed sites, No water, Vault/pit toilet, Tents only: $5, Boat-in, Open all year, Reservations accepted, Elev: 654ft/199m, Tel: 931-243-3136, Nearest town: Celina. GPS: 36.565641, -85.379754

18 • B3 | Floating Mill
Total sites: 111, RV sites: 66, Elec sites: 96, Water at site, Flush toilet, Free showers, RV dump, Tents: $22-24/RVs: $26-30, 2 full hookups, Open Apr-Oct, Max Length: 48ft, Reservations accepted, Elev: 676ft/206m, Tel: 931-858-4845, Nearest town: Silver Point. GPS: 36.044189, -85.762695

19 • B3 | Geiger Island
Dispersed sites, No water, Vault/pit toilet, Tents only: $5, Boat-in, Open all year, Reservations accepted, Elev: 654ft/199m, Tel: 931-243-3136, Nearest town: Celina. GPS: 36.603186, -85.321446

20 • B3 | Gunnels Camp
Total sites: 5, RV sites: 5, No water, Vault/pit toilet, Tent & RV camping: $5, Open all year, Reservations accepted, Elev: 646ft/197m, Tel: 931-243-3136, Nearest town: Byrdstown. GPS: 36.610078, -85.150008

21 • B3 | Hendrick's Creek
Dispersed sites, No water, Vault/pit toilet, Tents only: $5, Boat-in, Permit required, Open all year, Reservations accepted, Elev: 654ft/199m, Tel: 931-243-3136, Nearest town: Celina. GPS: 36.595835, -85.368492

22 • B3 | Hendrick's Creek
Dispersed sites, No water, Vault/pit toilet, Tents only: Free, Boat-in, Permit required, Reservations accepted, Elev: 654ft/199m. GPS: 36.614515, -85.371443

23 • B3 | Horse Trail
Dispersed sites, No water, No toilets, Tent & RV camping: Free, Elev: 512ft/156m, Nearest town: Granville. GPS: 36.316722, -85.793196

24 • B3 | Jackson Creek Island
Dispersed sites, No water, Vault/pit toilet, Tents only: $5, Boat-in, Open all year, Reservations accepted, Elev: 657ft/200m, Tel: 931-243-3136. GPS: 36.548165, -85.222357

25 • B3 | Jones Chapel
Dispersed sites, No water, Vault/pit toilet, Tents only: $5, Also boat-in sites, Open all year, Reservations accepted, Elev: 671ft/205m, Tel: 931-243-3136. GPS: 36.611444, -85.189879

26 • B3 | Jouett Creek Point
Dispersed sites, No water, Vault/pit toilet, Tents only: $5, Boat-in, Open all year, Reservations accepted, Elev: 643ft/196m, Tel: 931-243-3136. GPS: 36.585503, -85.259798

27 • B3 | Kemper Flats
Dispersed sites, No water, Vault/pit toilet, Tents only: $5, Boat-in, Open all year, Reservations accepted, Elev: 666ft/203m, Tel: 931-243-3136. GPS: 36.574517, -85.359149

28 • B3 | Lillydale
Total sites: 115, RV sites: 85, Elec sites: 84, Central water, Flush toilet, Free showers, RV dump, Tents: $18-22/RVs: $22-40, Stay limit: 14 days, Open Apr-Sep, Max Length: 76ft, Reservations accepted, Elev: 676ft/206m, Tel: 931-823-4155, Nearest town: Celina. GPS: 36.604421, -85.301405

29 • B3 | Long Branch
Total sites: 60, RV sites: 60, Elec sites: 60, Water at site, Flush toilet, Free showers, RV dump, Tent & RV camping: $26-30, 3 full hookups, Open Apr-Oct, Max Length: 156ft, Reservations accepted, Elev: 495ft/151m, Nearest town: Lancaster. GPS: 36.100123, -85.833384

30 • B3 | Mitchell Creek
Dispersed sites, No water, Vault/pit toilet, Tents only: Free, Boat-in, Permit required, Reservations accepted, Elev: 654ft/199m, Nearest town: Celina. GPS: 36.513254, -85.371976

31 • B3 | Mitchell Creek Boat-in
Dispersed sites, No water, Vault/pit toilet, Tents only: $3, Boat-in, Reservations accepted, Elev: 650ft/198m, Tel: 931-243-3136, Nearest town: Celina. GPS: 36.517665, -85.378821

32 • B3 | Moore Hollow Point
Dispersed sites, No water, Vault/pit toilet, Tents only: $5, Boat-in, Open all year, Reservations accepted, Elev: 681ft/208m, Tel:

931-243-3136, Nearest town: Peytonsburg. GPS: 36.613284, -85.339869

33 • B3 | Noel Island

Dispersed sites, No water, Vault/pit toilet, Tents only: $5, Boat-in, Reservations accepted, Elev: 661ft/201m, Tel: 931-243-3136, Nearest town: Celina. GPS: 36.599552, -85.287104

34 • B3 | Obey River

Total sites: 131, RV sites: 108, Elec sites: 72, Central water, Flush toilet, Free showers, RV dump, Tents: $22-32/RVs: $22-40, Stay limit: 14 days, Open Apr-Oct, Max Length: 91ft, Reservations accepted, Elev: 673ft/205m, Tel: 931-864-6388, Nearest town: Livingston. GPS: 36.530273, -85.169678

35 • B3 | Phillips Island

Dispersed sites, No water, Vault/pit toilet, Tents only: $5, Boat-in, Open all year, Reservations accepted, Elev: 665ft/203m, Tel: 931-243-3136, Nearest town: Celina. GPS: 36.606518, -85.287627

36 • B3 | Plankyard

Dispersed sites, No water, Vault/pit toilet, Tents only: $5, Also boat-in sites, Open all year, Reservations accepted, Elev: 661ft/201m, Tel: 931-243-3136, Nearest town: Celina. GPS: 36.538278, -85.173206

37 • B3 | Poole Knobs

Total sites: 86, RV sites: 78, Elec sites: 56, Central water, Flush toilet, Free showers, RV dump, Tents: $20-26/RVs: $20-40, Group site: $50, Open May-Sep, Max Length: 40ft, Reservations accepted, Elev: 597ft/182m, Tel: 615-459-6948, Nearest town: Lavergne. GPS: 36.056713, -86.518775

38 • B3 | Ragland Bottom

Total sites: 56, RV sites: 40, Elec sites: 40, Water at site, Flush toilet, Free showers, RV dump, Tents: $16-24/RVs: $26-30, 10 full hookups, Open Apr-Oct, Max Length: 125ft, Reservations accepted, Elev: 679ft/207m, Tel: 931-761-3616, Nearest town: Smithville. GPS: 35.977234, -85.722368

39 • B3 | Rayburn Point

Dispersed sites, No water, Vault/pit toilet, Tents only: $5, Boat-in, Open all year, Reservations accepted, Elev: 655ft/200m, Tel: 931-243-3136, Nearest town: Celina. GPS: 36.626802, -85.245951

40 • B3 | Red Oak Ridge A TH

Dispersed sites, No water, Vault/pit toilet, Tents only: $5, Open all year, Reservations accepted, Elev: 926ft/282m, Tel: 931-243-3136, Nearest town: Celina. GPS: 36.565587, -85.409719

41 • B3 | Roberts Hollow Point Boat-in

Dispersed sites, No water, Vault/pit toilet, Tents only: $5, Boat-in, Reservations accepted, Elev: 650ft/198m, Tel: 931-243-3136, Nearest town: Celina. GPS: 36.589165, -85.381103

42 • B3 | Roberts Hollow Point Boat-in

Dispersed sites, No water, Vault/pit toilet, Tents only: $5, Boat-in, Reservations accepted, Elev: 650ft/198m, Tel: 931-243-3136, Nearest town: Celina. GPS: 36.591615, -85.384274

43 • B3 | Salt Lick Creek

Total sites: 145, RV sites: 145, Elec sites: 145, Central water, Flush toilet, Free showers, RV dump, Tent & RV camping: $20-25, 28 full hookups, Open Apr-Oct, Max Length: 216ft, Reservations accepted, Elev: 577ft/176m, Tel: 931-678-4718, Nearest town: Carthage. GPS: 36.322021, -85.788818

44 • B3 | Seven Points

Total sites: 59, RV sites: 59, Elec sites: 59, Central water, Flush toilet, Free showers, RV dump, Tent & RV camping: $26-30, Open Apr-Oct, Max Length: 45ft, Reservations accepted, Elev: 532ft/162m, Tel: 615-889-1975, Nearest town: Hermitage. GPS: 36.133651, -86.572696

45 • B3 | Sewell Bend

Dispersed sites, No water, Vault/pit toilet, Tents only: $5, Boat-in, Open all year, Reservations accepted, Elev: 664ft/202m, Tel: 931-243-3136, Nearest town: Celina. GPS: 36.553538, -85.387594

46 • B3 | Sherman Hollow

Dispersed sites, No water, Vault/pit toilet, Tents only: $5, Boat-in, Open all year, Reservations accepted, Elev: 663ft/202m, Tel: 931-243-3136, Nearest town: Celina. GPS: 36.616397, -85.335719

47 • B3 | State Line Island

Dispersed sites, No water, Vault/pit toilet, Tents only: $5, Boat-in, Open all year, Reservations accepted, Elev: 659ft/201m, Tel: 931-243-3136, Nearest town: Celina. GPS: 36.624869, -85.285072

48 • B3 | Taylors Ford

Dispersed sites, No water, Vault/pit toilet, Tents only: $5, Open all year, Reservations accepted, Elev: 655ft/200m, Tel: 931-243-3136, Nearest town: Celina. GPS: 36.505011, -85.138303

49 • B3 | West Fork Ashburn Creek

Dispersed sites, No water, Vault/pit toilet, Tents only: $5, Boat-in, Open all year, Reservations accepted, Elev: 653ft/199m, Tel: 931-243-3136, Nearest town: Celina. GPS: 36.573678, -85.277454

50 • B3 | Willow Grove

Total sites: 81, RV sites: 60, Elec sites: 60, Central water, Flush toilet, Free showers, RV dump, Tents: $22/RVs: $32, Stay limit: 14 days, Open May-Sep, Max Length: 81ft, Reservations accepted, Elev: 669ft/204m, Tel: 931-243-3136, Nearest town: Oakley. GPS: 36.587402, -85.343750

Texas

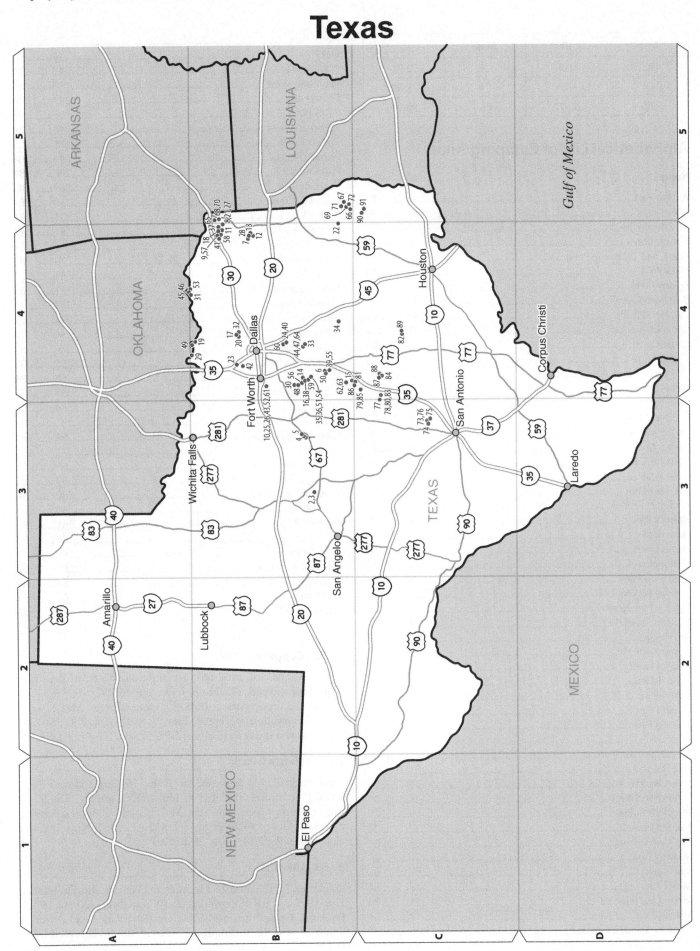

Map	ID	Map	ID
B3	1-5	C3	73-77
B4	6-64	C4	78-89
B5	65-72	C5	90-91

Alphabetical List of Camping Areas

Name	ID	Map
Airport Park	6	B4
Alley Creek	7	B4
Armstrong Creek	8	B4
Bassett Creek	9	B4
Bear Creek (Mustang Park)	10	B4
Black Point	11	B4
Brushy Creek	12	B4
Buckhorn Creek	13	B4
Canyon Park	73	C3
Cedar Breaks	78	C4
Cedar Creek	14	B4
Cedar Ridge	15	B4
Cedron Creek	16	B4
Clear Lake Park	17	B4
Clear Spring	65	B5
Copperas Creek	1	B3
Corely Area 2	18	B4
Cranes Mill	74	C3
Damsite Area	19	B4
Dana Peak	79	C4
East Fork Park	20	B4
Ebenezer Park	66	B5
Flatrock Park	2	B3
Flatwoods	21	B4
Hanks Creek	22	B4
Hickory Creek	23	B4
High View Park	24	B4
Holiday Park Main CG	25	B4
Holiday Park North End	26	B4
Jackson Creek Park	27	B4
Jim Hogg	80	C4
Johnson Creek	28	B4
Juniper Point	29	B4
Kimball Bend	30	B4
Lakeside	3	B3
Lamar Point	31	B4
Lavonia Park	32	B4
Liberty Hill	33	B4
Limestone Lake Park	34	B4
Live Oak Ridge	81	C4
Lofers Bend East	35	B4
Lofers Bend West	36	B4
Magnolia Ridge	90	C5
Malden Lake	37	B4
McCown Valley	38	B4
Midway Park	39	B4
Mill Creek	67	B5
Mott Park	40	B4
Mudd Lake (Blue Lake)	41	B4
Murrell Park	42	B4
Mustang Point	43	B4
North Park	75	C3
Oak Park	44	B4
Pat Mayse East	45	B4
Pat Mayse West	46	B4
Pecan Point	47	B4
Piney Point	68	B5
Plowman Creek	48	B4
Potters Creek	76	C3
Preston Bend	49	B4
Promontory	4	B3
Rayburn Park	69	B5
Reynolds Creek	50	B4
Riverside	51	B4
Rocky Creek Park	52	B4
Rocky Creek Park	82	C4
Rocky Point Park	70	B5
Russell Park	83	C4
San Augustine Park	71	B5
Sanders Cove	53	B4
Sandy Creek	91	C5
Soldiers Bluff	54	B4
Sowell Creek	5	B3
Speegleville Park	55	B4
Steele Creek	56	B4
Sulphur River Bank	57	B4
Taylor	84	C4
Tejas Camp	77	C3
Thomas Lake	58	B4
Twin Dikes	72	B5
Union Grove	85	C4
Walling Bend	59	B4
Waxahachie Creek	60	B4
Westcliff Park	86	C4
Westcreek Circle (Mustang Park)	61	B4
White Flint	62	B4
Willis Creek	87	C4
Wilson H. Fox Park	88	C4
Winkler Park	63	B4
Wolf Creek	64	B4
Yequa Creek Park	89	C4

1 • B3 | Copperas Creek

Total sites: 66, RV sites: 66, Elec sites: 66, Water at site, Flush toilet, Free showers, RV dump, Tents: $16-26/RVs: $16-38, 24 full hookups, 2 group sites: $100-$130, Open all year, Max Length: 140ft, Reservations accepted, Elev: 1184ft/361m, Tel: 254-879-2424, Nearest town: Comanche. GPS: 31.966797, -98.504395

2 • B3 | Flatrock Park

Total sites: 56, RV sites: 56, Elec sites: 56, Water at site, Flush toilet, Free showers, RV dump, Tent & RV camping: $20-26, 10 full hookups, Open May-Sep, Max Length: 80ft, Reservations accepted, Elev: 1909ft/582m, Tel: 432-625-2322, Nearest town: Coleman. GPS: 31.834104, -99.579901

3 • B3 | Lakeside

Total sites: 74, RV sites: 74, Elec sites: 68, Water at site, Flush toilet, Free showers, RV dump, Tent & RV camping: $20-30, 16 full hookups, Group sites: $90-$260, Use East Park Road entrance, Open all year, Max Length: 100ft, Reservations accepted, Elev:

1955ft/596m, Tel: 432-625-2322, Nearest town: Coleman. GPS: 31.842165, -99.578837

4 • B3 | Promontory

Total sites: 82, RV sites: 82, Elec sites: 61, Water at site, Flush toilet, Free showers, RV dump, Tents: $8/RVs: $16-20, 5 shelter sites - $22, Open Apr-Sep, Max Length: 140ft, Reservations accepted, Elev: 1194ft/364m, Tel: 254-879-2424, Nearest town: Comanche. GPS: 31.981934, -98.489258

5 • B3 | Sowell Creek

Total sites: 61, RV sites: 61, Elec sites: 61, Water at site, Flush toilet, Free showers, RV dump, Tents: $16-20/RVs: $16-26, Group site: $130, 14 full hookups, Open all year, Max Length: 110ft, Reservations accepted, Elev: 1201ft/366m, Tel: 254-879-2424, Nearest town: Proctor. GPS: 31.989502, -98.459717

6 • B4 | Airport Park

Total sites: 74, RV sites: 74, Elec sites: 59, Water at site, Flush toilet, Free showers, RV dump, Tents: $16/RVs: $28-32, 21 full hookups, Group site $150, Open all year, Reservations accepted, Elev: 505ft/154m, Tel: 254-756-5359, Nearest town: Waco. GPS: 31.597001, -97.238042

7 • B4 | Alley Creek

Total sites: 79, RV sites: 49, Elec sites: 49, Water at site, Flush toilet, Free showers, RV dump, Tents: $18/RVs: $28-32, Group site $175, Open Mar-Sep, Max Length: 80ft, Reservations accepted, Elev: 269ft/82m, Tel: 903-665-2336, Nearest town: Jefferson. GPS: 32.798383, -94.590036

8 • B4 | Armstrong Creek

Dispersed sites, No water, No toilets, Tent & RV camping: Free, Stay limit: 14 days, Reservations not accepted, Elev: 244ft/74m, Tel: 903-838-8781, Nearest town: Atlanta. GPS: 33.226278, -94.279362

9 • B4 | Bassett Creek

Dispersed sites, No water, No toilets, Tent & RV camping: Free, Nothing larger than truck camper, Stay limit: 14 days, Reservations not accepted, Elev: 246ft/75m, Tel: 903-838-8781, Nearest town: Naples. GPS: 33.285128, -94.495016

10 • B4 | Bear Creek (Mustang Park)

Total sites: 40, RV sites: 40, Elec sites: 40, Water at site, Flush toilet, Free showers, RV dump, Tent & RV camping: $28, 2 full hookups, Group site $125, Open Apr-Sep, Max Length: 85ft, Reservations accepted, Elev: 725ft/221m, Tel: 817-292-2400, Nearest town: Fort Worth. GPS: 32.609013, -97.488512

11 • B4 | Black Point

Dispersed sites, No water, No toilets, Tent & RV camping: Free, Stay limit: 14 days, Elev: 236ft/72m, Tel: 903-838-8781, Nearest town: Douglassville. GPS: 33.258229, -94.402746

12 • B4 | Brushy Creek

Total sites: 99, RV sites: 62, Elec sites: 74, Water at site, Flush toilet, Free showers, RV dump, Tents: $18-20/RVs: $28-32, Open Mar-Nov, Max Length: 180ft, Reservations accepted, Elev: 302ft/92m, Tel: 903-665-2336, Nearest town: Jefferson. GPS: 32.743556, -94.535561

13 • B4 | Buckhorn Creek

Total sites: 95, RV sites: 57, Elec sites: 57, Water at site, Flush toilet, Free showers, RV dump, Tents: $18/RVs: $28-32, Open all year, Max Length: 135ft, Reservations accepted, Elev: 282ft/86m, Tel: 903-665-2336, Nearest town: Jefferson. GPS: 32.756592, -94.495850

14 • B4 | Cedar Creek

Total sites: 20, RV sites: 20, Central water, Vault/pit toilet, No showers, No RV dump, Tent & RV camping: Free, Open all year, Reservations not accepted, Elev: 558ft/170m, Tel: 254-622-3332, Nearest town: Whitney. GPS: 31.990085, -97.373333

15 • B4 | Cedar Ridge

Total sites: 68, RV sites: 68, Elec sites: 68, Water at site, Flush toilet, Free showers, RV dump, Tents: $16/RVs: $24, Also 8 shelter sites $30, Group site $100-$175, Open all year, Max Length: 81ft, Reservations accepted, Elev: 669ft/204m, Tel: 254-939-2461, Nearest town: Belton. GPS: 31.169434, -97.442871

16 • B4 | Cedron Creek

Total sites: 45, RV sites: 45, Elec sites: 45, Water at site, Flush toilet, Free showers, RV dump, Tent & RV camping: $24-26, Group site $140, $14-$18 Oct-Mar, Open Apr-Sep, Max Length: 45ft, Reservations accepted, Elev: 594ft/181m, Tel: 254-694-3189, Nearest town: Whitney. GPS: 31.961914, -97.415283

17 • B4 | Clear Lake Park

Total sites: 23, RV sites: 23, Elec sites: 23, Water at site, Flush toilet, Free showers, RV dump, Tent & RV camping: $30, 23 full hookups, Group site $150, Open Apr-Sep, Max Length: 98ft, Reservations accepted, Elev: 518ft/158m, Tel: 972-442-3141, Nearest town: Princeton. GPS: 33.055375, -96.488121

18 • B4 | Corely Area 2

Dispersed sites, No water, No toilets, Tent & RV camping: Free, Stay limit: 14 days, Reservations not accepted, Elev: 243ft/74m, Tel: 903-838-8781, Nearest town: Naples. GPS: 33.271756, -94.404804

19 • B4 | Damsite Area

Total sites: 30, RV sites: 21, Elec sites: 21, Water at site, Flush toilet, Free showers, RV dump, Tents: $15/RVs: $20, Open Apr-Sep, Max Length: 65+ft, Reservations not accepted, Elev: 525ft/160m, Tel: 903-465-4990, Nearest town: Denison. GPS: 33.818233, -96.559938

20 • B4 | East Fork Park

Total sites: 62, RV sites: 50, Elec sites: 50, Water at site, Vault/pit toilet, No showers, RV dump, Tents: $14/RVs: $30, 11 equestrian sites, Group site $150, Open all year, Max Length: 60ft, Reservations accepted, Elev: 525ft/160m, Tel: 972-442-3141, Nearest town: Wylie. GPS: 33.038330, -96.511719

21 • B4 | Flatwoods

Dispersed sites, No water, No toilets, Tent & RV camping: Free, Stay limit: 14 days, Elev: 233ft/71m, Tel: 903-838-8781, Nearest town: Douglassville. GPS: 33.248267, -94.310504

22 • B4 | Hanks Creek

Total sites: 52, RV sites: 52, Elec sites: 52, Water at site, Flush toilet, Free showers, RV dump, Tent & RV camping: $26-28, 8 sites w/ screened shelter - $36, Group site $150, Open all year, Max Length: 120ft, Reservations accepted, Elev: 220ft/67m, Tel: 409-384-5716, Nearest town: Huntington. GPS: 31.272746, -94.401341

23 • B4 | Hickory Creek

Total sites: 131, RV sites: 121, Elec sites: 121, Water at site, Flush toilet, Free showers, RV dump, Tents: $14/RVs: $30, Stay limit: 14 days, Open all year, Max Length: 102ft, Reservations accepted, Elev: 551ft/168m, Tel: 469-645-9100, Nearest town: Lewisville. GPS: 33.106002, -97.042959

24 • B4 | High View Park

Total sites: 39, RV sites: 39, Elec sites: 39, Water at site, Flush toilet, Free showers, RV dump, Tent & RV camping: $14-16, Open all year, Max Length: 80ft, Reservations required, Elev: 436ft/133m, Tel: 972-875-5711, Nearest town: Ennis. GPS: 32.268048, -96.663908

25 • B4 | Holiday Park Main CG

Total sites: 64, RV sites: 64, Elec sites: 62, Water at site, No toilets, No showers, RV dump, Tents: $14/RVs: $14-28, Stay limit: 14 days, Open all year, Max Length: 143ft, Reservations accepted, Elev: 698ft/213m, Tel: 817-292-2400, Nearest town: Fort Worth. GPS: 32.618147, -97.496885

26 • B4 | Holiday Park North End

Total sites: 41, RV sites: 31, Elec sites: 17, Water at site, Flush toilet, Free showers, RV dump, Tents: $14/RVs: $28, Shelter sites: $40, Stay limit: 14 days, Open all year, Max Length: 200ft, Reservations accepted, Elev: 794ft/242m, Tel: 817-292-2400, Nearest town: Fort Worth. GPS: 32.625879, -97.482779

27 • B4 | Jackson Creek Park

Total sites: 20, RV sites: 20, No water, Vault/pit toilet, Tent & RV camping: Free, Stay limit: 14 days, Max Length: 25ft, Elev: 269ft/82m, Tel: 903-838-8781, Nearest town: Atlanta. GPS: 33.224198, -94.302568

28 • B4 | Johnson Creek

Total sites: 85, RV sites: 63, Elec sites: 73, Water at site, Flush toilet, Free showers, RV dump, Tents: $18-20/RVs: $28-32, Group site: $175, Open Mar-Dec, Max Length: 70ft, Reservations accepted, Elev: 322ft/98m, Tel: 903-665-2336, Nearest town: Jefferson. GPS: 32.782959, -94.550781

29 • B4 | Juniper Point

Total sites: 69, RV sites: 44, Elec sites: 44, Water at site, Flush toilet, Free showers, RV dump, Tents: $16/RVs: $22-24, Open all year, Max Length: 50ft, Reservations accepted, Elev: 643ft/196m, Tel: 903-523-4022, Nearest town: Whitesboro. GPS: 33.861754, -96.828865

30 • B4 | Kimball Bend

Total sites: 34, RV sites: 34, Elec sites: 34, Water at site, Flush toilet, Free showers, RV dump, Tent & RV camping: $26, Open all year, Max Length: 45ft, Reservations accepted, Elev: 554ft/169m, Tel: 254-622-3332, Nearest town: Whitney. GPS: 32.123743, -97.496311

31 • B4 | Lamar Point

Total sites: 9, RV sites: 9, No water, Vault/pit toilet, Tent & RV camping: $8, Open all year, Reservations not accepted, Elev: 522ft/159m, Tel: 903-732-3020, Nearest town: Paris. GPS: 33.825391, -95.628144

32 • B4 | Lavonia Park

Total sites: 49, RV sites: 34, Elec sites: 34, Water at site, Flush toilet, Free showers, RV dump, Tents: $14/RVs: $30, Open all year, Max Length: 65ft, Reservations accepted, Elev: 554ft/169m, Tel: 972-442-3141, Nearest town: Wylie. GPS: 33.042936, -96.444073

33 • B4 | Liberty Hill

Total sites: 102, RV sites: 99, Elec sites: 99, Water at site, Flush toilet, Free showers, RV dump, Tents: $18/RVs: $18-28, 6 full hookups, Group site $95, Open all year, Max Length: 150ft, Reservations accepted, Elev: 440ft/134m, Tel: 254-578-1431, Nearest town: Dawson. GPS: 31.945349, -96.711987

34 • B4 | Limestone Lake Park

Total sites: 20, RV sites: 20, Central water, Vault/pit toilet, No showers, No RV dump, Tent & RV camping: Free, No campfires, Reservations not accepted, Elev: 385ft/117m, Nearest town: Marquez. GPS: 31.340133, -96.309082

35 • B4 | Lofers Bend East

Total sites: 72, RV sites: 66, Elec sites: 66, Water at site, Flush toilet, Free showers, RV dump, Tent & RV camping: $12-24, Group site: $105, Open Apr-Sep, Max Length: 45ft, Reservations accepted, Elev: 574ft/175m, Tel: 254-694-3189, Nearest town: Whitney. GPS: 31.889548, -97.353073

36 • B4 | Lofers Bend West

Total sites: 74, RV sites: 51, Elec sites: 51, Water at site, Flush toilet, Free showers, RV dump, Tents: $12/RVs: $24-26, Group site: $80, Overnight shelters: $30, Open all year, Max Length: 45ft, Reservations accepted, Elev: 574ft/175m, Tel: 254-622-3332, Nearest town: Whitney. GPS: 31.881961, -97.366656

37 • B4 | Malden Lake

Total sites: 39, RV sites: 39, Elec sites: 39, Water at site, No toilets, No showers, RV dump, Tent & RV camping: $24-26, Open all year, Max Length: 55ft, Reservations required, Elev: 292ft/89m, Tel: 903-838-8781, Nearest town: Maud. GPS: 33.281257, -94.339571

38 • B4 | McCown Valley

Total sites: 100, RV sites: 87, Elec sites: 87, Water at site, Flush toilet, Free showers, RV dump, Tents: $12/RVs: $24-26, Overnight shelters: $30, 39 equestrian sites, Open all year, Max Length: 50ft, Reservations accepted, Elev: 587ft/179m, Tel: 254-694-3189, Nearest town: Whitney. GPS: 31.943954, -97.397344

39 • B4 | Midway Park

Total sites: 42, RV sites: 37, Elec sites: 37, Water at site, Flush toilet, Free showers, RV dump, Tents: $16/RVs: $28-32, 11 full hookups, Open all year, Max Length: 60ft, Reservations accepted, Elev: 518ft/158m, Tel: 254-756-5359, Nearest town: Waco. GPS: 31.524975, -97.226614

40 • B4 | Mott Park

Total sites: 40, RV sites: 34, Elec sites: 34, Water at site, Flush toilet, Free showers, RV dump, Tent & RV camping: $14, Group site: $80, Open Apr-Sep, Max Length: 140ft, Reservations required, Elev: 433ft/132m, Tel: 972-875-5711, Nearest town: Ennis. GPS: 32.259401, -96.662929

41 • B4 | Mudd Lake (Blue Lake)

Dispersed sites, No water, No toilets, Tent & RV camping: Free, Stay limit: 14 days, Reservations not accepted, Elev: 248ft/76m, Tel: 903-838-8781, Nearest town: Naples. GPS: 33.291499, -94.550663

42 • B4 | Murrell Park

Total sites: 22, RV sites: 0, Central water, Vault/pit toilet, No showers, No RV dump, Tents only: $10, Open all year, Reservations accepted, Elev: 568ft/173m, Tel: 817-865-2600, Nearest town: Grapevine. GPS: 32.994149, -97.087068

43 • B4 | Mustang Point

Total sites: 100, RV sites: 0, Central water, Flush toilet, No showers, No RV dump, Tents only: $14, Group site: $125, Open Apr-Sep, Reservations accepted, Elev: 722ft/220m, Tel: 817-292-2400, Nearest town: Fort Worth. GPS: 32.609405, -97.472859

44 • B4 | Oak Park

Total sites: 48, RV sites: 48, Elec sites: 48, Water at site, Flush toilet, Free showers, RV dump, Tents: $24/RVs: $24-28, Group site: $95, 6 full hookups, Open all year, Max Length: 110ft, Reservations accepted, Elev: 466ft/142m, Tel: 254-578-1431, Nearest town: Dawson. GPS: 31.966423, -96.695572

45 • B4 | Pat Mayse East

Total sites: 26, RV sites: 26, Elec sites: 26, Water at site, No toilets, No showers, RV dump, Tent & RV camping: $15, Open all year, Reservations not accepted, Elev: 518ft/158m, Tel: 903-732-3020, Nearest town: Paris. GPS: 33.843506, -95.587158

46 • B4 | Pat Mayse West

Total sites: 88, RV sites: 88, Elec sites: 83, Water at site, Flush toilet, Free showers, RV dump, Tent & RV camping: $12-18, Open all year, Max Length: 90ft, Reservations accepted, Elev: 502ft/153m, Tel: 903-732-3020, Nearest town: Paris. GPS: 33.843262, -95.605957

47 • B4 | Pecan Point

Total sites: 35, RV sites: 35, Elec sites: 5, Central water, Vault/pit toilet, No showers, RV dump, Tents: $12/RVs: $14, Open Apr-Sep, Max Length: 150ft, Reservations accepted, Elev: 443ft/135m, Tel: 254-578-1431, Nearest town: Dawson. GPS: 31.963411, -96.736102

48 • B4 | Plowman Creek

Total sites: 34, RV sites: 34, Elec sites: 22, Water at site, Flush toilet, Free showers, RV dump, Tents: $12/RVs: $24, 10 equestrian sites, Open all year, Max Length: 50ft, Reservations accepted, Elev: 568ft/173m, Tel: 254-622-3332, Nearest town: Whitney. GPS: 32.069207, -97.492315

49 • B4 | Preston Bend

Total sites: 34, RV sites: 34, Elec sites: 22, Water at site, Flush toilet, Free showers, RV dump, Tents: $16/RVs: $22-24, Open Apr-Sep, Max Length: 70ft, Reservations accepted, Elev: 653ft/199m, Tel: 903-465-4990, Nearest town: Denison. GPS: 33.876569, -96.643765

50 • B4 | Reynolds Creek

Total sites: 67, RV sites: 61, Elec sites: 61, Water at site, Flush toilet, Free showers, RV dump, Tents: $16/RVs: $28, 10 equestrian sites with W/E open all year, Open all year, Reservations accepted, Elev: 508ft/155m, Tel: 254-756-5359, Nearest town: Waco. GPS: 31.586275, -97.267439

51 • B4 | Riverside

Total sites: 5, RV sites: 5, No water, Vault/pit toilet, Tent & RV camping: Free, Reservations not accepted, Elev: 512ft/156m, Tel: 254-622-3332, Nearest town: Whitney. GPS: 31.868045, -97.367785

52 • B4 | Rocky Creek Park

Total sites: 11, RV sites: 11, Central water, Vault/pit toilet, No showers, RV dump, Tent & RV camping: $14, Open Apr-Sep, Max Length: 50ft, Reservations accepted, Elev: 722ft/220m, Tel: 817-292-2400, Nearest town: Fort Worth. GPS: 32.605191, -97.458054

53 • B4 | Sanders Cove

Total sites: 89, RV sites: 89, Elec sites: 85, Water at site, Flush toilet, Free showers, RV dump, Tents: $12/RVs: $12-22, Open all year, Max Length: 80ft, Reservations accepted, Elev: 508ft/155m, Tel: 903-732-3020, Nearest town: Paris. GPS: 33.838582, -95.539637

54 • B4 | Soldiers Bluff

Total sites: 14, RV sites: 14, No water, Vault/pit toilet, No showers, No RV dump, Tent & RV camping: Free, Open all year, Reservations not accepted, Elev: 574ft/175m, Tel: 254-622-3332, Nearest town: Whitney. GPS: 31.862041, -97.372373

55 • B4 | Speegleville Park

Total sites: 30, RV sites: 30, Elec sites: 30, Water at site, Flush toilet, Free showers, RV dump, Tent & RV camping: $28, 2 screened shelters: $32, Open all year, Reservations accepted, Elev: 486ft/148m, Tel: 254-756-5359, Nearest town: Waco. GPS: 31.557191, -97.240065

56 • B4 | Steele Creek

Total sites: 21, RV sites: 21, Central water, Vault/pit toilet, No showers, No RV dump, Tent & RV camping: Free, Reservations not accepted, Elev: 551ft/168m, Tel: 254-622-3332, Nearest town: Whitney. GPS: 32.005741, -97.451559

57 • B4 | Sulphur River Bank

Dispersed sites, No water, No toilets, Tents only: Free, Boat-in, Stay limit: 14 days, Reservations not accepted, Elev: 257ft/78m, Tel: 903-838-8781, Nearest town: Naples. GPS: 33.285702, -94.457882

58 • B4 | Thomas Lake

Dispersed sites, No water, Vault/pit toilet, Tent & RV camping: Free, Stay limit: 14 days, Open all year, Elev: 249ft/76m, Tel: 903-838-8781, Nearest town: Eagan. GPS: 33.266835, -94.470869

59 • B4 | Walling Bend

Total sites: 10, RV sites: 10, No water, Vault/pit toilet, Tent & RV camping: Free, Reservations not accepted, Elev: 550ft/168m, Tel: 254-622-3332, Nearest town: Waco. GPS: 31.897572, -97.397161

60 • B4 | Waxahachie Creek

Total sites: 76, RV sites: 69, Elec sites: 69, Water at site, Flush toilet, Free showers, RV dump, Tents: $14/RVs: $16-18, 4 equestrian sites & corrals, Open Apr-Sep, Max Length: 60ft, Reservations required, Elev: 450ft/137m, Tel: 972-875-5711, Nearest town: Ennis. GPS: 32.292361, -96.686697

61 • B4 | Westcreek Circle (Mustang Park)

Dispersed sites, No water, No toilets, Group site - walk-to, Permission required, Reservations required, Elev: 722ft/220m, Tel: 817-292-2400, Nearest town: Fort Worth. GPS: 32.602983, -97.501008

62 • B4 | White Flint

Total sites: 25, RV sites: 13, Elec sites: 13, Water at site, No toilets, No showers, RV dump, Tent & RV camping: $24, 12 shelter sites: $30, Open Mar-Sep, Max Length: 60ft, Reservations accepted, Elev: 627ft/191m, Tel: 254-939-2461, Nearest town: Temple. GPS: 31.231149, -97.472332

63 • B4 | Winkler Park

Total sites: 14, RV sites: 14, Water at site, Flush toilet, Free showers, No RV dump, Tent & RV camping: $14, Open Mar-Sep, Max Length: 75ft, Reservations accepted, Elev: 604ft/184m, Tel: 254-939-2461, Nearest town: Temple. GPS: 31.250983, -97.472691

64 • B4 | Wolf Creek

Total sites: 73, RV sites: 73, Elec sites: 50, Water at site, Flush toilet, Free showers, RV dump, Tents: $16/RVs: $24, Group site: $95, Open Apr-Sep, Max Length: 120ft, Reservations accepted, Elev: 456ft/139m, Tel: 254-578-1431, Nearest town: Dawson. GPS: 31.963733, -96.720307

65 • B5 | Clear Spring

Total sites: 114, RV sites: 102, Elec sites: 102, Water at site, Flush toilet, Free showers, RV dump, Tents: $14/RVs: $24-32, Group site $26-$90, $32 sites have screened shelter, Open all year, Max Length: 85ft, Reservations accepted, Elev: 285ft/87m, Tel: 903-838-8781, Nearest town: Texarkana. GPS: 33.354469, -94.187934

66 • B5 | Ebenezer Park

Total sites: 40, RV sites: 40, Elec sites: 13, Central water, Vault/pit toilet, No showers, RV dump, Tents: $14/RVs: $26-28, 10 equestrian sites with E/W open all year, Open all year, Max Length: 155ft, Reservations accepted, Elev: 226ft/69m, Tel: 409-384-5716, Nearest town: Jasper. GPS: 31.070141, -94.124442

67 • B5 | Mill Creek

Total sites: 110, RV sites: 110, Elec sites: 110, Water at site, Flush toilet, Free showers, RV dump, Tent & RV camping: $26-28, Open all year, Max Length: 63ft, Reservations accepted, Elev: 184ft/56m, Tel: 409-384-5716, Nearest town: Brookeland. GPS: 31.153320, -94.007568

68 • B5 | Piney Point

Total sites: 68, RV sites: 48, Elec sites: 48, Water at site, Flush toilet, Free showers, RV dump, Tents: $14/RVs: $24-26, Open Mar-Sep, Max Length: 55ft, Reservations required, Elev: 341ft/104m, Tel: 903-838-8781, Nearest town: Texarkana. GPS: 33.300049, -94.169922

69 • B5 | Rayburn Park

Total sites: 46, RV sites: 46, Elec sites: 24, Water at site, Flush toilet, Free showers, RV dump, Tents: $14/RVs: $26-28, Open all year, Max Length: 98ft, Reservations accepted, Elev: 226ft/69m, Tel: 409-384-5716, Nearest town: Pineland. GPS: 31.108643, -94.106689

70 • B5 | Rocky Point Park

Total sites: 124, RV sites: 124, Elec sites: 124, Water at site, Flush toilet, Free showers, RV dump, Tent & RV camping: $24-28, 15 full hookups, Open all year, Max Length: 98ft, Reservations required, Elev: 276ft/84m, Tel: 903-838-8781, Nearest town: Texarkana. GPS: 33.288818, -94.172363

71 • B5 | San Augustine Park

Total sites: 100, RV sites: 95, Elec sites: 100, Water at site, Flush toilet, Free showers, RV dump, Tents: $16/RVs: $26, Open all year, Max Length: 104ft, Reservations accepted, Elev: 223ft/68m, Tel: 409-384-5716, Nearest town: Pineland. GPS: 31.199201, -94.079078

72 • B5 | Twin Dikes

Total sites: 43, RV sites: 43, Elec sites: 19, Water at site, Flush toilet, Free showers, RV dump, Tents: $14/RVs: $26-28, Overnight shelter: $38, Open all year, Max Length: 156ft, Reservations accepted, Elev: 167ft/51m, Tel: 409-384-5716, Nearest town: Jasper. GPS: 31.071476, -94.055893

73 • C3 | Canyon Park

Total sites: 150, RV sites: 0, Central water, Vault/pit toilet, No showers, No RV dump, Tents only: $12, Open Apr-Sep, Reservations not accepted, Elev: 965ft/294m, Tel: 830-964-3341, Nearest town: New Braunfels. GPS: 29.896484, -98.234375

74 • C3 | Cranes Mill

Total sites: 64, RV sites: 30, Elec sites: 59, Central water, Flush toilet, Free showers, RV dump, Tents: $24/RVs: $30, Group sites: $100-$130, full hookup sites, Open all year, Max Length: 80ft, Reservations accepted, Elev: 932ft/284m, Tel: 830-964-3341, Nearest town: Sattler. GPS: 29.889648, -98.291992

75 • C3 | North Park
Total sites: 19, RV sites: 0, No water, Vault/pit toilet, No showers, No RV dump, Tents only: $8-12, Fri-Sat only, Open May-Sep, Reservations not accepted, Elev: 1014ft/309m, Tel: 830-964-3341, Nearest town: New Braunfels. GPS: 29.874268, -98.205566

76 • C3 | Potters Creek
Total sites: 125, RV sites: 115, Elec sites: 115, Water at site, Flush toilet, Free showers, RV dump, Tents: $24/RVs: $30, Screened shelters available: $45, Open all year, Max Length: 60ft, Reservations accepted, Elev: 958ft/292m, Tel: 830-964-3341, Nearest town: New Braunfels. GPS: 29.905762, -98.266602

77 • C3 | Tejas Camp
Total sites: 12, RV sites: 0, Central water, Vault/pit toilet, No showers, No RV dump, Tents only: $6, Group site: $14, Open all year, Reservations accepted, Elev: 820ft/250m, Tel: 512-819-9046, Nearest town: Georgetown. GPS: 30.696291, -97.827271

78 • C4 | Cedar Breaks
Total sites: 64, RV sites: 64, Elec sites: 64, Water at site, Flush toilet, Free showers, RV dump, Tent & RV camping: $26, Open all year, Max Length: 55ft, Reservations accepted, Elev: 840ft/256m, Tel: 512-819-9046, Nearest town: Georgetown. GPS: 30.673129, -97.737671

79 • C4 | Dana Peak
Total sites: 33, RV sites: 20, Elec sites: 20, Water at site, Flush toilet, Free showers, RV dump, Tents: $12-18/RVs: $24, Open Mar-Sep, Max Length: 91ft, Reservations accepted, Elev: 653ft/199m, Tel: 254-939-2461, Nearest town: Belton. GPS: 31.024414, -97.605225

80 • C4 | Jim Hogg
Total sites: 148, RV sites: 148, Elec sites: 148, Water at site, Flush toilet, Free showers, RV dump, Tent & RV camping: $22-26, 5 group shelters $32-$40, Sites w/ screened shelters: $32-$40, Open all year, Max Length: 55ft, Reservations accepted, Elev: 853ft/260m, Tel: 512-819-9046, Nearest town: Georgetown. GPS: 30.683924, -97.740682

81 • C4 | Live Oak Ridge
Total sites: 48, RV sites: 48, Elec sites: 48, Water at site, Flush toilet, Free showers, RV dump, Tent & RV camping: $20-24, Open all year, Max Length: 90ft, Reservations accepted, Elev: 676ft/206m, Tel: 254-939-2461, Nearest town: Belton. GPS: 31.116639, -97.476111

82 • C4 | Rocky Creek Park
Total sites: 192, RV sites: 157, Elec sites: 192, Water at site, Flush toilet, Free showers, RV dump, Tents: $24-26/RVs: $24-28, Open all year, Max Length: 111ft, Reservations accepted, Elev: 282ft/86m, Tel: 979-596-1622, Nearest town: Somerville. GPS: 30.298584, -96.568604

83 • C4 | Russell Park
Total sites: 27, RV sites: 0, Central water, Flush toilet, No showers, No RV dump, Tents only: $12, 3 group sites: $60-$75, 10 sites w/ screened shelter - $24, Open all year, Reservations accepted, Elev: 866ft/264m, Tel: 512-930-5253, Nearest town: Georgetown. GPS: 30.675105, -97.757494

84 • C4 | Taylor
Total sites: 48, RV sites: 48, Elec sites: 48, Water at site, Flush toilet, Free showers, RV dump, Tent & RV camping: $22-26, Open Apr-Sep, Max Length: 50ft, Reservations accepted, Elev: 548ft/167m, Tel: 512-859-2668, Nearest town: New Braunfels. GPS: 30.670992, -97.368361

85 • C4 | Union Grove
Total sites: 37, RV sites: 30, Elec sites: 37, Water at site, Flush toilet, Free showers, RV dump, Tents: $18/RVs: $24, Screened shelters: $30, Open all year, Max Length: 85ft, Reservations accepted, Elev: 686ft/209m, Tel: 254-939-2461, Nearest town: Belton. GPS: 31.011230, -97.620361

86 • C4 | Westcliff Park
Total sites: 31, RV sites: 27, Elec sites: 27, Water at site, Flush toilet, Free showers, RV dump, Tents: $14-18/RVs: $24, Open Mar-Sep, Max Length: 70ft, Reservations accepted, Elev: 610ft/186m, Tel: 254-939-2461, Nearest town: Temple. GPS: 31.116379, -97.519839

87 • C4 | Willis Creek
Total sites: 37, RV sites: 37, Elec sites: 27, Water at site, Flush toilet, Free showers, RV dump, Tent & RV camping: $22-26, 4 full hookups, Group site $50, 10 equestrian sites (no hookups) $10, Open all year, Max Length: 50ft, Reservations accepted, Elev: 525ft/160m, Tel: 512-859-2668, Nearest town: Granger. GPS: 30.695399, -97.388896

88 • C4 | Wilson H. Fox Park
Total sites: 58, RV sites: 58, Elec sites: 58, Water at site, Flush toilet, Free showers, RV dump, Tent & RV camping: $22-26, 5 shelter sites: $36, Open all year, Max Length: 50ft, Reservations accepted, Elev: 551ft/168m, Tel: 512-859-2668, Nearest town: Granger. GPS: 30.684407, -97.349121

89 • C4 | Yequa Creek Park
Total sites: 82, RV sites: 82, Elec sites: 65, Water at site, Flush toilet, Free showers, RV dump, Tents: $18/RVs: $26-28, Open all year, Max Length: 104ft, Reservations accepted, Elev: 249ft/76m, Tel: 979-596-1622, Nearest town: Somerville. GPS: 30.307146, -96.540386

90 • C5 | Magnolia Ridge
Total sites: 41, RV sites: 39, Elec sites: 39, Water at site, Flush toilet, Free showers, RV dump, Tents: $10/RVs: $18-20, Group site $30-$45, Open all year, Max Length: 184ft, Reservations required, Elev: 131ft/40m, Tel: 409-429-3491, Nearest town: Jasper. GPS: 30.879328, -94.233057

91 • C5 | Sandy Creek
Total sites: 76, RV sites: 76, Elec sites: 71, Water at site, Flush toilet, Free showers, RV dump, Tents: $10/RVs: $18-20, Shelter: $25, Open all year, Max Length: 200ft, Reservations accepted, Elev: 144ft/44m, Tel: 409-429-3491, Nearest town: Jasper. GPS: 30.827643, -94.154196

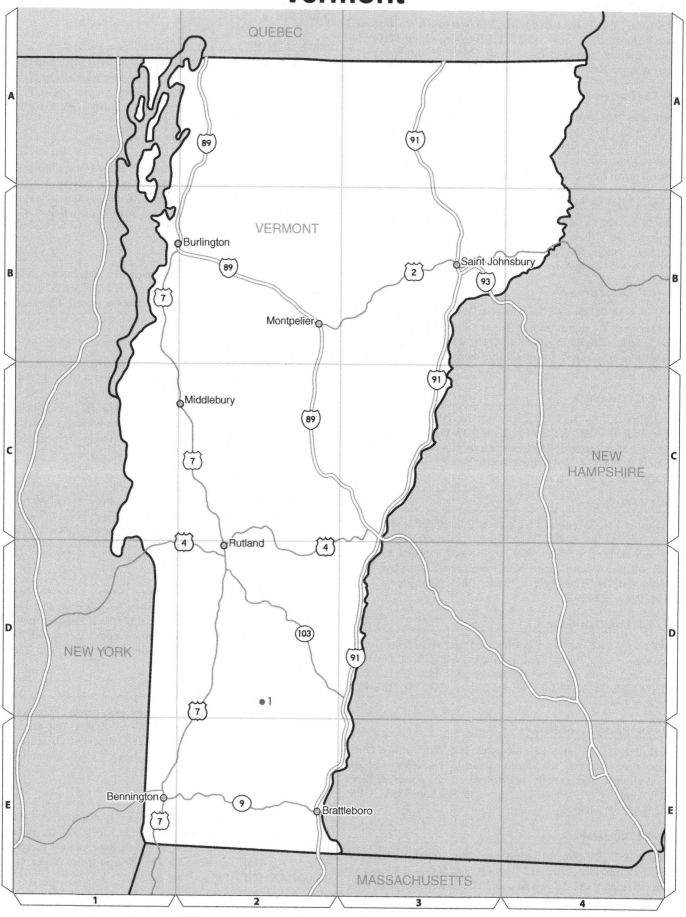

Map	ID	Map	ID
D2	1		

Alphabetical List of Camping Areas

Name   **ID**   **Map**

Winhall Brook .... 1 .... D2

1 • D2 | Winhall Brook

Total sites: 111, RV sites: 111, Elec sites: 23, Central water, Flush toilet, Free showers, RV dump, Tents: $20/RVs: $20-26, 14 lean-to's: $24, Open May-Oct, Max Length: 85ft, Reservations accepted, Elev: 1083ft/330m, Tel: 802-824-4570, Nearest town: Jamaica. GPS: 43.161938, -72.808438

Virginia

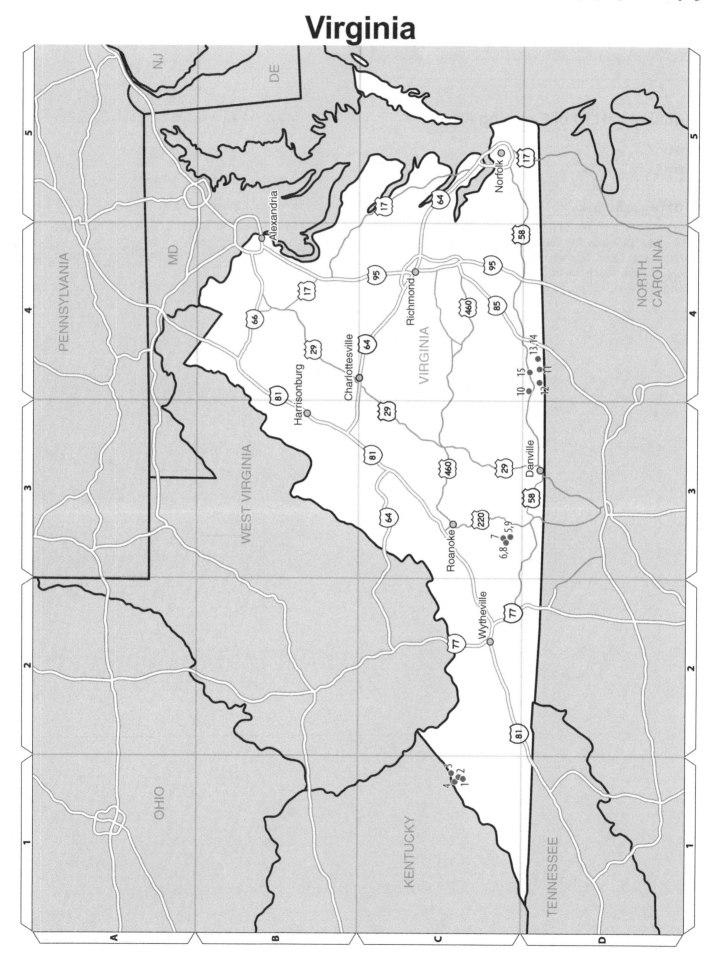

Map	ID	Map	ID
C1	1-4	D4	10-15
C3	5-9		

Alphabetical List of Camping Areas

Name	ID	Map
Buffalo Park	10	D4
Cranes Nest 1	1	C1
Cranes Nest 3	2	C1
Goose Point	5	C3
Horseshoe Point	6	C3
Ivy Hill	11	D4
Jamison Mill Park	7	C3
Longwood	12	D4
Lower Twin	3	C1
Mines Branch	8	C3
North Bend	13	D4
North Bend - Piney Woods Group	14	D4
Pound River	4	C1
Rudds Creek	15	D4
Salthouse Branch	9	C3

1 • C1 | Cranes Nest 1

Total sites: 19, RV sites: 16, Elec sites: 16, Central water, Flush toilet, Free showers, RV dump, Tents: $24/RVs: $28, Open May-Sep, Max Length: 40ft, Reservations accepted, Elev: 1447ft/441m, Tel: 276-835-9544, Nearest town: Clintwood. GPS: 37.150148, -82.409726

2 • C1 | Cranes Nest 3

Dispersed sites, Central water, Vault/pit toilet, Tents only: Free, Open May-Sep, Reservations not accepted, Elev: 1437ft/438m, Tel: 276-835-9544, Nearest town: Clintwood. GPS: 37.171435, -82.404527

3 • C1 | Lower Twin

Total sites: 33, RV sites: 33, Elec sites: 15, Central water, Flush toilet, Free showers, RV dump, Tents: $24/RVs: $28, Open May-Sep, Reservations accepted, Elev: 1581ft/482m, Tel: 276-835-9544, Nearest town: Haysi. GPS: 37.231005, -82.374106

4 • C1 | Pound River

Total sites: 27, RV sites: 27, Central water, Flush toilet, Free showers, RV dump, Tent & RV camping: $30, Open May-Sep, Max Length: 40ft, Reservations accepted, Elev: 1444ft/440m, Tel: 276-835-9544, Nearest town: Clintwood. GPS: 37.195806, -82.440646

5 • C3 | Goose Point

Total sites: 63, RV sites: 63, Elec sites: 53, Water at site, Flush toilet, Free showers, RV dump, Tents: $20/RVs: $28, Open Mar-Oct, Max Length: 82ft, Reservations accepted, Elev: 1010ft/308m, Tel: 276-629-1847, Nearest town: Martinsville. GPS: 36.803956, -80.052349

6 • C3 | Horseshoe Point

Total sites: 49, RV sites: 49, Elec sites: 15, Water at site, Flush toilet, Free showers, RV dump, Tent & RV camping: $20-25, Open May-Sep, Max Length: 38ft, Reservations accepted, Elev: 1024ft/312m, Tel: 540-365-7385, Nearest town: Martinsville. GPS: 36.834044, -80.073268

7 • C3 | Jamison Mill Park

Total sites: 12, RV sites: 12, Elec sites: 5, Water at site, Flush toilet, Free showers, RV dump, Tents: $20/RVs: $25, Open Apr-Oct, Reservations not accepted, Elev: 1043ft/318m, Tel: 276-629-2703, Nearest town: Henry. GPS: 36.850830, -80.064941

8 • C3 | Mines Branch

Dispersed sites, Vault/pit toilet, Tent & RV camping: Fee unk, Elev: 1112ft/339m, Nearest town: Bassett. GPS: 36.842198, -80.107325

9 • C3 | Salthouse Branch

Total sites: 84, RV sites: 58, Elec sites: 44, Water at site, Flush toilet, Free showers, RV dump, Tents: $20/RVs: $28, Open Apr-Oct, Max Length: 132ft, Reservations accepted, Elev: 1073ft/327m, Tel: 540-365-7005, Nearest town: Henry. GPS: 36.813772, -80.038396

10 • D4 | Buffalo Park

Total sites: 21, RV sites: 21, Elec sites: 11, Central water, Flush toilet, Free showers, RV dump, Tents: $20/RVs: $28, Open May-Sep, Max Length: 40ft, Reservations accepted, Elev: 335ft/102m, Tel: 434-738-6143, Nearest town: Clarksville. GPS: 36.661013, -78.628516

11 • D4 | Ivy Hill

Total sites: 25, RV sites: 25, Central water, No toilets, No showers, RV dump, Tent & RV camping: $10, Open May-Sep, Max Length: 32ft, Reservations not accepted, Elev: 302ft/92m, Nearest town: Townsville NC. GPS: 36.575369, -78.419171

12 • D4 | Longwood

Total sites: 66, RV sites: 66, Elec sites: 34, Central water, Flush toilet, Free showers, RV dump, Tents: $20/RVs: $28, Open Apr-Oct, Max Length: 45ft, Reservations accepted, Elev: 354ft/108m, Tel: 434-374-2711, Nearest town: Clarksville. GPS: 36.576720, -78.549767

13 • D4 | North Bend

Total sites: 244, RV sites: 244, Elec sites: 138, Central water, Flush toilet, Free showers, RV dump, Tents: $20/RVs: $28, Open all year, Max Length: 50ft, Reservations accepted, Elev: 361ft/110m, Tel: 434-738-0059, Nearest town: Boydton. GPS: 36.588612, -78.319608

14 • D4 | North Bend - Piney Woods Group

Total sites: 1, Central water, Vault/pit toilet, No showers, No RV dump, Group site: $125, Open all year, Reservations accepted, Elev: 325ft/99m, Tel: 434-738-0059, Nearest town: Boydton. GPS: 36.588619, -78.308116

15 • D4 | Rudds Creek

Total sites: 99, RV sites: 99, Elec sites: 75, Central water, Flush toilet, Free showers, RV dump, Tents: $20/RVs: $28, Outside showers, Open Apr-Oct, Max Length: 45ft, Reservations accepted, Elev: 338ft/103m, Tel: 434-738-6827, Nearest town: Boydton. GPS: 36.656257, -78.441978

Washington

Map	ID	Map	ID
C4	1-7	D3	22-24
C5	8-21	D4	25-26

Alphabetical List of Camping Areas

Name	ID	Map
Avery Park	22	D3
Ayer Boat Basin	1	C4
Big Flat HMU	2	C4
Blyton Landing	8	C5
Charbonneau Park	3	C4
Chief Timothy Park	9	C5
Devil's Bench	4	C4
Fishhook Park	5	C4
Hood Park	6	C4
Illia Landing	10	C5
Lambi Creek	11	C5
Little Goose Dam North	12	C5
Little Goose Dam South	13	C5
Little Goose Landing	14	C5
Lower Granite Lock and Dam	15	C5
Nisqually John Landing	16	C5
Offield Landing	17	C5
Paradise Park	25	D4
Plymouth Park	26	D4
Riparia Park	18	C5
Roosevelt Park	23	D3
Sundale Park	24	D3
Texas Rapids	19	C5
Wawawai Landing	20	C5
Willow Landing	21	C5
Windust	7	C4

1 • C4 | Ayer Boat Basin

Dispersed sites, No water, Vault/pit toilet, Tent & RV camping: Free, Open all year, Max Length: 40ft, Reservations not accepted, Elev: 545ft/166m, Tel: 509-282-3219, Nearest town: Ayers. GPS: 46.585975, -118.367966

2 • C4 | Big Flat HMU

Dispersed sites, No water, Vault/pit toilet, Tent & RV camping: Free, Open all year, Reservations not accepted, Elev: 502ft/153m, Tel: 509-547-2048, Nearest town: Burbank. GPS: 46.294521, -118.792344

3 • C4 | Charbonneau Park

Total sites: 52, RV sites: 52, Elec sites: 52, Water at site, Flush toilet, Free showers, RV dump, Tents: $26-30/RVs: $26-36, 15 full hookups, Open May-Sep, Max Length: 142ft, Reservations accepted, Elev: 479ft/146m, Tel: 509-547-2048, Nearest town: Pasco. GPS: 46.259535, -118.845321

4 • C4 | Devil's Bench

Total sites: 6, RV sites: 6, No water, Vault/pit toilet, No showers, No RV dump, Tent & RV camping: Free, Open all year, Reservations not accepted, Elev: 584ft/178m, Tel: 509-282-3219, Nearest town: Kahlotus. GPS: 46.567474, -118.537404

5 • C4 | Fishhook Park

Total sites: 52, RV sites: 41, Elec sites: 41, Central water, Flush toilet, Free showers, RV dump, Tents: $22/RVs: $32-35, 2 group tent sites: $44, Open May-Sep, Max Length: 133ft, Reservations accepted, Elev: 479ft/146m, Tel: 509-547-2048, Nearest town: Pasco. GPS: 46.314697, -118.767090

6 • C4 | Hood Park

Total sites: 67, RV sites: 67, Elec sites: 67, Central water, Flush toilet, Free showers, RV dump, Tent & RV camping: $30, Open May-Sep, Max Length: 105ft, Reservations accepted, Elev: 381ft/116m, Tel: 509-547-2048, Nearest town: Pasco. GPS: 46.216054, -119.013085

7 • C4 | Windust

Total sites: 24, RV sites: 20, Central water, Vault/pit toilet, No showers, RV dump, Tent & RV camping: $10, Also walk-to sites, 4 walk-to sites, Open May-Aug, Max Length: 40ft, Reservations not accepted, Elev: 476ft/145m, Tel: 509-547-2048, Nearest town: Pasco. GPS: 46.534258, -118.578314

8 • C5 | Blyton Landing

Dispersed sites, No water, Vault/pit toilet, Tent & RV camping: Free, Open all year, Reservations not accepted, Elev: 761ft/232m, Tel: 509-751-0240, Nearest town: West Clarkston. GPS: 46.559246, -117.270804

9 • C5 | Chief Timothy Park

Total sites: 66, RV sites: 50, Elec sites: 33, Water at site, Flush toilet, Free showers, RV dump, Tents: $24/RVs: $25-46, 25 full hookups, RV dump fee: Yes, Golden Age and Access Passports are not accepted, Concessionaire, Max Length: 40ft, Reservations accepted, Elev: 755ft/230m, Tel: 509-758-9580, Nearest town: Clarkston. GPS: 46.415638, -117.193024

10 • C5 | Illia Landing

Dispersed sites, Central water, Vault/pit toilet, No showers, No RV dump, Tent & RV camping: Free, Open all year, Reservations not accepted, Elev: 643ft/196m, Tel: 509-843-2214, Nearest town: Pomeroy. GPS: 46.696473, -117.471492

11 • C5 | Lambi Creek

Total sites: 6, RV sites: 6, No water, Vault/pit toilet, No showers, No RV dump, Tent & RV camping: Free, Open all year, Max Length: 18ft, Reservations not accepted, Elev: 660ft/201m, Nearest town: Pomeroy. GPS: 46.680028, -117.501517

12 • C5 | Little Goose Dam North

Dispersed sites, No water, Vault/pit toilet, Tent & RV camping: Free, Open all year, Reservations not accepted, Elev: 547ft/167m, Tel: 509-751-0240, Nearest town: Starbuck. GPS: 46.587083, -118.035968

13 • C5 | Little Goose Dam South

Dispersed sites, No water, Vault/pit toilet, No tents/RVs: Free, Reservations not accepted, Elev: 553ft/169m, Tel: 509-751-0240, Nearest town: Starbuck. GPS: 46.579407, -118.043583

14 • C5 | Little Goose Landing

Total sites: 4, RV sites: 4, No water, Vault/pit toilet, Tent & RV camping: Free, Open all year, Elev: 607ft/185m, Tel: 509-751-0240, Nearest town: Starbuck. GPS: 46.585664, -118.006097

15 • C5 | Lower Granite Lock and Dam

Dispersed sites, No water, Vault/pit toilet, Tent & RV camping: Free, Elev: 655ft/200m, Tel: 509-843-1493, Nearest town: West Clarkston. GPS: 46.664922, -117.433902

16 • C5 | Nisqually John Landing

Dispersed sites, No water, Vault/pit toilet, Tent & RV camping: Free, Open all year, Elev: 764ft/233m, Tel: 509-751-0240, Nearest town: Lewiston, ID. GPS: 46.476857, -117.235060

17 • C5 | Offield Landing

Dispersed sites, No water, Vault/pit toilet, Tent & RV camping: Free, Open all year, Elev: 748ft/228m, Tel: 509-397-6413, Nearest town: Pomeroy. GPS: 46.652655, -117.418236

18 • C5 | Riparia Park

Dispersed sites, No water, Vault/pit toilet, Tent & RV camping: Free, No wood fires Jun-Oct, Open all year, Max Length: 40ft, Reservations not accepted, Elev: 538ft/164m, Tel: 509-282-3219, Nearest town: Hay. GPS: 46.577182, -118.090553

19 • C5 | Texas Rapids

Dispersed sites, No water, Flush toilet, Tent & RV camping: Free, Open all year, Reservations not accepted, Elev: 581ft/177m, Tel: 509-282-3219, Nearest town: Hay. GPS: 46.578826, -118.058079

20 • C5 | Wawawai Landing

Dispersed sites, No water, Vault/pit toilet, Tent & RV camping: Free, Open all year, Elev: 745ft/227m, Tel: 509-751-0240, Nearest town: Pullman. GPS: 46.630525, -117.379952

21 • C5 | Willow Landing

Dispersed sites, No water, Vault/pit toilet, Tent & RV camping: Free, Open all year, Reservations not accepted, Elev: 633ft/193m, Tel: 509-751-0240, Nearest town: Starbuck. GPS: 46.681858, -117.749517

22 • D3 | Avery Park

Dispersed sites, No water, Vault/pit toilet, Tent & RV camping: Free, Stay limit: 7 days, Open Apr-Oct, Reservations not accepted, Elev: 210ft/64m, Tel: 541-506-7819, Nearest town: Wishram. GPS: 45.662814, -121.036197

23 • D3 | Roosevelt Park

Dispersed sites, Central water, Vault/pit toilet, Tent & RV camping: Free, Tent Camping Fri-Sat-Sun evenings only, Stay limit: 7 days, Open Apr-Oct, Reservations not accepted, Elev: 266ft/81m, Tel: 541-506-7819, Nearest town: Roosevelt. GPS: 45.731855, -120.222176

24 • D3 | Sundale Park

Dispersed sites, No water, Vault/pit toilet, Tent & RV camping: Free, No public use during commercial treaty fishing seasons, Stay limit: 7 days, Open all year, Reservations not accepted, Elev: 269ft/82m, Tel: 503-296-1181, Nearest town: Kennewick. GPS: 45.719066, -120.315282

25 • D4 | Paradise Park

Dispersed sites, No water, Vault/pit toilet, Group site: $50, Stay limit: 14 days, Open Apr-Oct, Reservations required, Elev: 276ft/84m, Tel: 509-783-1270, Nearest town: Plymouth. GPS: 45.922686, -119.408068

26 • D4 | Plymouth Park

Total sites: 32, RV sites: 32, Elec sites: 32, Water at site, Flush toilet, Free showers, RV dump, Tents: $22-30/RVs: $30-35, 12 full hookups, Stay limit: 14 days, Open Apr-Oct, Max Length: 55ft, Reservations accepted, Elev: 285ft/87m, Tel: 541-506-7819, Nearest town: Plymouth. GPS: 45.933237, -119.345875

West Virginia

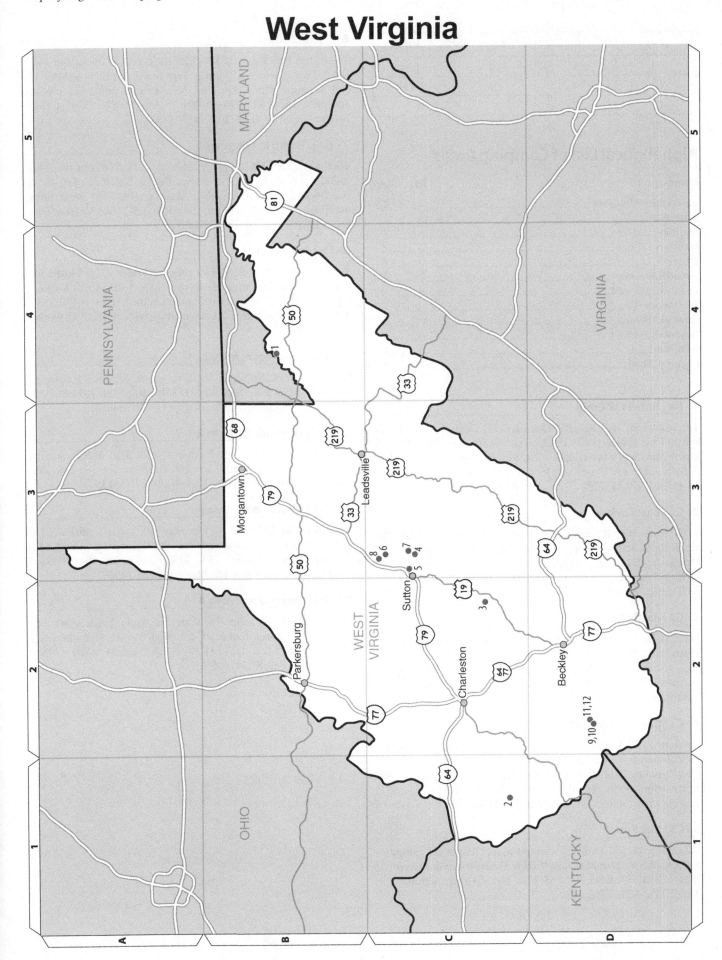

Map	ID	Map	ID
B4	1	C3	4-8
C1	2	D2	9-12
C2	3		

Alphabetical List of Camping Areas

Name	ID	Map
Bakers Run - Mill Creek	4	C3
Battle Run	3	C2
Bee Run	5	C3
Bulltown	6	C3
East Fork	2	C1
Gerald R. Freeman	7	C3
Guyandotte Area 1	9	D2
Guyandotte Area 2	10	D2
Guyandotte Area 3	11	D2
Guyandotte Area 4	12	D2
Riffle Run	8	C3
Robert W Craig	1	B4

1 • B4 | Robert W Craig

Total sites: 81, RV sites: 81, Elec sites: 72, Central water, Flush toilet, Free showers, RV dump, Tent & RV camping: $22-26, Open May-Sep, Max Length: 72ft, Reservations accepted, Elev: 2054ft/626m, Tel: 304-355-2346, Nearest town: Elk Garden. GPS: 39.417006, -79.115738

2 • C1 | East Fork

Total sites: 166, RV sites: 166, Elec sites: 145, Water at site, Flush toilet, Free showers, RV dump, Tent & RV camping: $28, Open May-Oct, Max Length: 68ft, Reservations accepted, Elev: 889ft/271m, Tel: 304-849-5000, Nearest town: East Lynn. GPS: 38.072191, -82.298651

3 • C2 | Battle Run

Total sites: 117, RV sites: 110, Elec sites: 110, Central water, Flush toilet, Free showers, RV dump, Tents: $24/RVs: $34, Also walk-to sites, Open May-Oct, Max Length: 90ft, Reservations accepted, Elev: 1657ft/505m, Tel: 304-872-3459, Nearest town: Summerville. GPS: 38.222373, -80.906796

4 • C3 | Bakers Run - Mill Creek

Total sites: 79, RV sites: 79, Elec sites: 34, Central water, Flush toilet, Free showers, RV dump, Tent & RV camping: $20-28, Narrow/steep/winding road, Near RR, Open May-Oct, Max Length: 58ft, Reservations not accepted, Elev: 915ft/279m, Tel: 304-765-5631, Nearest town: Sutton. GPS: 38.635010, -80.574951

5 • C3 | Bee Run

Total sites: 12, RV sites: 12, Vault/pit toilet, Tent & RV camping: $10, Open May-Dec, Max Length: 20ft, Reservations not accepted, Elev: 1290ft/393m, Tel: 304-765-2816, Nearest town: Sutton. GPS: 38.667335, -80.677768

6 • C3 | Bulltown

Total sites: 196, RV sites: 196, Elec sites: 196, Water at site, Flush toilet, Free showers, RV dump, Tent & RV camping: $28-40, 133 full hookups, Open Apr-Nov, Max Length: 98ft, Reservations accepted, Elev: 833ft/254m, Tel: 304-452-8006, Nearest town: Burnsville. GPS: 38.797202, -80.574783

7 • C3 | Gerald R. Freeman

Total sites: 159, RV sites: 159, Elec sites: 74, Water at site, Flush toilet, Free showers, RV dump, Tents: $24/RVs: $30-40, 34 full hookups, Open Apr-Nov, Max Length: 75ft, Reservations accepted, Elev: 938ft/286m, Tel: 304-765-7756, Nearest town: Sutton. GPS: 38.670336, -80.548077

8 • C3 | Riffle Run

Total sites: 60, RV sites: 54, Elec sites: 54, Water at site, Flush toilet, Free showers, RV dump, Tents: $16/RVs: $30, 54 full hookups, Open Apr-Nov, Reservations not accepted, Elev: 935ft/285m, Tel: 304-853-2583, Nearest town: Burnsville. GPS: 38.839594, -80.606354

9 • D2 | Guyandotte Area 1

Dispersed sites, No water, Vault/pit toilet, Tent & RV camping: Fee unk, Open May-Sep, Elev: 1135ft/346m, Tel: 304-399-5353, Nearest town: Gilbert. GPS: 37.596143, -81.764599

10 • D2 | Guyandotte Area 2

Dispersed sites, No water, Vault/pit toilet, Tent & RV camping: Fee unk, Open May-Sep, Elev: 1063ft/324m, Tel: 304-399-5353, Nearest town: Gilbert. GPS: 37.598724, -81.755135

11 • D2 | Guyandotte Area 3

Total sites: 20, RV sites: 20, Elec sites: 20, Water available, Flush toilet, Free showers, RV dump, Tent & RV camping: $16-24, 5 full hookups, Open May-Sep, Elev: 1132ft/345m, Tel: 304-399-5353, Nearest town: Gilbert. GPS: 37.606063, -81.749687

12 • D2 | Guyandotte Area 4

Total sites: 18, RV sites: 18, Water available, Flush toilet, Free showers, RV dump, Tent & RV camping: $16-24, Open May-Sep, Elev: 1184ft/361m, Tel: 304-399-5353, Nearest town: Gilbert. GPS: 37.611255, -81.741496

Wisconsin

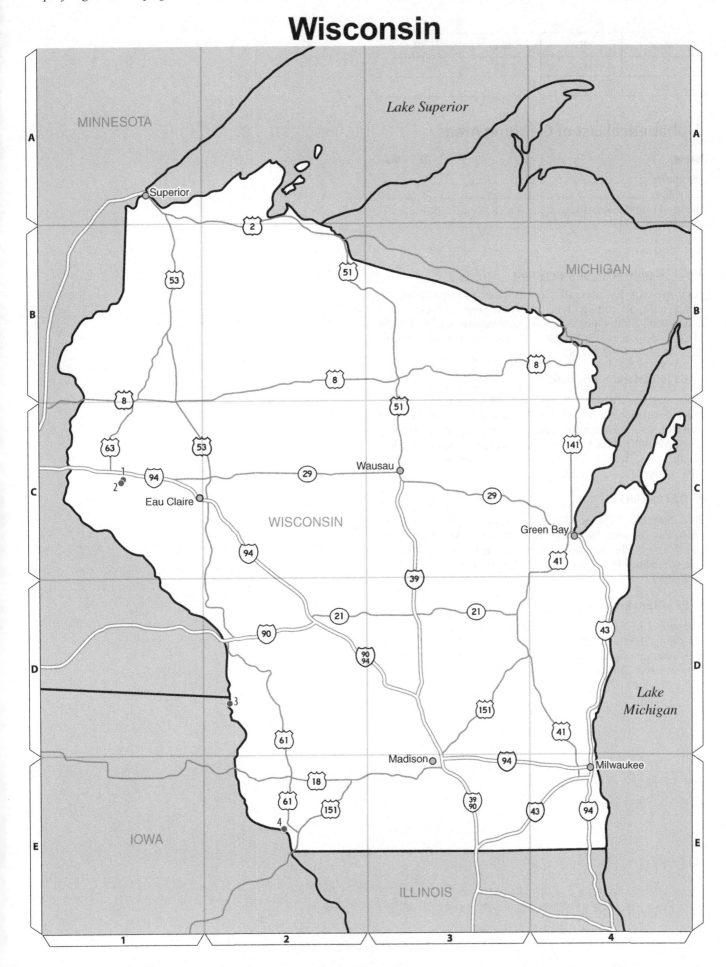

Map	ID	Map	ID
C1	1-2	E2	4
D2	3		

Alphabetical List of Camping Areas

Name	ID	Map
Blackhawk	3	D2
Grant River	4	E2
Highland Ridge Equestrian	1	C1
Highland Ridge Main	2	C1

1 • C1 | Highland Ridge Equestrian

Total sites: 10, RV sites: 10, Central water, Vault/pit toilet, No showers, No RV dump, Tent & RV camping: $20, Generator hours: 0600-2200, Open Apr-Nov, Reservations accepted, Elev: 1142ft/348m, Tel: 715-778-5562, Nearest town: Spring Valley. GPS: 44.879298, -92.239388

2 • C1 | Highland Ridge Main

Total sites: 36, RV sites: 28, Elec sites: 28, Central water, Flush toilet, Free showers, RV dump, Tents: $20/RVs: $20-24, Also walk-to sites, 7 , Fee for RV dump, Generator hours: 0600-2200, Open May-Oct, Max Length: 30ft, Reservations accepted, Elev: 1092ft/333m, Tel: 715-778-5562, Nearest town: Spring Valley. GPS: 44.869225, -92.244268

3 • D2 | Blackhawk

Total sites: 175, RV sites: 175, Elec sites: 73, Central water, Flush toilet, Pay showers, RV dump, Tents: $18/RVs: $26, Open Apr-Oct, Max Length: 99ft, Reservations accepted, Elev: 643ft/196m, Tel: 608-648-3314, Nearest town: DeSoto. GPS: 43.456787, -91.225830

4 • E2 | Grant River

Total sites: 73, RV sites: 63, Central water, Flush toilet, Free showers, RV dump, Tents: $14/RVs: $20, Open May-Oct, Max Length: 55ft, Reservations accepted, Elev: 617ft/188m, Tel: 800-645-0248, Nearest town: Dubuque IA. GPS: 42.649793, -90.697924

Made in the USA
Middletown, DE
24 October 2023

41285010R00066